Scratches

EUROPEAN SOURCES

Series Editors
Russell Epprecht and Sylvère Lotringer

RULES OF THE GAME

I

Scratches

Michel Leiris

Translated by Lydia Davis

Paragon House
New York

First American edition, 1991
Published in the United States by
Paragon House
90 Fifth Avenue
New York, NY 10011
English Translation Copyright © 1991 by Lydia Davis

Originally published in French under the title La Règle du jeu I: Biffures by Editions Gallimard in 1948.
Copyright © 1948, renewed © 1975 by Editions Gallimard

Library of Congress Cataloging-in-Publication Data

Leiris, Michel, 1901–1990
[Règle du jeu. English]
Rules of the game I: Scratches / by Michel Leiris; translated by Lydia Davis.
— 1st American ed.
p.   cm.
Translation of: La Règle du jeu I: Biffures
Contents: 1. Scratches
ISBN 1-55778-399-3 (v. 1) : $22.95
1. Leiris, Michel, 1901–1990   —Biography.   2. Poets, French—
20th
century—Biography.   3. Anthropologists—France—Biography.
4. Surrealism (Literature)—France.   I. Title.
PQ2623.E424Z47513   1991
848'.91209—dc20
[B]   91-9573
                                                    CIP

Manufactured in the United States of America
10   9   8   7   6   5   4   3   2   1

for Zette

Contents

Translator's Note

As poet, early Surrealist, critic and essayist, eminent anthropologist, author of over twenty books, and until recently curator at the Musée de l'Homme in Paris, Michel Leiris enjoys a solid reputation in France and in the history of French letters. His early associates and, in some cases, lifelong close friends, formed a stellar group that included Max Jacob, Georges Bataille, Picasso, Sartre, Beauvoir, Juan Gris, Dubuffet, Aimé Césaire, André Masson, Giacometti, and Miró. His work has had a marked influence on Foucault and Levi-Strauss, among many others.

Yet, because of that curious lag in which an important foreign work may first appear in English after a lapse of decades, Leiris is only now beginning to become known here to readers outside the small but devoted group that has followed his work for many years. Aside from some critical and anthropological essays, the first important literary work of his to appear in English came out when he was already sixty-two years old. Hailed at that time by Susan Sontag as a "brilliant autobiographical narrative," *Manhood* (in Richard Howard's translation) may be regarded as the prologue to Leiris's monumental thirty-five-year-long project of self-exploration, *Rules of the Game*, which opens with *Scratches*, the first of four volumes. Although this book was composed some fifty years ago, its urgency, its surprising originality, its scathing and often humorous honesty give it a freshness and immediacy equal to such earlier, yet still "contemporary" personal explorations as Rousseau's *Confessions* and Montaigne's essays.

What does Leiris himself mean by the "rules of the game"? When asked to describe it, he has said that his aim in writing the book was to discover a *savoir-vivre*, a mode of living that would have a place for both his poetics and his personal morality, for "I can scarcely see the literary use of speech as anything but a means of sharpening one's consciousness in order to be more—and in a better way—alive." But *La Règle du jeu* can also be translated "the rule of the *I*," and in this sense his search, his investigation also exemplifies Michel Foucault's reflection that a writer does not simply create an oeuvre in books—his principal oeuvre is ultimately himself writing those books.

Just as he had, some ten years earlier, dared to introduce a subjective approach into his major anthropological work, *L'Afrique fantôme*, an extraordinary journal of his stay in North Africa, here in *Rules of the Game* he dares to apply a rigorously analytical, objective, ethnographical approach to his study of himself. In *Scratches* he examines his inventory of memories, explores the language of his childhood, weaves anecdotes from his private life in with his old and recent ideas—and in the end, he has scrutinized what was familiar so mercilessly, and from such an odd angle, that its familiarity drops away and it blossoms into something exotic. Of course, such a project, of "exposing as thoroughly as possible the sample of humanity that he is," as he says, is anything but safe, for, as Edmond Jabès has suggested about Leiris, writing about oneself entails vulnerability before the other. *

In the case of Leiris we feel far more acutely what occurs to us reading any form of autobiography: that its author will never be able to complete the work he has begun. Not only was Leiris horrified very early on by the prospect of his own death, reading signs of mortality everywhere, even in such apparently innocent sounds as the rasping of an unknown insect in the night, he also considered his autobiographical writings to be, in part, attempts to exorcise this horror. Both his horrified anticipation and his life work ended in 1990 with his death at the age of eighty-nine.

Two interesting problems occur in translating Leiris. One is his style, in which, as James Clifford has said, "One senses a certain hostility and fascination for syntax. The well-formed utterance, al-

* See *Sulfur 15*, Los Angeles, 1986, for a selection of writings by and about Michel Leiris.

ways a drastic selection of linguistic possibilities, is made to seem
awkward, to stagger under excessive demands of meaning, allusion or
qualification. Leiris's most complex constructions show a baroque
process of thought, association, and analysis occurring *in writing*. He
is suspicious of summary, peremptory expressions, preferring elaborate, careful, self-limiting performances. But there is also a subver-
sion in this precision . . ."* This deliberate overload on Leiris's part
inevitably tempts the translator to go too far in the direction of a
similar deliberate awkwardness. The second is that certain of Leiris's
words must be retained in French, and not only because he himself so
stipulated, remarking that "unlike a novel, an autobiography has its
historic truth."*

Leiris's life was not an American or English life, of course, and the
language of that life was not English. Certain words, phrases, labels,
titles, or remarks which fell upon his ears—oft-repeated family tags
like *la maison d'en face* ("the house across the street"), or punning
clusters that gave rise to subliminal childhood identifications or the
vocabulary of a private language, such as *Mors, alphabet Morse, morse*,
and *mors* (respectively a make of car, the Morse code, "walrus," and the
Latin for "death")—are, for him, not only sounds of sentimental
importance but also so many knots where the threads of his re-
membrances and associations, ideas and moods, come together either
tidily or untidily from every direction of his past and present. This
new, English text—not the "same" text as the one Michel Leiris
wrote—must therefore be tied back to that original with these same
knots, so that the two texts may be part of the same weave.

—Lydia Davis, 1991

* Quoted from a letter to Leiris's French publisher.

Scratches

"...Reusement!"

Onto the pitiless floor (of the living room or the dining room? onto a
fitted carpet with faded floral patterns or a rug with some other design
on which I inscribed palaces, landscapes, continents, a true kaleidoscope delightful to me in my childishness, for I designed fairyland
constructions on it as if it were a canvas for some thousand and one
nights that hadn't yet been revealed to me by the pages of any book in
those days? or a bare floor, waxed wood with darker lineaments,
cleanly cut by the rigid, black grooves from which I sometimes liked
to pull up tufts of dust with a pin when I was lucky enough to find one
that had fallen from the dressmaker's hands during the day?) onto the
irreproachable, soulless, floor of the room (velvety or ligneous, dressed
up in its Sunday best or stripped bare, favoring excursions of the
imagination or more mechanical games), in the living or dining room,
in shadow or light (depending on whether it was the part of the house
where the furniture was usually protected by dust sheets and its modest
riches were often screened from the sun by the bars of the shutters), in
the special precinct accessible only to the grownups—a tranquil cave
for the somnolent piano—or in the more common place that contained
the large, many-leaved table around which all or part of the family
would gather for the ritual of daily meals, the soldier had fallen.

A soldier made of lead or papier-mâché. A delicately shaped and
colored figurine or one of those sloppily rough-cast little men splashed
all over with blue, red, white, and black, whose bodies, when they
break, appear to be made of some poor, dubious material, whitish or
earth-colored.

A new soldier or an old one. One that I had set up earlier alongside his fellows—or others of different designs, a heteroclite army!—on a good solid table or a light pedestal stand perhaps ornamented with curios or animal figures such as long-beaked storks, if this stand was actually one of those "stork tables" which (as the name shows) can only be decorated with storks.

Probably a French soldier. And it had fallen, slipped from my awkward hands, which were still incapable even of writing simple lines in a notebook.

The important thing was not that a *soldier* had fallen, that it was a military figure and not some other creature. At that time, I don't think the word "soldier" corresponded to anything very precise for me. No doubt I barely knew that you could recognize a French soldier by his red trousers. Perhaps I had already gone into raptures before the window of the Meurdefroy grocery on Rue d'Auteuil over an advertising poster portraying a scene in a mess hall or canteen whose protagonists—played by cutout cardboard figures—were men dressed in fatigue coats or wearing blue tunics and red pants. Perhaps I had already fixed my eyes on this comical animated scene with its clashing colors as I was being taken up Rue d'Auteuil for a walk in the Bois. But I certainly didn't yet have any special interest in "soldiers." I didn't care at all whether I was well informed about the different uniforms, and I had only a small set of soldiers, not the rich collection I would have later, which especially included tin soldiers (bought a few at a time, in oval boxes of thin wood that cost 13, 19, 28, or 32 *sous* depending on their size) and of which the brightest jewel was a troop of medieval warriors—horsemen in gold and silver armor—facing one another in a tournament, lances pointed and mounts at a gallop.

The important thing was not that a soldier had fallen; I had no definite response to the word "soldier." What mattered was that something belonging to me had fallen and the thing that belonged to me was a toy, part of a closed world that you shut up in boxes when you were done with them. It was part of this marvelous, separate world whose elements, through their shape and color, contrast so strongly with the real world, at the same time that they represent perhaps its sharpest features. A world apart, superadded onto everyday life just as engraved initials are added onto metal drinking cups and watch charms onto watch chains; an intense world, like everything in nature that gives the impression of being *something for show*:

butterflies, poppies in wheat fields, shells, stars in the sky, and even mosses and lichens, which are like decorations on rocks and tree trunks.

One of my toys had fallen—and it hardly mattered which: enough that it was a *toy*. In great danger of being broken, because the fall had been direct and the height of a table from the ground, even a simple pedestal table, is far from negligible, when the fall of a toy is involved.

Because of my clumsiness—the initial cause of the fall—one of my toys came within an inch of being broken. One of my toys, which meant one of the elements of the world I was most closely attached to in those days.

I bent down quickly, picked up the fallen soldier, felt it all over and looked at it. It wasn't broken, and I was very glad. Which I expressed by shouting, ". . . *reusement!*"*

Someone older than I—my mother or older s ister or brother—happened to be with me in this ill-defined room—living room or dining room, formal room or family room—in this place which was simply my play place at the time. Someone more experienced than I, less ignorant, who heard my exclamation and pointed out to me that I should say *heureusement* and not, as I had said, ". . . *reusement!*"

This remark cut short my joy or rather—disconcerting me for a moment—immediately replaced my joy, which had at first completely filled my thoughts, with an odd feeling, a feeling whose strangeness I can barely manage to fathom now.

One doesn't say . . . *reusement* but *heureusement*. This word, which I had used until then without any awareness of its real meaning but simply as an interjection, was related to *heureux*, and the magical power of this relation suddenly inserted it into a whole sequence of precise meanings. Suddenly to perceive in its entirety a word that I had always mangled before felt like a discovery, as though a veil had suddenly been torn away or some truth had exploded. This vague utterance—which until now had been completely private and in some sense closed—had suddenly and fortuitously been promoted to the role of a link in a whole semantic cycle. Now it was no longer something of my own: it was part of a reality that was the language of my brothers, my sister, and my parents. It had changed from something belonging to me into something communal and open. There it

* ". . . Reusement!"—from *heureusement*: happily, fortunately, luckily.

was, in a flash, transformed into something shared or perhaps *socialized*. Now it was no longer a confused exclamation escaping from my lips—still visceral, like a laugh or a shout—but one of thousands of other constituent elements of the language, of this vast instrument of communication whose life outside me, filled with strangeness, I had been allowed to glimpse through the chance remark of an older child or adult concerning my exclamation after the soldier fell on the dining room floor or the living room rug.

The lead or papier-mâché soldier had just fallen onto the floor of the dining room or living room. I had cried out ". . . *reusement!*" I had been corrected. For a moment I was dazed, seized by a sort of vertigo. Because this word, which I had said incorrectly and had just discovered was not really what I had thought it was before then, enabled me to sense obscurely—through the sort of deviation or displacement it impressed on my mind—how articulated language, the arachnean tissue of my relations with others, went beyond me, thrusting its mysterious antennae in all directions.

Songs

When you don't know how to read, when you haven't yet systematically learned the longer or shorter lists of words in one of the
anthologies intended for schoolchildren in the lowest grades to enrich
their vocabulary by teaching them new words in each lesson (words
grouped according to meaning and not arranged in alphabetical order
as they are in lexicons and dictionaries), when you haven't yet been
initiated into the great mystery of reading or are still a beginner and
have just barely entered it, the only way you perceive words is by
hearing them; and because of this they assume strange forms that
will be difficult to recognize when you see them written black on
white. How many oral monsters are dreamed up in this way! How
many preposterous creations, existing on a scale that will later seem
fantastic!

If ordinary language seems full of pitfalls (how many words and
expressions are transformed or distorted in their meanings and give
rise to troubling images! . . . like that of a *weeping cookie*, or a cookie
whose rippled surface is sweating, an image created by the colloquial expression *pleurer comme une Madeleine** for a child who doesn't
yet know about the repentant saint); if the most common speech,
the speech he hears every day, proves to be full of enigmas and difficulties for the unlettered child, then what about sung language, in
which rhythm—a special way of linking words—and the music

---

* To cry one's eyes out, lit. "to cry like Mary Magdalen"; but a *madeleine* is
also a cookie.

itself mischievously spread confusion and turn the proffered phrase into a pronouncement as obscure as any that ever issued from an oracle's lips!

One of the simplest examples is *dansons la capucine,** where it isn't a matter of dancing a female Capuchin monk (even less, of dancing a dance introduced by the Capuchin monks) but of dancing a flower.

In this case, no monster is created, and it is also completely natural for a round dance to be compared to the shape of a flower. I wasn't very baffled, either, for example, when I heard the spinster I had to call Aunt Adèle (later—perhaps because she was very corpulent?—I always associated her name, like a rhyme, with *citadelle*), when I heard this spinster, who was not a relative of ours but the real or adopted daughter of the owners of a house in Nemours that my father and mother rented for the summer at that time, sing to her parrot, shut up in a cage whose roundness could also have evoked the idea of a citadelle:

> *Quand je bois du vin clairet*
> *Tout tourne, tout tourne,*
> *Quand je bois du vin clairet*
> *Tout tourne, tout tourne*
> *Au cabaret.*

> When I drink pale red wine
> It all spins round, it all spins round,
> When I drink pale red wine
> It all spins round, it all spins round
> In the cabaret.

Clairet seemed not a qualifier of the wine but the name of the parrot. Singing like a ventriloquist—any one of whose innumerable voices is always intolerable to listen to because one senses that it is entirely fabricated (including even his natural voice, which is also upsetting, in the end, because in contrast to the others it has such a false ring)—the idiot bird waddled round and round like a drunkard behind his metal bars until, with his wrinkled foot or curved beak (a false Mardi Gras nose attached to his artificial voice for some sinister carnival), he took hold of the tidbit that was given him as a reward for the performance after he alternately mumbled and screeched a few fragments of the song:

* *Dansons la capucine*: let's dance the capucine; *capucine*: nasturtium.

Quand je bois du vin, Clairet!
Tout tourne, tout tourne
Au cabaret!

When I drink some wine, Clairet!
It all spins round, it all spins round
In the cabaret!

As for the cabaret in which everything was turning around, as in the head of the wine drinker (who ended up becoming confused with the so-called Clairet himself), what else could that really have been but the cage, the round coop where the parrot, dressed in stunning green, was staggering about? And all these images rolled around together in my head: Aunt Adèle, round as a tower, pretending to be drunk in front of her parrot in his round cage and only calling him *Jacquot* when she asked him if he had had a good lunch, as though this name could only be used for the ritual question about food and for everything else—especially everything to do with drink—the acid-colored bird with the vicious beak should never be called anything but *Clairet*.

This bird, with his drunken waddling and aggressive livery (the color of the cloth on a billiard table, like the famous suit in a story I was told: a certain stern father ordered it for his son and forced him to wear until it was threadbare because the son had a habit of hanging about in cafés, and one day, as he was playing billiards, he had clumsily torn the billiard cloth: whence the anger of the café owner and the need to repay him for the damage done, which was what motivated the harsh behavior of the father, equally mindful of morality and economy), this parrot with his stylish name—very much the jolly, amorous 18th-century soldier with the blustering moustache of a member of the *gardes-Françaises*—had nothing about him, either, however odd he was, that could put him in the category of monsters, those creatures of ill-defined shape with no clear adherence to any group, those sudden abstractions who have plummeted from a sky frosted over with a confusion of ideas or clouded over with nightmares. A quaint, exotic bird clothed all in green, he fit naturally into the domestic landscape, where he functioned as an accessory and one scarcely noticed his costume, which was perhaps not much more garish than the bright sundresses that enveloped the *embonpoint* of the fat spinster I called Aunt Adèle.

This spinster's own aunt and uncle, a couple of old horticulturists known as *les Tréforts*, already provided me with a name I could have fun speculating about freely with my brothers. So did the place where they all lived, Chaintréauville, which partook of a cat—or rather a multitude of cats, enough to throng an entire city. The *Très-forts* of *Chats-tréauville*.*

However, it was a song my second brother knew that opened a door to another world for me more effectively than any of these verbal rattles, which clinked like a waffle man's wheel or a zoo turnstile. This other world was also one made up of words, but nothing farcical leered out from it. It was untainted by puns and drew its emotive power from the very mist of words of which it was formed, an indecipherable nebulousness.

> *Blaise qui partait,*
> *En guerre s'en allait,*
>
> Blaise was leaving,
> Going off to war,

sang my brother; but that was not what I heard. Between his lips and my ears, the second line changed, and what reached me, the problem I had to solve, was:

> *Blaise qui partait*
> *En berçant la laisse*
>
> Blaise was leaving,
> Rocking the beach†

A fragment of a very old-fashioned and unremarkable song from the *Dragons de Villars* was thus transformed by my ears into a mystery to be solved.

What could this *laisse* be, that was going to be rocked? And who was this Blaise who "rocked the beach," and whose name, if one simply removed the initial consonant and changed a voiced fricative into an unvoiced fricative, yielded the word designating the unknown thing that he should be rocking, as though for all eternity there had been a link between this name and this object, and as though the foreordained task of this man named Blaise, as the very texture of his name indicated, was to rock the *laisse*? There wasn't any versifier's or linguist's subtlety involved, then, in the confused perception I had of

* "Very-Stout-Folk of Cat-Town."
† *Laisse*: on a beach, the strip of sand between high- and low-water marks.

the relationship of assonance between the two words. First there was the mystery of the "beach," and it was this mystery that extended to the name of Blaise, by virtue of the very structure of the sentence (in which Blaise was in the position of the subject) and, more obscurely but just as effectively, by virtue of this play of assonances, the dim sparkle of foam beneath which were revealed the machinations of an unmanifested power.

If I listen carefully—to try to rediscover or reinvent the echo that brought to my ears, or to my understanding, the message, mumbled rather than articulated, that emanated from what I later thought was one of the mouths of the marvelous thing itself—I hear the word *Blaise* resonate like something profoundly sad and pale as a chalky cliff. Nothing can be associated with this Blaise, whose name, dissyllabic though it is, is endlessly drawn out, but the monotonous gesture of rocking. He rocks, he rocks endlessly, just as the sea—according to the cliché—never tires of rocking the foot of the cliff. He rocks tirelessly, and the "beach" that he does not stop rocking is perhaps none other than the pure object of this rocking, or perhaps the particular quality that, among all the others, distinguishes such a rocking. *Bercer la laisse*, as one would *ronger son frein* [champ at the bit], or *broyer du noir* [eat one's heart out], or *battre la chamade* [beat a retreat]: more than an image of a certain way of rocking, a figure of speech that doesn't correspond to any physical action but only to the fog of a whitish state of boredom, even more colorless than the most plastery Gervais cream cheese. "To rock the beach": the only action poor Blaise could take, the only mental attitude he could assume, Blaise who was leaving and whose silhouette would soon appear against the gray cliff. Leaving, with the monotonous and tired beat of his feet . . . not even a beat, but a murmur . . . the formless murmur of his untiring lips that said over and over:

> *Blaise qui partait*
> *En berçant la laisse,*
> *Blaise qui partait . . .*

> Blaise was leaving,
> Rocking the beach,
> Blaise was leaving . . .

The hold that songs have always had on me—whether they go back to the very earliest times, like the ones I remember hearing when I was a child, or are quite fresh and, conversely, powerful because of this very freshness, which is free of all the dross that time accumulates— may in part result, if not from such unintentional disguises of words, at least from something closely related to the pun. A play that occurs between tune and words such that the tune, intruding into the words, sometimes appears synonymous with them, miraculously capable of intensifying their meaning, and sometimes keeps to its own part except to tangle their thread or amalgamate into insoluble enigmas the rhythm, the sound, and the significative value of the words and melody. In this way, exchanges take place between the properly musical phrase and the purely verbal music of the phrase: conjunctions followed by breaks after a longer or shorter interval, momentarily parallel paces or diverging steps that suddenly prove to be confluent. And in the text itself an irrefutable fragmentation occurs, that coincides only partially with the meaning and injects into the crystalline parcels or groups of words cropping up from the surface of this harmonious chaos a more intense viridity, an unexpected combination of mirrors, lenses, and prisms shattering the light in order to make it rise up again from the negative summit of its blackest depths. It's incredible, it's more baffling than any of the experiments described in books of physics-for-fun!

Along with the already special luster of the words—changed into pearls by the very fact of being strung in couplets—is yet another luster that takes their potential for magic as far as possible: the luster into which the flow of music plunges words, whether its waves disperse and shatter them, allowing the nacreous globe of a jellyfish to appear here and there, or just the opposite happens: the pearls and the waves join their ill-assorted limbs tightly in a long, glistening loop. Reduced to shards, which captivate our eyes with the gleaming of their broken edges and the strangeness of their angles, or simply resolved into the fluidity of a line, which we follow from note to note, from syllable to syllable, phrases steeped in music acquire a special sheen that separates them from ordinary language, surrounds them with a halo of magnificent isolation. A more effective treatment than commonplace typographical artifices, whatever the attraction for eye and mind of, say, italics, large type, footnotes, words marked with asterisks, or even the blank spaces poets use, which split up the sentence and consequently allow the written words to emerge— thicker and more active chemical bodies because they are just now being born—from the invisibility of the page.

The same kind of special nature was attached to certain words in a religious allegory I was told during my first communion retreat. According to this tale, the most fervent prayers are written in the book of God in gold, whereas others, less fervent, are written in silver, and still others—those recited in a perfunctory way—are written in ordinary ink or not written at all. And more generally—like these prayers, in which what mattered was not their greater or lesser degree of fervor but the distinctive silver or gold ink in which they were written—in a vaster domain that paralleled the realm of discourse and extended almost to the whole world, everything also became special that was qualified in one way or another by a special appellation in which a proper noun figured, a proper noun that in effect became its *name* and turned it into a sort of person, a being endowed with its own life, provided with its own face: as, for instance, Falières phosphatine, Flavigny anise, Bar-le-Duc jams, sticks of apple-flavored Rouen sugar candy, and other medicines such as Manceau syrup, Ramy compounds, "soothing balm," ipecacuanha (in this case, the pharmaceutical name functioned as a person's name)—entities that emerged, because of the reference points formed by their names (indications of provenance, scientific terms, or simply trademarks), from the indistinct fog of things that in the world as a whole did not have the benefit of being immediately called to one's attention this way by a *distinctive mark* that acted as a stigma or seal.

The object of this passage—which seems contestable to me even after a quick rereading, or at least overly subtle and not entirely free of those evasions thanks to which the uncertainties of one's thinking are masked by the flashiness of one's words, and what tends to be mere verbal clarity is substituted for clarity of ideas—is to introduce a fragment of song that I hesitate to bring forward because the charm that invests it is, in my opinion, a little too particular and personal for me to be able to reveal its one line right away, without the sort of preparation that forms a bridge between the author's intimate emotion and the reader's consciousness, or rather that creates between the two of them the indispensable conducting medium in which a current has some chance of being created, a series of waves some chance of being propagated by the apparently cold and inert little pebble that lies hidden from everyone in a corner of the author's head or heart. Because for the writer, this is the whole point: to transmit into the head or heart of another person the concretions that have been deposited by his present or past life in the depths of his own head or heart and that have had value only for him until then; to communicate something in order to make it more valuable, to let it circulate, so that once it has been cast out to others it will come back to him a little more magical, like the shields of the Northwest American Indians, which are endowed with greater and greater value the more often they have been the object of ceremonial exchanges. But even the most ordinary exchange can't take place without a minimum of ceremony. Whence these ostentations of writing, these enticements, this swaggering, all these artifices, which are as entirely natural as a peacock spreading its tail or the various stratagems of courtship.

If I have a memory in my head, and it extends in all directions through emotional ramifications, it is not a foreign body to be extirpated. Even though it has come to me from outside, even though it is the result of an absolutely fortuitous conjunction of circumstances, it is nonetheless an integral part of me; it has become my substance just like the food from outside me that I eat. Even more so! Insofar as this memory remains an image—an image that is circumscribed and separate, as it is supposed to be—it tends to reverse roles and pose as a mirror, as though in relation to it I lose all real consistency and now find it to be, in fact, a solid thing—the only solid thing I look at and that throws my reflection back at me. There is a paradox to this kind of memory: in it I find the purest expression of myself, to the very extent that it struck me by the strangeness it harbored within it. . . .

"As odd as it is strange,"—as we sometimes said jokingly in my family—very foreign and very strange was this line from the duet in *Manon*, as I heard it sung by my sister, a girl already in long skirts.

> *Adieu, notre petite table!*
> Farewell, our little table!

says Manon, conscientiously pronouncing the silent *e* separating the last two *t*'s of the series of three, the last two of which seem to be merely the lurching echo of the first, over which the tongue has stumbled. *Ti-te-ta.* The *e* of *te*, between the *i* of *ti* and the *a* of *ta*, far from being skipped over, is sufficiently prominent so that the syllable *te* derives a sort of consistency from it, thickens and tends to metamorphose into an object, and forsaking the adjective *petit*, clings to the noun *table*, which designates a solid body, a mass made of heavy wood whose attractive force is greater than that of the adjective *petit*, which hasn't even the particle of reality of a slight breath of air. So here is our table changed into *tetable*, into *totable*, having become a masculine noun naming some peculiar instrument or other: an *étable*, a *retable*, a *totem*, a washbasin with water that is either *potable* or *non potable*,* all the vocables that come to my mind right now to label an indefinite thing of which I only know that it was an object, a thing occupying a bit of space in a room where Des Grieux and Manon were saying farewell to each other, a thing that was at once well and truly a table and a little more than a table, for to it was added—like an extra leaf—the peculiar quality that transformed it completely and that was inexplicably expressed by the prefixing of the *te* torn from *petite*.

One of the scenes that comes after the great leave-taking occurs, no longer in a room, but at the Saint Sulpice seminary. It is quite clear that there are prayer stools here (since seminary means church), which suggests the presence of other pieces of furniture that can be moved, that can scrape or bump their feet when they are shifted around, like pedestal tables; their backs are often covered in faded velvet, just as you often see shoddy looking cloths on pedestal tables. Yet the object called a *tetable* is not a prayer stool, and it is perhaps not a pedestal table either, even though the tripping of the first syllable describes very precisely the noise of the feet of a pedestal table knocking or scratching when you pull it across the floor to move it. Here I see Des Grieux in a short black soutane, silk stockings, shoes with buckles, and an abbot's white bands, his two hands resting on the back of his prayer stool, his eyes slightly raised—as though he is looking piously toward the vault of the church—and I listen to the word *tetable*, peremptory in the air of the room where the real table rests balanced on its four feet, the table that Des Grieux, in the Saint Sulpice seminary, must be dreaming of as of his only authentic tabernacle. I listen to this word, *tetable*, but I know very well I won't find any solution. It will remain a *tetable*, neither a pedestal table nor a prayer stool, and it won't be given a definite form, either by the fact that this object is the central piece of furniture in the room, which it seems to sum up entirely, or by the fact that the word that evokes this object and the object itself can be transported, simply by a man's memory, to another point in space: to a church in Saint Sulpice, near a prayer stool, surrounded by organ sounds. Does the word *tetable*, then, derive its magic from the fact that although it partakes of the table and

* Stable; altarpiece; totem; drinkable; and non-drinkable.

resonates like the wood of the prayer stool as it is moved across the flagstones, it designates nothing, even though it seems to signify something, and remains a label applied to pure nothingness or to an object forever incomprehensible? Some element of thing-in-itself probably trails after these words, which seem to correspond to a precise reality but are actually without any kind of meaning. Hence their *revelatory* air, since they are by definition formulas for what can least be formed, names for extraordinary entities that populate a world beyond our laws.

This awareness, produced by a mere word, of the untimely existence of an object—one that remains undefined but is no less an almost palpable thing, vocabulary being so invested with authority—this irritating awareness (like the search for a memory that at moments you think you're about to grasp but that keeps eluding you) is perhaps not so very different, despite its futility, from what people feel who persist in an eager, if faithless, quest of the absolute.

I often used to have dreams whose details I couldn't remember. They were like objects of which I knew only the angles in their most abstract form, their measurement in degrees. One of these angles would appear in my memory, but despite my efforts, it would remain bare and fail to assume any substance. I perceived only its sharpness; it was like the elbow of a passerby poking me in the ribs without my having the time or opportunity to catch a glimpse of the stranger before he lost himself in the crowd. Trying to revive the dream, to make it take on mass and color, lift it from the flat and dead geometry that, in its disloyal way, was all it amounted to; injecting into it, as a breath of new life, the very vague atmosphere that was all I had left of what had been essential to it; wearing down the fragments of setting, characters, and events that my memory, with some effort, managed to summon up here and there, for a moment; feeling them dissolve even before I had a chance to readjust them; resuming this work an indefinite number of times and under conditions that deteriorated each time (because the atmosphere dissolved little by little or became tainted, and the fragments themselves, having been worn down, dwindled away or were falsified, and soon what I would have seen take shape in my head, if I had gone on any longer, would have been a completely fabricated dream, with no tangible content); thinking of that in bed before getting up, or in my bath (where I have always liked to daydream), or outdoors, at work, at the table; chewing all this over again without having the courage to spit it out before my certainty of not accomplishing anything was evidenced by an almost physical feeling of nausea—because of such dreams, this was how I sometimes spent an entire day.

At present I find myself in the same sort of state as I try to bring back to life, under the tip of my pen, what is really no more than a set of needle points, the rather particular layer of memories that I am trying to prospect here. Very sharp needles whose steel glimmers will fascinate me all the more the finer their points, the better suited for perforating and more impalpable they are. Or less cruel needles of which I would only ask that they draw music from the almost imperceptible grooves carved on my heart, grooves whose brief trans-formation into melody would be the only thing capable of briefly saving me.

Likewise, if I try to give substance to this present moment—to this very *presence*—it immediately hides, becomes indistinct; and every-thing I say about it, not being able—with good reason!—to address it directly (whereas I would like to cry out to it . . .), all I invent to bring it to reality—or bring it back to reality—becomes the most futile chitchat. I line up sentences, collect words and figures of speech, but what gets caught in each of these traps is always the shadow and not the prey. Whether I am hunting the present fugitive instant, a memory that has crumbled into dust, or those imaginary objects that seem to hide behind false windows of words painted in trompe l'oeil on the facade of my mind, I am always seeking the same game: that precious thing, the only real thing, which frequently appears in my dreams in the form of a wonderful record of American Negro music I recall hearing but remember only very confusedly, a record I know is somewhere in my possession but can't manage to find even though I try stacks of records.

Whether it is a memory precisely located in the past, an old imaginary creation that may, for all I know, be taking shape at this very instant, or a present moment: in the end, the goal hardly matters. Because when I hunt, my efforts always take place in the present. This tense race is no doubt the only affecting element in all my strivings here, and now that it has become its own object, is probably what constitutes—both in the clenched gesture of writing and in the relaxed posture of dreaming—the strange series of so-norous vibrations whose vague perception fascinates me so.

In Court Dress

We lived on Rue Michel-Ange. The name of the concierge, who went off to work every morning in the silver-buttoned uniform of a gas company employee or a bank messenger, was Monsieur Poisson.* His children, of course, were the "little fishes."

After passing through an ordinary sort of vestibule and crossing the glassed-in courtyard (a kind of greenhouse or aquarium onto which the concierge's lodge looked out), we went up three stories. Then we were "at home."

There was a recessed cupboard in my older brother's room, and it was here, among other things belonging to us, that my phonograph was kept—a cylinder phonograph with a horn. I often played it, not only taking pleasure in hearing the cylinders but also—almost touching them with my nose—in smelling their wax. One of the most worn, most often played, was the Consecration March from Meyerbeer's *Le Prophète* performed by the band of the Garde Républicaine, "conducted by Parès," as a voice announced at the beginning of the piece. I was fascinated by it because of the brightness of the brass instruments, which evoked something pompous, as did the uniforms I imagined the musicians were wearing, with their white straps and their red or gold lanyards and shoulder knots. If, at the point I've reached today, what is ordinarily considered sacred almost always seems to me annoyingly redundant or excessively solemn, it is perhaps in part because of that Consecration March, whose pomp, for me, left

Poisson: fish.

its mark on words like *sacre* [consecration], *sacrement* [sacrament], and *sacré* [sacred], and imprinted forever the ideas they labeled with this element of ceremony, fanfare, and procession, which fascinated me in the past but no longer fascinates me.

I also very much liked Figaro's great aria in *The Barber of Seville*. I had such trouble understanding the words that I always thought at least part of it was sung in a foreign language. *"Un bar-e-bier . . . de qualité, de qualité, de qualité!"* [a ba-er-ber of quality]. Those were the only more or less understandable bits I grasped. My enjoyment was all the keener because they came to me like a series of problematic pebbly islands jutting up out of a stream that rushed along but also meandered indescribably. As for Figaro's name itself, it had a taste that delighted me—the taste of the fat pale cherries called *bigarreaux*, which are very nearly its homonym.

There was one cylinder, however, that intrigued me more than any of the others, even though it wasn't my favorite, and this was "The Reading of the Report," a monologue by the comic soldier Polin, a simple recitation whose only musical element was a short cavalry bugle call in the beginning.

There was a barracks on Boulevard Suchet, near the racecourse and the Auteuil station, and sometimes I saw soldiers drilling there. They wore white, rather dirty fatigues, and the coarse, rumpled cloth gave them a clumsy look. Sometimes they had piled up their rifles, making airy pyramids whose ridges were formed of the crisscrossing tips of the weapons. Like the signs of writing, each letter of which is also a complicated assemblage, these diagrams lay in a line on the flat surface where the drilling was taking place; next to the louts performing their maneuvers, they were marvels of delicacy.

The drilling grounds lay alongside the fortifications, and it was here I situated the scene narrated by Polin in his monologue. A few hundred yards farther down, at the intersection of the boulevard and an avenue leading to the Bois, was the place where on Sunday they set up the entrance turnstiles to the public enclosures of the racecourse. A spot which, to my mother's dismay, would be littered with losing pari-mutuel tickets, discarded pink programs, old newspapers, and all sorts of crumpled paper following race days. No matter how conscientiously the groundsmen of the Bois de Boulogne did their job, some rubbish always remained because there had been such a large crowd of bettors.

At the Boulevard Suchet barracks, the walls were filthy, the windows were all identical, there was an iron gate, and, I believe, two sentry-boxes—*guérites*, or more prettily *guerites*, which was also the diminutive of *Marguerite*, the name of a first cousin of mine. Most importantly, there were soldiers in this barracks, creatures with large feet, moustaches, and peaked caps, and I knew that some day I would be one of them. I only saw them from a distance, but when they marched together as a company I could hear that liquid noise of footsteps that was so well imitated in those days at the movie theater in the Grands Magasins Dufayel, which was famous for the ingenuity of the sound accompanying its movies, reels that were in some instances gray and in others poorly colored and for the most part relied on special effects, presenting either brief comic scenes or episodic adventure stories in the manner of Châtelet or the novels of Jules Verne.

I don't really know what the soldiers were doing: they marched, they stopped, they performed maneuvers, they froze in place. An NCO in a black tunic and red knickerbockers walked around observing them and giving them orders. The drilling ground was completely level, all of bare earth; it had for a backdrop—just as the beach has the sea—the yellow-green lawn of the fortifications. Beneath a sky that was now gray, now blue, the shouted commands fluttered about like graceless birds.

This happened in what was called, it seems to me, a "bastion." *Bastion*: a place I could only imagine, a little later, surrounded by gabions, wickerwork cylinders of a kind, filled with earth, like the ones I had seen on some of the covers of a series of notebooks depicting episodes from the War of 1870 in faded colors: the Battle of Rezonville (with the German horsemen all in white, wearing pointed helmets and breastplates), the militia of Grevelotte, the cuirassiers of Reischoffen (the latter wore pointed goatees and long moustaches, whereas the former had cleanshaven chins, though their lips were covered with a thick coiled fringe of hair). There was nothing about the drilling ground—this bare space, this lifeless, geometrically bounded plain—to suggest the confusion of a real battlefield, which would teem with soldiers very different from the poor "*militaires*" I was watching.

There was the embankment slope of the fortifications. There were the piles of arms, the twin sentry boxes, the barracks gate. There were the glossy turnstiles of the race course. And most importantly, emblem of the drilling ground, there were the *paranroizeuses*, whose

name—rustic, rainy, splashing, and floundering—was perfectly
suited to this not very alluring place situated by the side of a road
that also had its graceless civilian aspect—Boulevard Suchet.
Paranroizeuses: an essence of white fatigues, studded army boots, the
liquid sound of footsteps, and awkward maneuvers.

This probably had to be something that could be found somewhere
at the far end of the drilling ground. Something like a palisade or a
row of turnstiles. *Passer au falot, au tourniquet.**

I did not learn these expressions until later. At that time the only
turnstiles I knew were the ones leading to the racecourse and the
drums of the waffle men or "pleasure vendors" who sold their feather-
light delicacies in the avenues near the greenhouses of the city of Paris
for one or two sous, though for reasons of hygiene, I was only very
rarely allowed to taste them. *Paranroizeuses* had nothing to do with the
large drums carried by these waffle vendors, these adolescent boys in
caps; they had nothing to do with the greenhouses of the city of Paris,
which were vast and hermetically sealed and located in a park closed
to the public where I was never taken. They also had nothing to do
with the adjoining garden with its well-raked alleys and beautiful off-
limits lawns, whose main attraction was the gardener who watered
them, dragging behind him his long train of hoses. Nor did it refer to
the tollgate next to the little house in which the customs men stood in
their dark blue tunics, armed only with their narrow, wooden-
handled iron bars, the probes they used for discovering illegal goods.
Paranroizeuses were, quite simply, something military that Polin
talked about in his monologue, something I thought was an organic
part of the piece of ground where, from time to time, I saw the
soldiers performing their maneuvers. There were *paranroizeuses*, just as
there are palisades, barricades, municipal street sweepers, pavers,
rammers, roadmenders' shovels or wheelbarrows, and innumerable
other different kinds of objects, utilitarian or not.

Even though I instinctively put them in the category of tools
involved in the demarcation or repair of the road system, I absolutely
didn't know what *paranroizeuses* were. The trooper imitated by Polin
said himself, at the end of the monologue, "*Paranroizeuses* . . . I don't
even have a clue what these here *paranroizeuses* are!"

The monologue was about a soldier who was punished, a cavalryman

---

* To be courtmartialed: lit. "to be put under the guardhouse lantern, to be
sent through the turnstile."

who was put in the guardroom and made to sleep on the floor because he had grumbled about or murmured *paranroizeuses* apparently the same way M. Jourdain writes prose, since "he didn't even have a clue what these here *paranroizeuses* were" and wondered, with a bewilderment fully equal to mine, what mistake he had been guilty of.

The only thing that was clear was that he had grumbled, that he had spoken against *paranroizeuses*, that he had objected to them—in short, that he had behaved like a soldier who didn't know how to put a brave face on things and was even incapable of keeping his mouth shut in the presence of his superiors. "Grumbling about the *paranroizeuses*," speaking out against the drilling grounds—this was certainly something punishable.

Maybe I had the vague idea that this soldier who didn't know what *paranroizeuses* were—and who didn't have the excuse I had, of being a child—was only a raw recruit, and the most ignorant sort of person. It wasn't for nothing that he spoke with that peasant accent. No doubt the word was one whose meaning you don't know until you've finished your military service, when you're grown up, a big person who can understand puns, a man who has access to all words, especially "curses." But I knew this one wasn't a curse. At the very most, a few curses had slipped out in the midst of the grumbling. . . .

As I heard it, this word made somewhat the same noise of rain falling that street sprinklers made; it had something runny or rusty about it, but something sparkling too, like the points, gilded in the old days, that capped each of the long bars, in parallel echelons, of the tollgate. But it was such a vague sparkling, a gilding so corroded by humidity and so decayed that one might just as well compare the metallic protuberances that spring out from the leather of studded shoe soles to sidereal spots. On the one hand there was a glimmer that turned one's thoughts toward the most noble things: everything associated with tournaments, kings, and Frankish chieftains raised high on their shields; on the other, there was the croaking and miry place where that same diphthong *oi* got stuck: everything to do with a Zouave's breeches, *patois patoisant* and *ouailles* from the *paroisse* of *Fouillis-les-Oies.**

Long after—but without having had to do my military service or even reach the age when one likes to show off an illusory collection of slang words picked up here and there—I discovered the key to

* Babbling dialect and minister's flock from the parish of "Middle-of-Nowhere."

paranroizeuses. Not the key that would have allowed me to handle that tool or unbolt that gate (since there was no tool or gate), but the explanation of the word. *Paranroizeuses* was actually *"paroles oiseuses"* [idle chatter] pronounced with the appropriate comic accent, the foolish, sniveling accent of the cavalryman with his large hand-kerchief caricatured by Polin. A soldier from a cavalry squadron complains of having been punished for having been so indiscreet as to murmur *"des paroles oiseuses"* when "he doesn't even have a clue what this here idle chatter might be!"—those were the secrets of *"paran-roizeuses."*

From our walks in the Bois, in the *"jardin de la Ville,"* and along Boulevard Suchet, we would return to Rue Michel-Ange, which was a street without mystery, except for its resemblance to my name; I could see my own name in it, slightly distorted, transformed into *mikel* instead of the hissing *Michel* I was used to. Our building was mostly surrounded by private houses, but behind it was an immense garden with gravel, big trees, and a vast structure with red tiled roofs that was the Jewish school. When people talked about the place they said, "at the Jews'." The Jews were the high school boys I saw walking in groups of two, three, or more at their recreation hours, when they went out into the garden. There was nothing especially remarkable about them, no sign indicating the slightest relation between these schoolchildren's indistinct forms and the people who, according to church history, had tortured Christ. They were simply big boys dressed in navy blue and wearing visored caps, responsible for the uproar we heard at certain times of the day, composed of the sounds of feet walking or running over the gravel and voices calling back and forth in the excitement of a game, voices whose crisscrossing wove a dense clamor prolonged in a muted way by the monotonous murmur of numerous conversations.

As far as I can remember, our street had a wood surface. I think on one occasion it was covered with straw because someone in a nearby house was dying. The street was actually not very busy, and it was hardly worth the trouble to muffle the impact the horses' shoes made on it. But even the sound of one hackney coach must be enough to disturb someone who is dying, and anyway, isn't the straw on the road the initial display of ostentation that precedes the opening of the funeral rites? Then the flowers and wreaths burst into blossom, and they seem to be simply the ripening of the straw that was laid down for the dying.

Sometimes the outside bell of one of the neighboring houses would ring. One Easter Sunday (*Pâques* [Easter] was a name that crunched like sugar, with a nicely circumflexed *â* like a round egg in one's mouth, an egg decorated with scallops) I ran to the balcony because I thought the bells themselves had just arrived, bringing presents. But what could I have expected from such a sour tinkling? At best some mint pastilles, sweets I loathed. But this wasn't the arrival of any mystical bells. Only the tinkling of a doorbell. There weren't any beribboned eggs on the balcony; there wasn't a perceptible trace of any visit or any present whatsoever.

Whether or not the balcony had presents on it, I was drawn to it because of the spectacle of the street, though it wasn't very lively, and also because of the balcony's iron ornaments, which I loved to touch with my hands, my feet, even my tongue, when I would press my lips against the slightly dusty and corroded railing and savor the faintly metallic taste. I sometimes amused myself following the circumvolutions of the design with my index finger, trying different routes but never succeeding in what I wanted to do—to discover a very long arabesque that would allow my finger to travel over a large part, at least, of the openwork barrier that stood, for my own peace of mind and the relative peace of mind of my parents, between me and empty space.

From the balcony, I would look not only at the street but at the other balconies, especially the ones on the building that faced ours, which was much more interesting to me because of its bulk, large number of windows, and position opposite us than structures farther away or simply of smaller dimensions, like the private houses. I've never ceased to be struck by the large number of windows even a building of modest proportions can contain. What is odd about a building is that it should be punctured, pierced with openings and riddled with little cells whereas, seen at a glance, it looks like a compact block and seems impenetrable, massive, like a boulder or a slab of stone.

I was familiar with every segment of the "house across the street," knowing that on a certain floor there was a balcony that ran the length of the facade, that on another there were windows, each of which had a separate and narrower balcony, and that on another there were windows without any balconies at all so that one could only see the upper halves of the people who lived there, if they chanced to rest their elbows on the windowsill and lean out. The image I have retained of those torsos is dark and motionless; and this absence of light, this lack of motion, makes me think they must, almost always, have belonged to old people.

The ironwork of our own balcony—in one of the windows in the dining room, which was the room in our house where we did everything and where I usually liked to be—responded to the kicks I sometimes gave it, while I bit the railing with my teeth, with a dull sound and a vibration that pleasantly irritated my gums. I felt it tremble right down to its fastenings. My parents didn't like this very much, always thinking that some day I might lean too far over and fall out the window. They didn't know that what interested me more than anything was the balcony itself, the way it looked and what it was made of, and I probably would never have thought of using these ornaments as steps to climb up on—they kept me sufficiently occupied with all the twists and turns of form I could find in them.

Very different from these front balconies were the windows in the back, which looked out on an open courtyard and beyond it the Jews' garden. These were the sorts of windows without balconies that children can't look out of without some effort, obliged either to kneel on the sill—a tiring position, and painful after a while, because it cuts into their knees—or boldly sit between the sill and the rail, which makes them dizzy and can lead to remonstrances from their parents, who always think they might fall. The rail on these windows was not made of iron but wood, and had a distinctly disagreeable taste of paint when licked.

On this back side of the house there was, however, one spot that had some attraction—a sort of small platform made entirely of metal onto which the kitchen opened on one side (separated from it only by a French window) and on the other side the servants' W.C.s. Confined by a balustrade formed of plain vertical bars connected by a railing, the platform consisted of a thin sheet of iron laid over and supported by crossbars. When one stood on it and moved a little, one could feel it trembling under one's feet. From there, one could take in the courtyard in its entire length. On the right was the shaded park of the Jews, and at the far end one saw, lower than our house, the house next door, which was a family pension whose rather dingy back formed a boundary of our courtyard. At night I would see, much farther off, an intense red glow coming from the illuminated sign of the factory that made ZIGZAG cigarette papers, built on the odd-numbered side of the boulevard, which had a series of arcades all along it supporting the tracks of the belt railway from the Auteuil-Boulogne train station to the Auteuil viaduct crossing the Seine and connecting the manufacturing district of Javel to the now bourgeois neighborhood of Point-du-Jour. Point-du-Jour: a neighborhood whose name might have evoked the cheerful image of the coming of dawn, but instead, in part because of the scorn that the people of Auteuil had for it, since it was poorer than their own neighborhood, had an indecisive aspect, a slightly hangdog, grayish hue. Point-du-Jour, *pointe du jour*: the far far east, the crack of dawn, the hinterlands, a hopelessly suburban district, a borderline where the beginning of day merged with the end of night, the eternally equivocal moment when streetlamps and night-lights are turned off, in rooms thronged with the various constructions dreamed by sleepers, as well as in the streets where buildings survey from their great height the empty roads and sidewalks. Point-du-Jour: a far distant point pushed by the cozily padded neighborhood of Auteuil toward remote places like Issy-les-Moulineaux and Billancourt, thrown out beyond the Barrière and entered, with a great clanging noise, by two-car trams.

From the metal platform overlooking the courtyard of our building, I often watched that red glow. It gave part of the sky such a sinister appearance that I couldn't help thinking it was the glow of a fire, even after I was told that it came from the word "Zigzag" composed of a group of incandescent electric light bulbs.

Of the things associated with fire, I knew nothing about the smoke, flames, heaps of debris, or charred bodies that were the physical expression of the "disaster"; I knew only about firemen. I had seen them go by a number of times, with their helmets of polished brass, their leather jackets, and their red painted engine. More often, I had heard the "*pinpon*" sound of the horn. Once I had even chanced to see a fireman from very close up, a flesh-and-blood fireman who appeared one day framed in the front doorway of our apartment, which opened onto the landing of the big staircase: "Don't be afraid, Madame, don't be afraid!" he said to my sister, who had already made me put on my coat and was getting ready to take me outside because a chimney fire had broken out in the building, and since my mother was gone for the afternoon, my sister was responsible for the household. It gave me a strange feeling to know that there was a fire in our house and to see that the firemen had stopped right in front of our carriage entrance. Usually they only went past the house. They remained offstage; the sound of their horn was one of the sounds from outdoors that had nothing to do with me. Their clothing also set them apart: besides the helmet, they wore a wide red belt with a black strip in the middle bearing two brass rings—in the language of the profession, this was known as "a fire belt." And the way they slid down a pole instead of using the stairs to get down from where they lived! These experts in disasters and rigid streams of water coming out of fire-hose nozzles, these inhabitants of dormitories that had to resemble roosts of some sort—not to mention their colleagues in theaters, lying in wait behind the flats—really had very strange ways.

The two colors of the belt, the brassy glint of the helmet (not caldron red, like the vast basins in which jams are cooked, but a pale yellow, more delicate and more acid, its gemlike precision contrasting with the serpentine delirium of the flames), the jacket of shining black leather, the boots, and all the many other elements that went to form a panoply or coat of arms: the pump, the ax, the red-painted automobile, the command whistle, and the flames, and the smoke, and the splashing water. But every coat of arms—even a municipal one— is accompanied by a motto; every panoply has a manufacturer's mark or a price tag; every display of cheap goods is identified by some writing on a strip of calico; every railway terminus includes the mention of a station name; every shop has a sign. Everything stored in my memory that corresponds to the idea of fire (the glow emanating from the Zigzag factory, the fireman appearing in the doorway, the two-noted horn of the engines) remains linked—like the cancellation mark over the design on a postage stamp or the caption under a funny drawing in the newspaper—to a brief scrap of language. It is hardly a group of words, and much less than a phrase, because the chain is composed of three links only: three rings, of which the middle one— almost nonexistent—plays the role of simple connective. "*Habillé-en-cour*" [in-court-dress]: between the past participle of the verb *habiller* and the common noun *cour* (which can just as well be the court of the Sun King as that of King Pétaud* or even that of our building) the preposition *en* keeps modestly in its place, serving not as a caption to any image with well or ill defined features but performing the very humble function of an abstract articulation of speech.

There was once a fire at Billancourt. At Billancourt—meaning in a spot that was part of the indefinite area extending beyond Point-du-

* King Pétaud's court; a house misruled, where everyone is master, Pétaud being a legendary figure of the 16th century whose name is probably derived from *pet*, fart.

Jour. I think this was at a time when a relative of my father's was living in our house, a person very vaguely and distantly related by marriage whom my brothers and I called Uncle Prosper, or Uncle P., in keeping with a family custom. Prosper had lived in Madagascar for several years. A sergeant in the colonial army, he had come to Paris on leave, and the rest he was taking now was quite well deserved, because according to him he had conquered the whole island and fought some hard battles as the righthand man, if not actually the aide-de-camp, of Gallieni. He was a very tall, ungainly fellow, one of whose favorite games was to catch hold of me under the arms and lift me up at arm's length almost to the ceiling until I whimpered that I was dizzy. Another weakness of his, besides the childish bragging that marked all his conversation, was a tendency to sponge off others. He also displayed a distinct liking for aperitifs (a custom in the tropics, whence he had also brought back a case of malaria) and skirts. No doubt he smoked like a sapper or the bearded Zoave who was employed at that time as an advertisement for the Algerian company that manufactured Job cigarettes and cigarette papers. To us children, ignorant as we were of that famous trinity—wine, love, and tobacco—he was above all the man who had waged a difficult campaign against savages while sharing the tent of his leader Gallieni and, an even rarer piece of luck, had been allowed to see Queen Ranavalo from close up.

Apart from his great size, his high color, his black moustache and imperial, what I found most imposing about Prosper was his dark blue uniform and his sergeant's stripes. A giant dressed this way could only be an important person. A little later, during the summer holidays I spent in the country with my parents, I thought of him, and of the torrid climate of Madagascar, every time I was made to put on a cap with a sun curtain in the back when I went outdoors, something believed to be indispensable for protecting me from the sun in the country.

Prosper's usual headgear was not a cap with a sun curtain, still less a tropical helmet, but a very ordinary kepi with a black visor, on the front of which a sailor's anchor was embroidered. I'm quite sure that Prosper also wore a wide belt with a thick brass buckle, very different from the firemen's belts, which were of the kind worn by gymnastics associations rather than the martial sort—like the firemen themselves, actually: bastard creatures who partook at once of the police officer, the soldier, and the acrobat, with something of the chimney

sweep, the street sweeper, and the municipal watercart man thrown in
as well. In addition to so many and various qualities, the firemen had
the quality of being essentially certified rescuers, to which their black
and red had to testify, just as Uncle P.'s anchor, stripes, and belt
testified to his position as faithful aide-de-camp of a great colonial
leader. While awaiting new campaigns Uncle P., the proud reenlisted
soldier, delighted in the prestige that his martial past earned him
among servant girls and tried out gallantries he had learned in the
court of Ranavalo on the lowliest seamstresses.

I could not imagine, either clearly or confusedly, this Madagascar
where he had lived. It was too far away for me, too much of another
world. I only knew that there were Madagascans and sunlight there.
Certainly, the name *Billancourt* gave me a much more positive feeling
of the exotic. For Billancourt was situated at the far reaches; but they
were the far reaches of my world, whereas Madagascar's only connection was with the faraway world of the "soldier pages" published by
Epinal, large colored pages that most often showed long series of
portraits of soldiers in uniform with all sorts of arms from all countries, but sometimes also historic tableaux such as scenes from the
Boer War or other phases of the colonial conquest.

When I was told there had been a fire at Billancourt, at first I didn't
really understand. *Billancourt*, a name that trailed over the skylights,
the weathervanes, and the courtyards like smoke from a factory, like
the squeaking of a tram rolling along its rails, and whose three
syllables knocked against one another sadly the way the few thick sous
collected by a beggar chink together in the bottom of the wooden
bowl that he shakes in the hope of exciting the compassion of the
heedless people. A *Billancourt*—what immediately struck me most
about these syllables was their clean tonality, and I transformed them
into these three words: *habillé en cour*. It wasn't a question of a court
costume—of this I was always convinced: both Louis XIV and Queen
Ranavalo had very little to do with what came trailing along with the
name *Billancourt*. If it was a question of dressing in court dress, this
clothing could not have anything at all in common with fancy ball
dress, the kind of outfit you put on to go parading down galleries
reflected many times over in mirrors, or through enclosed verandas
with doors wide open in search of a breeze that isn't there, when black
statues draped in gaudy fabric melt into the water. To be in court dress
was to be dressed in a way that was comfortable for running fast, for
using maximum speed to get to places where people were shouting

"au feu!" [fire!] or *"au secours!"* [help!]. Without any doubt, the gymnastic firemen's red and black belt was the essential detail that defined being in court dress.

When I thought of this red and black belt I wondered if Sergeant Prosper hadn't bloodied his dark blue tunic running, elbows next to his sides, to Billancourt where duty called him, if not as certified rescuer, at least as a reenlisted noncommissioned officer and hard-as-nails survivor of Madagascar. But I wasn't very sure of it. Point-du-Jour, Issy-les-Moulineaux, and Billancourt were such special places, and everything associated with fire engines and firemen happened so much at the edge of the normal world!

Perhaps it was simply the concierge, dressed in court dress and no longer as a bank messenger, who started this race? Perhaps it was not Uncle Prosper but a completely different relative, or someone who happened to be visiting our apartment, which one reached by climbing three stories after crossing a vestibule and a courtyard? Perhaps it was young Poisson, the oldest son of the concierge, a boy who had come home one evening with his eye swollen and bloody because he had fallen getting off the tram? Perhaps it was only the firemen? And of course, in the end I knew that it was only they, when the ambiguity that had so delighted me was cleared up, and I realized that no one needed to put on court dress because we were only talking about Billancourt.

We learned a little later that the fire had been in the Ripolin factories. In the Paris metro stations in those days were large posters in glowing colors showing three painters in white blouses and straw hats, almost life-size. Each one held a can of Ripolin paint; they were standing in single file, their backs slightly bent, and writing with their paintbrushes, the first on a wall, each of the other two on the back of the one in front of him, a few lines about the high quality of Ripolin paint.

Afterward, what I always thought when I stood on my lofty iron platform looking in the approximate direction of Point-du-Jour at the luminous sign of the Zigzag cigarette papers was how the innumerable cans of Ripolin paint stored in the factories must have burst into flame.

Point-du-Jour, *paranroizeuses*, Billancourt: barriers, borders, or limits, openworks of curving iron or scallops of arcades and houses. Through this latticework, I would glimpse something flickering, zigzags of lightning inscribed on a screen that was neither night nor day.

Alphabet

The French word *alphabet* is a yellowish color and sticks to your teeth in a delicate, dense paste that smells of petit-beurre cookies because one variety of Olibet cookies is—or might be—petit-beurres. This, of course, was the case only once I learned to read, acquired certain notions of orthography, and was able to distinguish the *bê* of *gibet* or *quolibet*, for example, from that of a *bai* horse.

Alphabet is also endowed with a form and a weight because it is an object: the little book in which capital and lower case letters were written, with examples of words beginning with each of the twenty-five letters, some of which were printed and some written in cursive, with beautiful strokes, downstrokes and upstrokes, sometimes straight up and down, sometimes sloping.

Alphabet is, in short, something you hold in your mouth when you pronounce it out loud or silently: what is called a concrete word, which fills with a perceptible content the cavity surrounded by your throat, tongue, teeth and palate.

Alphabet is consequently a thing with its own opacity and consistency. Not only a thready assemblage of lines—straight lines, curved, or broken—it is also a body just as solid as the bodies that make up four o'clock tea, and as substantial as the host, the god that believers can touch and eat.

I look at the alphabet: a succession of symbols on pages or a small book that I study, a slender collection of white pages where various linear constructions stand out in black, constructions I must assimilate at all costs.

I pronounce it: I am immediately imbued with its flavor, more effectively than if I had had the thing within reach of my hand or in my field of vision.

I get closer to anything I look at if I take it into my mouth by saying its name. The same is true of *alphabet*, which I can't pronounce without chewing a little of language itself in a concentrated form.

In contrast to the word *alphabet*, there is the thing, and the thing *alphabet* responds dutifully as soon as the word is spoken. And yet, this thing we're talking about is twofold: the strictly intellectual entity corresponding to the code of signs that allows us to transcribe spoken language into visible images; and the object *alphabet*, the book—bound in leather, boards, or just paper—in which this code of signs is written down. Between the light scaffolding of letters and the thickened space that is the book an osmosis takes place. The two, however, remain distinct, and I know very well that what tastes of petit-beurre is not the impalpable structure of joists that forms the characters but the object *alphabet*, which is oblong and sometimes clothed in a yellow cover.

If I think that when I say *alphabet* I am eating language, the illusion takes place by way of the book, this book whose materiality remains a ballast when I join together the primary elements of writing, which themselves lead me to the tongue, of which they are the algebraic summary or the broken reflection. This is no miracle, nothing to make a fuss about: from the word *alphabet*, which is more than anything else a taste, since it rhymes with the brand name Olibet, I have gone on to the spelling book, a thing to be seen and touched, then to the alphabet as a group of exclusively optical signs, finally to this thing of the mouth and the ear that is physically language, thus completing the circle and coming back to the organ of taste from which a play of assonance had started me off. At the same time, the tongue that moves in the mouth, a ballerina clothed in pink mucous membrane, has been replaced by the tongue as instrument of the mind, a choreographic scoring of the thoughts in which their twirling, their leaping, their movements from one side of the stage to the other are conventionally fixed.

Signs that signify, buccal games one savors, and leaves of a book one leafs through, the alphabet and the ABC's aren't the same: the alphabet nobler, the ABC's more vulgar. A matter of placing them respectively according to how clean they are. Spotted with gray fingerprints, ABC's only applies to the little book one learns from. Associated with school, it always smells more or less strongly of old ink or paper; it can't be separated from these physical elements—sediments of the classroom. The alphabet, on the other hand, takes flight or runs off with vast strides: letters with the motions of fencers, with scalloped wings, with stone terraces; a group of figures lining up like partners in a game or knocking into each other and changing places like dice thrown down on a table with their many changeable faces in a black and white geometry.

Cubes of bone with edges slightly blunted, sides pocked with cuplets arranged according to a meticulous order: by ones, by twos, by threes, by fours, by fives, by sixes—either there is one central spot isolated in the whiteness of the surface or enclosed evenly by four identical spots; or two spots are opposed (with sometimes a third in the middle) as the ends of a diagonal; or two pairs, marking the four corners, establish a frame with an empty middle (where nothing is marked); or two parallel rows of three underline with black spots the indistinct lines of two edges—the dice, hard masses wrested from the fluidity of space, frankly present their sixfold possibility of signs (each of which is oriented according to whether the surface faces the zenith, the nadir, or one of the cardinal points) and possess all the prominence, all the truth of things attached to the physical world but endowed with autonomy and mobility. It is because of their compactness, the palpable manifestness they give the forms of chance as soon as they have shot forth from the leather cup, that—with the same implication of sudden disclosure as the phrases *coup de foudre* [lightning bolt], *coup de théâtre* [dramatic turn of events], or *coup du ciel* [blow from heaven]—one can speak of a *coup de dés* [throw of the dice]. Even though language offers us a rich selection of other expressions— from *coup de sang* [apoplectic fit] to *coup de vent* [gust of wind], from *coup de mer* [heavy sea] to *coup de feu* [gunshot], from *coup de tête* [head butt in wrestling] to *tout à coup* [all of a sudden]—in my opinion, none of these alloys of words (of which *coup* is the parent metal) will strike the flint in the brain as vigorously as the homologous expression by which one describes this event, childishly simple though it is. The impact made by the three ivory projectiles on the wooden table when they come out of their smoky blunderbuss, then the immobilization of the lilliputian avalanche in a trinity of cubes each offering to the sky—like a riddled target—the mathematical count of the black spots with which its upper surface is pitted.

More insidious, less dramatic, in any case less summary than the dice's *coup de tonnerre* [clap of thunder] is the alphabet's *coup de sonde* [cast of the lead in sounding a depth of water]. But here it is no longer a question of *coup* as blast or stroke, and by means of a simple figure of speech one can also, when speaking of the alphabet, refer to the *coup de filet* [cast of a net]. For if a dice game, even more than a game of cards—which is less sudden and has a much more complex and nuanced collection of signs—appears to be a succession of crises, this is not at all true of the alphabet. The alphabet always remains obediently embedded in the white page, and if it should happen that the letters come to life, intermingle, or oppose one another, find themselves washed by various different currents, and see their straight lines change into the flat trajectories of bullets, their curves into skids, their closed lines into the flights of boomerangs out and back or the paths of circuits, this is the fault of the spectator alone—craving metaphorical equivalences, or perhaps just learning to read—who projects onto the printed characters a flood of forces that is his alone but is nevertheless enough to give life to these depthless signs locked in a two-dimensional typographical world.

On the one hand, then, are the dice: solid ciphers swept up, released, in a single exciting motion; on the other hand is the alphabet, which is also a ciphered message but which demands that one decipher it patiently, beyond any game or drama, and almost, even, without moving at all. On the one hand, the fixed quantity of black spots the white cube throws up at our eyes once its course has been arrested; on the other, the dark sign that stands out against the page and moves darkly in the field of our vision, even though neither the page nor the sign are or have been subjected to the slightest displacement.

Between the number thrown by the hand, which has made itself an instrument of chance, and the character drawn or printed by that same hand (acting directly or using a machine as an intermediary) with a prearranged goal, there lies, obviously, the abyss that separates a significant act complete in itself (the act of a man who makes a decision, crosses the Rubicon, causes "the die to be cast") from an operation that consists in fabricating a tool destined for important practical ends but in itself without interest. Yet in this case the appearance of the tool remains enigmatic enough so that it becomes a key releasing the springs of our imagination and causing a garden to open before us, filled with every variety of flora and fauna (as though, being the very type of the *sign*, it had to be a sign that could stand for anything). So that in the end, this gap—which one would have thought insurmountable—is almost eliminated. Starting from the two opposite poles of play and knowledge, the little bones by means of which destiny becomes material and the letters or material marks destined to ossify thought, to fix for the log book all adventures or experiences, come together again inasmuch as they are emblems of our struggle with fate: the first, as image, in some sense prophetic, of the tide that is carrying us away; the second, as compass for orienting our daydreaming and trap in which to catch the winds we really need to tame, in one way or another, if we don't want to let ourselves be blindly carried away.

However, going back up the verbal slope I have just descended, in order to look at it more closely, I must acknowledge that I haven't detected any noteworthy convergence here between letters and dice: once it is agreed that a value as sign will be attributed to each thing—that the group of all visible things will be treated, in fact, as a cryptography—it is pure tautology and wordplay to pretend to reveal a close connection between a particular fragment of the world and the letters of the alphabet. If I find myself at a loss, I will always be able to claim that what they have in common is that they are "signs," disregarding what is hidden underneath and not taking into account this detail—namely, that where signification is concerned, the letters of the alphabet are old offenders, and even professionals. . . . Which is all the more reason not to make too much of their resemblance to dice, the ancient method of divination, each combination of which asks nothing more than to be interpreted.

Signs invented to answer the needs of the moment, signs about which we can say that what they were already inclined to be is only extended when we take them for symbols of something other than what they are conventionally attached to: the characters of the alphabet lend themselves better than any sort of natural peculiarity of handwriting style to the exercise of our perspicacity. It is as though the efforts we made when we were very small children to assimilate this code have forever marked its various figures with such mystery that it is impossible for us to admit that, knowing how to read, we have exhausted its content and there is no longer any point in our studying the most secret recesses of its structure in the hopes that they will contain the revelation that the advent of the capacity to *read* used to make us hope for.

Thus, letters do not remain "dead letters," but are washed by the sap of a precious kabbala, which jars them from their dogmatic immobility and fills them with life, to the very tips of their branches. Quite naturally, the *A* changes into a Jacob's ladder (or the double ladder of a house painter); the *I* (a soldier standing at attention) into a column of fire or clouds, the *O* into the original spheroid of the world, the *S* into a path or a serpent, the *Z* into lightning that can only be Zeus's or Jehovah's.

Other letters incorporate to different degrees the content of certain words of which they are the first letter: *V* folds in two as it flaps its wings because of the word *vautour* [vulture] or into a stomach emptied by hunger because of *vorace* [voracious], into a crater if we think of *Vésuve* [Vesuvius] or simply *volcan* [volcano]; *R* assumes the rough outline of a *roc* [rock]; *B* the pot-bellied shape of *Bibendum* (that fat gentleman whose manner of breathing causes him to swell up and deflate so horrifyingly), the thick-lipped pout of *bébé* [baby] or the soft [*molle*] look of a *bémol* [B-flat]; *P* the loftiness of a *potence* [gallows] or a *prince*; *M* the majesty of *mort* [death] or *mère* [mother]; *C* the concavity of *cavernes*, *conques* [conchs], or the *coquilles* [shells] of breakable eggs.

Others—given their shapes, their names, or some of the uses they are put to—seem like accessories to some action at once simple and tragic: *X*, which is really the cross one makes on something whose secret one will never penetrate and is also the rack on which this unnamed thing is tied down, to be broken alive or else quartered; *H*, which is the homonym of *hache* [ax], and looks like a guillotine formed of two uprights between which the transverse blade slides down; *Y*, which is like a tree trunk extending into two thick, bare branches reaching toward the sky, or like the one fragment of portico left from a ruined Greek city.

Others, just the opposite, have a bohemian air, parading mountebanks dressed in a variety of cheap finery and striving only to look picturesque: *G*, a great Florentine lord wearing a doublet with puffed sleeves, whose fist rests at a level with his hip, close to the heavy basket hilt of his sword or the handle of his dagger; *K*, in whom a sort of corner has lodged, or who has been devastated by a blow from a pickaxe, the middle of his face staved in, so that now it looks broken, like that of a *fée Carabosse* [evil spirit] with a profoundly depressed mouth and hollowed out nostrils between his monstrously protuberant forehead and chin; *Q*, with the round and jovial face of a lover of easy wordplays, his double chin resting on the little knot in his tie; *Q*, also a letter that, when spelled, has something cutting about it like the blow of the ax that made this deep furrow, splitting the primordial globe into two buttocks; *W*, evoker of English words like *tramway, wattman* [tram driver], *wagon* [railway car], and, because it looks like a part of some mechanism, associated with every modern means of locomotion.

And finally, some letters remain relatively anodine constructions: *D*, the obese; *E*, the hooked tenon; *F* overhanging; *J*, the fishhook or inverted crozier; *L*, the legless chair, a seat planted directly on the ground; *N*, the beginning of a zigzag-shaped contrivance; *T*, the only pillar supporting an architrave; *U*, a vase with a rounded bottom seen in cross section. Here, only the shape matters. Only sight is involved. The character is not enhanced by any pilfering of the words in which it appears, nor does it become confused with the sound it is supposed to indicate, as is the case for *S* whose hissing matches its serpentine shape; or *R*, which makes a hoarse and rocky rolling sound at the same time as it stands up straight like a scarped rockface; or *V*, a *vol véloce* [swift flight] rending the air or a *glaive* [sword] with keen-edged tip, plunging its vibrating blade between the other characters.

Within the alphabet, therefore, elements of different provenances come together. As a system of writing, it is primarily a catalogue of visual signs addressed to the eyes, proposing a stock of images to them. But as a transcription of language, it also corresponds with the sound components of the latter and because of this acquires a value for the ear, with each character becoming the formal equivalent of a real or supposed sound and no longer merely a figure to be seized by vision alone. Finally, since it is a method of writing words, sonorous signs of things or ideas, it also receives from its immemorial commerce with these things and ideas a little something with which to overwhelm the intellect by creating the illusion that some providential action, occurring during the development of spoken language to make it into the adequate expression of the true nature of things, also had a role in the constitution of written language and made letters—even though they are no more than arbitrarily chosen references—into the clothing, even the body of these words, themselves in a strictly intimate relationship (and this, for all eternity) with the very heart of things.

If the pivot of the word *ravine*, for example, is the sound *v*, this is because *v* is by nature a cutting sound, and a ravine is a cut, consequently predestined to be designated by a word gravitating around that consonant, which is also represented by a letter whose shape, reduced to a sharp angle, itself partakes of a thing that is cut or split, a thing that pricks or slices; and it shows the ravine in cross section, therefore made visible, made explicit in its essence. Similarly, in the word *mort* [death], the only vowel is *o*, whose sound is prolonged the way the peal of a bell resounds from one end of a covered arcade to the other, while the circle representing this vowel yawns in the very middle of the word like the mouth of a tunnel, the opening of a drain-pipe, or the entrance to any sort of underground corridor that can become a channel for propagating echoes.

Summarizing *ravine* and *mort*, there is also the word *gouffre* [gulf], which opens with the muffled explosion of *hou*, an exclamation of fear. Following this stifled cry—which the preceding *g* manages, with some difficulty, to turn into something like an articulated syllable—is a doubled *f*, the image of a fall accelerated, multiplied by itself into a sort of *fortissimo* of terror marked by this double *f*, like the sign indicating an intensification of stress on a musical score.

On the other hand, the word *calme* is in fact perfectly calm, as serene in texture as a lake. The median *l* grows its lone tree here, between the foothills of *m* and the syllable *ca*, the solid cube of a small hut.

This game could go on for a long time, and there would be nothing to stop me from pulling quantities of words out of the dictionary one by one, as I have been doing, if I didn't know that underlying all this was something deceitful, which is to attribute to language, after the fact, special qualities that, ever since the time I learned to read and write, to use these auditory or visual signs for clearly defined ends (whether utilitarian or not), have been almost completely lost, since language has been reduced, for me, to the purely human role of an instrument. For no matter how much one might wish it, language is not a coded telegram sent us by the ambassador of an absolute remoteness. It is not a police file that one can go through in order to inform oneself about the private life of things, nor even the packet of descriptions comprising, in a physical way, the catalogue of all the diverse elements grasped by our thought. Far humbler than that, it could really be compared to a collection of nails and studs—tiny things made out of scrap iron that allow us to do the job of metal fitters and bring together, in an apparently logical whole, the thou-sands and thousands of disparate materials warehoused in our heads: the equipment of a tool box, whose attraction is perhaps analogous to the attraction I used to feel, in fact, to the hammer, screwdriver, pliers, cold chisel, folding wooden yardstick, nails of different sizes, wire, spikes, and pincers my father used—mediocre handyman though he was—for the little maintenance jobs he did on that great mechanism which was the house. And at the very most, I will be able to inject into words the mystery so readily assumed in our eyes by prehistoric objects, which are themselves simply tools but derive a certain glory from their decrepitude and our relative ignorance about their origins and their exact function in ancient times, close to behaving like simple people in practically all countries who think that boulders actually shaped by the hands of men fell from heaven and who call axes of polished flint "lightning stones."

I pronounce the word "tool" and conjure up the "tool box," the yellow pine parallelapiped representing a kit, not for traveling but, quite the contrary, the complete set of tools indispensable to the sedentary life one led throughout the impecunious year in one's house or apartment, in rooms provided with locks and protective plates around doorknobs, lit with gas or electricity, and, some of them (such as the kitchen or bathroom or W.C.'s) outfitted with a system of water pipes. Enclosed in this "tool box" is the equipment of a man of modest means whose life is similarly enclosed in a place that is also of modest dimensions, either a drawer or a box, depending on whether the place is one floor of an apartment building or a separate house. The idea of this equipment—also a panoply—is eminently satisfying and reassuring. A long time ago, I dreamed of a sort of *vade mecum* that would contain in a small space the impedimenta of objects and knowledge strictly useful for the practice as well as the theory of life. Perhaps a little of that feeling was assuaged when as a child, I saw the letters of the alphabet (keys to yet further keys, since they open books to us) physically realized in the form of sculpted characters in signs or, even more precisely, edible letters, noodles that were meant to go in broth. Each of whose isolated particles represented an element of the alphabet, just as other brands of noodles (or simply other kinds) were shaped like stars or long or short threads.

Wasn't the act of eating *A*'s, *B*'s, *C*'s, *D*'s . . . made of a substance with a rather soft consistency and whitish color, endowed with their own flavor at the same time as they were complemented by the taste of the soup, whether I ate them one by one—recognizing each sign in passing—or in whole spoonfuls, in large indistinct heaps, a way of performing an operation that belongs somewhere in the domain of magic, a way of tasting the fruit of the tree of knowledge, absorbing the very imagery of the secret and becoming like a god, even if it inevitably resulted (through too much gluttony, for want of the nobler sort of greed I would be tempted to attribute today, in this retrospective reconstruction, to the young "greedy-guts" I was then) in a plain and simple case of indigestion? However little awareness I might have had of what such an accident could represent metaphorically, I can still remember my surprise one evening when, no doubt not feeling very well and having gulped down too hastily a little too much soup, I suddenly brought back up, to the great detriment of the tablecloth and the deep, two-handled basket set near me, an endless series of letters I hadn't incorporated, which remained as legible as the bold-faced characters that spell out, if not the headlines, at least the subheads of a big daily paper.

Like the word *alphabet*, which tastes of cookie, these noodles shaped into letters of more or less rounded configuration played a part in suggesting to me that one of the basic characteristics of language (which only takes on reality when it sculpts itself in one's mouth) was that it could be mixed with saliva, kneaded by the tongue and teeth, eaten and savored. "Not to mince words," to be "foul-mouthed," to speak in a tone that is bitter, sour, sweet, or honeyed: each of these expressions shows in its own way how speech remains attached, for all of us, to its place of origin, the cavity of the mouth.

If from the point of view of logic alone, the alphabet belongs to the domain of sight, vowels and consonants, which are noises that reach the ear after having issued from the mouth, definitely belong to the domain of hearing but are also involved to some extent with taste, since it is in the cavern of the throat and under the vault of the palate, where the stalagmite tongue alternately rises and sinks, that the movements of air are born that go to make the flesh of the vowels and consonants, deities fomented in this grotto, cooking over a low flame as though within the walls of an alchemical athanor. Nothing prevents us from adding to the visual kaleidoscope of characters an auditory or even gustatory kaleidoscope. For the pleasure to be complete, all that will be lacking will be touch and smell.

As for the sense of taste, it will be satisfied by the vowels rather than the consonants, out of all the various sounds represented by letters. Next to the thick vowels, such as *a* and *o*, the first of which makes you think of *pois cassés* [puree of split peas] and the second, *pommes de terre* [potatoes] (two heavy dishes, pleasant to stuff into one's mouth and eat in great quantity), there are neutral vowels, such as *e* and the range of *ē*'s, simple garnishing vowels that remind you of bread. As for *i* and *u*, more acid and lighter, the first will taste of *citron* [lemon] and the second of *légumes verts* [green vegetables]; while if one insists on having meats, one will probably have to have resort to the consonants, which are less substantial, certainly, than the vowels but the only ones equipped with the musculature necessary for describing a denser, sharper quality, more pronounced in animal food than in most of the foods chosen from the plant kingdom (with the exception of the fruits).

As for smell, we will start by leaving to one side the so-called nasalized vowels (detestable wordplay!), those transcribed in French by the groups of letters *an*, *en*, *in*, *un*, *on*, which have the inelegance of organic fragrances (excretions, secretions . . .) and correspond to something represented in a parallel way, in the domain of taste, by dishes such as cheese, stews, sauerkraut, or high game. Flowers will be found in the vicinity of *i* and *u*, while a number of other quasi natural fragrances will be expression by consonants, such as *f* and *v*, which (perhaps because of the words *ferment* or *vin* [wine]) are connected with all sorts of alcoholic or fermented drinks.

Where sensations of touch are concerned, the amorphous vowels contrast with the consonants, some of which are blunt (*j*, *l*, *m*, *n*), and others pointed or angular to different degrees, such as *g* and *k*, which are irregular edges of broken minerals; *s*, *x*, and *z*, which are springs that relax; *b*, *d*, *p*, and *t*, which cut and thrust; *r*, which files down and corrodes; *f* and *v*, which are as sharp as razors and sometimes also as ambiguously soft as the velvet you feel when you caress a hen's flesh with the tips of your fingernails. Further, the semivowel *w* corresponds to the idea of something oily to the touch, which, from a culinary point of view, would be related to honey, butter, and other foods that accompany meals, whereas *y*—the other semivowel—deliberately turns away from solid substances toward the cool wetness of springs, tears dimming eyes, and diluvian rains pouring over roadways.

I am only amusing myself here, and I take very few of these correspondences seriously, meaning that very few force themselves on me as being obvious. Yet it seems that this particular correspondence bears further investigation. It is not for nothing that consonants such as *l* and *r* are ordinarily characterized as "liquid," nor is it by chance that people speak of *mouillure** in connection with all consonants that

* *Mouillure*: palatalization, lit. "wetting."

follow a soft *y*. In the same way, couldn't we point out more than one analogy between the motions we make pronouncing certain consonants and those we make consuming certain dishes? Similarly, it was by starting from objective data that people finally identified relations between sounds and colors, giving a rational foundation to a large proportion of those correspondences which for centuries had had only a mystical or poetic justification.

True, what use is it to try to find logical excuses for the fact that something in me is quite simply responding to the particular appetite I have for things to do with language? Even if I swear I am not a fool, that I don't take words for anything else but what they are, and that in my eyes the sonorous material we use for speaking has no more value in itself than the series of symbols with which we write—apart from that assigned to them, in each language, by convention—I will constantly overreach the limits I have tried to impose on myself and will use any pretext to treat language, practically, as though it were a means of revelation. The more lively my pleasure in playing with language, the stronger my tendency to see in these language games crucial experiences of a sort, as though I were incapable of resigning myself to the fact that my game is only a game I could only fully appreciate by attributing an almost religious importance to it.

In this wonderstruck attitude toward what is merely an expressive process, I recognize a habit I acquired in my childhood when I was learning to read, groping my way forward through that antechamber of all the other bodies of knowledge and advancing, as I went, not from simplification to simplification but from one feeling of astonishment to the next.

Because for the child who is being taught to read, it is not only the form of the letters that is surprising. If this child's mind is at all inclined toward the mysterious, if he likes—or, simply, is led by the very course of his studies—to ask himself questions, once the first barrier of enigmas is crossed, the real problems will loom up—the ones posed, no longer by letters in themselves (isolated figures that had to be identified) but by the groups of letters one spells out, by the meaningless particles of sound formed by the printed characters (such as *ba, be, bo, bu*), which one may at first imagine to be the constitutive materials of written words that will later have to be deciphered but are really, as one will eventually find out, abstract elements, syllables for pure "reading" that can never, or almost never, be joined together to make either words one already knows or new words added one by

one—like newly discovered members of a family—to the already
familiar vocabulary words.

Known as orthography, this code with its curious principles, this
set of rules to a baroque game, this disconcerting *credo* actually exists,
and it not only says that a sound pronounced *o*, for instance, should be
written *eau* or *haut*, but that it should be impossible—with rare
exceptions—to construct real words by combining the primary
monosyllables as one would assemble the variously patterned blocks of
a cubic picture puzzle, creating just one of its possible pictures. The
first few pages of spelling books (even though they contain only the
simplest exercises) barely manage to include even a few sentences
entirely constructed from these elements in their native form added to
one another altogether unchanged: *de la pâ-te de ju-ju-be* [jujube paste]
is the only phrase I can remember that was free of excess weight
(except for the circumflex accent over the *a*) and unobscured by any
equivalence substituting for a single letter a number of letters representing one and the same sound.

This would still be nothing if there weren't also letters that occupied a place apart. These are the doubles of other letters (or combinations of other letters) whose usefulness, however, it is hard to see
exactly, unless we agree that some words, precisely because of what
they contain, must be marked in some way to show they harbor
something unusual or particularly important that splits open the
husk or the blister of an unexpected protrusion.

Besides the letters with diaereses—which seem to represent vowels
endowed with such a special stridency—there is the letter people call
the "*c* cedilla" when they spell a word, and also the one called "*o, e* in *o*"
which is a double of *eu* just as the *c* cedilla is the double of *s* when the
latter consonant does not occur between two vowels.

With its lower appendage (a little pig's tail or a crank like the one
used by the owner of the store at the corner of Rue Michel-Ange and
Rue d'Auteuil to maneuver the awning that protected his stall), the *ç*
appears to be a perfected instrument, equipped as it is with this
cedilla which gives it its peculiar character and is added to the simple
c in certain cases to modify its value and transform it into a soft *c*,
changing it from the equivalent of a *k* to the double of an *s*. As for *oe*—
which we find in words like *oeuf, oeil, noeud, boeuf,* and *oesophage*
[esophagus] (the last of which is very disturbing when it is preceded
by the article, for then one can hear *les ophages* as one says *les intestins*
[intestines] or *les entrailles* [entrails] instead of *l' "eu"sophage*)—as for *oe*

with its circumvolutions, its two letters prisoners of each other, inextricably knotted and tangled, its mission seems to be to create a confused image of a labyrinth, of the original chaos and a life hidden in the folds of the darkest organic depths. As an adolescent, you recognize it in the names of certain Greek heros—Oedipus, Philopoemen—where it expresses their archaic and exotic quality, just as the *ae* in *rosae*, when you decline *rosa*, "rose," immediately takes you into an ancient, remote world of resounding bronze and crystal opened up to you when you study Latin.

Poles apart from these characters born of the coupling of two letters—especially *oe*, which is definitely more visceral, in a closer relationship with the belly and heavy parts of one's being, than *ae* because of the circularity lent it by the *o* and because of its thicker sonority—we have *ï*, *ü*, and *ë*, whose diaereses, those mysteriously suspended twin dots, mark the singular nature of signs thus placed in lofty isolation, which must be read by disregarding what surrounds them or, in the particular case of *ë*, mark the singular nature of an odd variety of silent *e*, which, in the word *ciguë* [hemlock], for example (pronounced as not one but two syllables), seems to be there only to show that hidden in this apparently benign flower is a subtle touch of poison. As it happens, what we have here is no longer a labyrinthine letter or a Gordian knot illustrating the arcana of death and birth, but characters that, each in its own way, express pure, sharp sounds, whether the *ë* lets us know that the *u* preceding it retains its absolute value and is not a simple conventional letter added by artifice to a *g* to show that it is gutteral, or whether the *ï* or the *ü* appear after another vowel, from which they remain clearly separated by the irritating gap of a hiatus. These last two letters, crowned—as by the insignia of an ambiguous power—by the duality of the diaeresis, were the starting point for some of the strangest itineraries I ever followed in my childhood through the crowds of will-o'-the-wisps and phantasms emanating from the quagmires of language.

Once I was past the stage of the spelling book, my first reader was a little *Sacred History*, as was appropriate to the deliberately "right-minded" nature of the small boarding school I attended. It opened with Genesis: "God created the world in six days and on the seventh he rested." Here it was told how light and darkness were separated ("Let there be light, and there was light"), how the sun, moon, and stars were hung in the celestial vault, then how the various animals were created: "birds that fly in the air," "fish that swim in the water," and, finally, man, whom God made in his image and called Adam, and to whom he gave Eve for a companion. Perhaps it was on a spring or summer morning, as hot as an incubator or an oven, that I stumbled through this text for the first time? "The sun is in my eyes," I said to the schoolmistress, my eyes dimming apparently with sorrow, though she was a good-natured young woman who corrected with angelic patience the mistakes I made in reading, the mistakes I was trying to excuse with the fact that I was sitting next to the window and was dazzled by the glare striking my eyes. The truth was that the still very new powers of those eyes must have been unequal to my discovery of the world at that moment, a discovery that paralleled my newly engendered discovery of knowledge, as though the story I was reading of the creation of the world was merely, on another level, the story of what was happening in me: the first foundations of knowledge were being laid down under the vigilant eye of the school-mistress, who watched over my reading in the same way that God, looking down from his eternity, had presided over the primeval stumbling progress of things and drummed into the different species their various lessons before leaving them all alone in the garden—or playground—that was the setting for the original sin. Genesis: the shaping of nature and man in their earliest youth. Can one imagine a choice of reading more astutely appropriate to the earliest shaping of a child's mind than this ancient and rough-hewn ABC of the world's childhood?

Whether the sun coming in through the window and casting a harsh light on the page I was reading actually did tire my eyes to the point of drawing a few tears that clouded my vision and hampered me in my work of deciphering, already extremely arduous in itself, or whether, quite the opposite, the very difficulty that the arduousness of my task put me in was the cause of these tears, and my gaze had come into conjunction with the rays of the sun simply because my eyes, trying to avoid the difficulty, had left the page for the window and looked out, it was through a veil of tears complicated by an iridescent filigree that the short, sober lines reached me, the lines that told about the origin of our surroundings and the origin of the rules we obey. And it was in this way that first and foremost, by the pain my reading caused me, I was given a patent illustration of the biblical maxim that man was obliged to "earn his bread by the sweat of his brow" and condemned, almost from the outset, to obtain nothing except through anxiety or effort. Driven then and there from the earthly

paradise of earliest childhood—blessed precinct in which I lived on
an almost equal footing with the still unclassified parts of my surrounding world as our first parents lived with the plants and
animals—I embarked, under the rule of that lay archangel, the
schoolmistress, upon the cruel conquest of this *I*, which first had to
become expert in the art of naming things. Applying myself in all
innocence, I didn't know that each of the words I was being taught to
recognize in its printed form was—more than a method of making me
better able to exercise a practical mastery over them—a ring of ink or
a trench intended to isolate them from one another and separate them
from me by relegating them to the periphery and determining, like
the rectangles of white cardboard on which a host writes the names of
his guests at table, their respective positions in relation to the central
point which I was. Much more: I had as yet tasted too little of the
fruits of the Tree of Knowledge to see the possibility of such discrimi-
nations, and with every phrase I read, so spellbound was I by the
words, I seemed to touch with my finger a vast segment of nature.
Only later would I know them for exactly what they were and would
not brood about them except as old and disloyal memories of a time
when they seemed to have been copied from the very physiognomy of
things, when they seemed confused with them, and indicative of a
rudimentary communication between them and me. *Dieu* would
gradually cease to be a name as obvious as the name *Eugène*, for
example, which was my father's and seemed to me to resemble him
like a portrait; Adam would no longer partake, except by a fluke, of
chiendent [couch grass or dog's tooth grass] or *brosse à dents* [tooth-
brush] (images of what was uncouth about primitive man or the
animal skin girded around his loins); *Paradis* would almost completely lose its asparagus flavor, which it got from the combination of
the earthly paradise, a sort of kitchen garden smelling pleasantly of
compost, and the external form of white asparagus, organ pipes
gathered in bunches or candles topped with mauve flames, reminding
one of angels wrapped in the white fur of their long hieratic robes and
carrying a plumage of muted, mingled rainbow colors on their shoulders. That time of my life, when everything I read was Scripture, the
gospel whose absolute truth could not be questioned, passed too
swiftly, I feel now. In those days, God was certainly the Word, this
word was god, and this god was incarnate in things. But now it is as
though "god" were taking revenge for being no more than a matter of
language, a word among other words, and as though ideas, words,
things, and I myself were all going off in our own different directions.

Having trusted the persuasive whispering of the serpent, having eaten the apple and committed the *péché* [sin] (the word for which, close to the word *pêche* [peach], suits it since a piece of "forbidden fruit" was the corpus delicti), Adam and Eve were then—like two children punished for their disobedience—driven out of Paradise, the green grove that I never imagined as a virgin forest but as a clump of trees (hardly even a small woods) such as one finds in so-called "English-style" gardens where they are supposed to evoke, in a conventional way, the idea of freedom and wilderness. Misfortunes never come singly: the offense of the parents was soon followed by that of their older son Caïn, whose name foredoomed him, since it seemed that all his wickedness, his hateful character, and his hard-as-flint aggressiveness, in contrast to the kindness of the handsome and good Abel, was contained in this *Caïn*, which was more precipitous than a *caillou* [stone, rock, pebble] and whose ending grated in a hostile way—the way a solid object with points and edges rubs against another solid that also has points and edges—whereas the word *caillou*, however rough it may seem at first, finally resolves itself into something damp, polished, almost soft, like a pebble that has been rolled about, worked and reworked for a long time by the waters of a stream.

In *Caïn*, the diaeresis marking the *i* corresponds to a sort of rictus, a curling up of the chops revealing two pointed canines that jut out over the other teeth. But in the name *Moïse*, the same sign seems very different. I didn't recognize it right away in the name of the prophet who led his people to the promised land. For some time, I thought that *Moïse* should be pronounced *Moisse*, and as soon as I knew a little geography that word sounded to me like an echo of the very euphonic name of *Seine-et-Oise*, the department that surrounds the densely populated agglomeration of the Seine with a slightly more countrylike belt, an area containing a few wooded spots and watered by not only the Seine but also its tributary, the Oise. In *Moïse*, even correctly pronounced, there is the flow of a cool river and the suppleness of *osier* [willow]: it was in the bottom of a cradle—which was a wickerwork basket lined with resin or pitch—that the child prophet was placed to be abandoned to the will of the river; it was in the hollow of a *moïse*—since nowadays that word is used to designate a certain kind of cradle—that *Moïse* was put, left to the hazards of his watery adventure in a bed made of interwoven rushes whose name partakes both of the fluidity of water and the elasticity of the reeds that grow close by river banks. If the name *Moïse* remains so very alive in me—snagged there by so many ramifications—this may be because of the displacement that made me perceive it more acutely when I had corrected my first reading and saw that the pronunciation *Moisse* was wrong. These two words—*Moïse* and *Moisse*, each of which is like the distorted and deflected reflection of the other—increase in power by the very fact of this tiny difference, which begins to look like a lesion or a grimace and makes us more sharply aware of their sonorous content when they are thus confronted and seem to caricature each other. All this power—once *Moisse* is acknowledged to be wrong and then crossed out, in some sense annihilated—reverts to *Moïse* alone, which at the same time assumes the various resonances that prolonged the other word. Now Moses' cradle, instead of floating on the Nile, drifts down the Oise, and now this river—like the departments it waters—is for me indissolubly linked to the idea of the strands of willow that I assume the cradle was made of, a hypothesis based perhaps only on the fact that *Moïse* and *osier* are assonant; so that in the end *Oise* seems to me like a radical and *osier* one of its possible derivatives. I am inevitably gripped by a certain emotion every time I read or hear one of those names, *Oise* and *Seine-et-Oise*, so deep are the roots that have been put down in me—and continue to be put down—by the old associations radiating out from *sauvé des eaux* [saved from the waters].

Sauvé des eaux: *Moïse*; *Sauveur* [savior] of mankind: Christ or Messiah—whom one could also call *sauveteur* [rescuer, lifesaver], given, the peculiar involvement he has with rivers and lakes, as evidenced by his baptism by immersion in the River Jordan, his walking on the waters, the miracle of the fish, and—an actual instance of rescuing—his quelling of the storm that threatened the disciples' boat on Lake Tiberias.

Before all this, there was the flood.

The rain fell for forty days and forty nights, and Noah in his ark waited with the pairs of animals for God to be ready to show that his wrath was appeased by drawing, with a magisterial stroke of his brush on a *firmament* synonymous with *ciel* [sky, heaven], and rhyming strangely with *maman* [mama] and *diamant* [diamond], the outline of an overturned hull, called an *arc-en-ciel* [rainbow], a luminous and reversed diagram of the old wooden ark that also prefigured the Ark of the Covenant before which David was to dance. The distance from this ark to those arches is not very great. If one is the celestial reflection of the nautical ark, thenceforth useless and now transfigured, it is also a pledge of peace and thus comes together with the other Ark, since both the earthly Ark and the ark of the sea—just as much as the arc in the sky—are signs of a divine covenant. So that this ark and those arches form a chain, like the arches of a bridge, or rather of an aqueduct through which what would be channeled would be precisely the waters of the flood.

Here again, as I attempt to revive memories—doping them in some sense or applying to them something equivalent to the artificial respiration by means of which one tries to bring the drowned back to life—I see that some words especially begin to quiver, particles of all this that seem to me somehow the most alive. I see them call out to one another, form groups, establish a reciprocation of affinities that go from one to another, from that other to another, from the last back to the first, and I'm inclined to think that they have become a refuge (just as Noah's ark became the refuge for representatives of the different animal species) for everything that can emerge now, endowed with some warmth, from the great mass of cold water that has gathered in my head as the years have gone by. In the same way, and without leaving the company of the Semitic peoples, I could speak of *tranche-syllabes*, oral dust clouds blown from a distant country or century and rising—sole vestiges of a disaster—into the Arab sky when, several years after the period of the *Sacred History*, I listened to a French teacher read aloud in class Victor Hugo's *Djinns*, including these two lines (at the moment when the poem, after having been let loose like the swarm of djinns, calms down):

> *D'etranges syllabes*
> *Nous viennent encor*
>
> Strange syllables
> Still come to us

and, before reading the text myself and realizing my mistake, I imagined that these *étranges syllabes* were *tranche-syllabes*,* slices or bits of syllables chopped up small or cut with a knife—pathetic bottle-imps of sound—that continued to linger in the air after the genies had turned into a hurricane.

Once the vast waters of the flood had been reabsorbed, the land appeared again, and other punishments followed: the destruction of the Tower of Babel, which I imagined to be like the labyrinth

---

* *Tranche-syllabes*: "cut-syllables" or "syllable-cuttings" or "syllable-cutters."

depicted in one of the squares of a game of snakes-and-ladders we played (a sort of conical tower with a spiral ramp running all around it); followed by the "confusion of languages," a spiritual disorder in which men spoke—playing blindman's bluff in the maze of their mumblings and each becoming tangled in the chaos of his own mind—but no longer understood one another. This universal incoherence would be in part remedied, afterward, when the Holy Spirit, descending on the head of the apostles in the form of little tongues of flame and remaining poised there like a row of Saint Elmo's fires on the tips of a row of masts, infused into them the gift of languages. This day would be the day of *Pentecôte** with rotisserie fires about to change into a harrow encircling your ribs. The mineralization of Lot's wife, who looked back over her shoulder as she was fleeing the burning city of Sodom and turned into a *statue de sel* [statue of salt], a sculpture made of rock salt or perhaps sea salt, a representation of someone actually petrified by amazement, unless we are talking about a *statue de selle* [saddle statue], as we would say *statue équestre* [equestrian statue] or *portrait en pied* [full-length portrait]?

After disobedience, which was punished in the person of Adam, what is being punished here is curiosity, another fault of children. As for pride, the moving force of the Tower of Babel episode and one of the seven capital sins, we won't know what it is until later, when we are taught not to despise "poor children," which implies that we have already assimilated a number of notions about the social order.

More accessible than the exact nature of pride was the exact nature of the sins Jacob committed against Esau. To buy the primogeniture from his starving brother with a plate of lentils, to extort the blessing from his blind and dying father by putting on an animal skin so as to be taken for that older brother whose distinctive mark was to be dreadfully hairy, are tricks you can understand very early if you have brothers and are the youngest, and if one of your main desires is to acquire as much importance as the older children. Didn't this skin of an animal, moreover, whose fur old Isaac felt with his faltering hands, confer on Jacob a bestial nature, so that his mother could quite rightly have called him a *grosse bête* [big fool, nitwit, lit. "great animal"], as my mother called me when I had done or said some piece of foolishness? Don't we come upon that same skin of a *bête* or *grosse bête* in the first syllable of the name *Bethléem*, the village in which the infant god

* Pentecost: a name containing the words *pente*: slope and *côte*: rib, coast, or slope.

was born and whose inns were certainly less hospitable than the one in the game of snakes-and-ladders, a square in which the piece arriving there by the hazard of the dice is obliged to stay for a more or less extended visit? *Bethléem*: the village that contains the good warmth of a heavy breathing animal in the *crèche de Noël*. *Noël*: a word with a diaeresis, a crest that hardens the second vowel like a frost and shoots its dazzling double point toward the stable where "Baby Jesus," lying naked in the straw, is asleep between the ox and the ass, that ox which is, perhaps, an article of prepared food more than an animal, and that ass whose female (or more precisely whose feminine form, *ânesse*) comes very close, in the minds of children, who are always on the lookout for a bad pun, to the *aînesse* [seniority, primogeniture] that passed from the less human of Isaac's two sons to his younger brother, who was more fragile but astute enough to steal it from him. And in the name of the usurper *Esaü* we come upon the diaeresis once again.

If for me the effect of the diaeresis in *Noël* is, most of all, that of a double point (or let's say two points of ice, since it is cold at the end of December) or a pair of stars (that is, one for the Magi, the other for the shepherds), the diaeresis in *Esaü* is the most delicate part of a piece of precision machinery.

In my childhood, the Hebrew name of *Esaü* seemed to me for a time inextricably involved with two pieces of furniture belonging to my sister. This sister was actually a first cousin who had been raised from a very early age by my parents; but they had thought it preferable to hide from my brothers and me the fact that she was only a close relative and not of the same flesh and blood until we were older, so that she wouldn't seem in the least a stranger to us. This is of no importance in relation to what I now propose to tell; all the same, if I add as a reminder that she was about thirteen years older than I (the number of apostles plus Christ, the thirteenth guest at the Last Supper) and that, whatever the real degree of our consanguinity, her role was that of a *soeur ainée* [older sister] whose *aînesse* was actually marked enough to establish—between these two people leading parallel lives in the care of the same heads of family—a separate relationship and to represent, given that this gap was almost as great as the gap separating two generations, a special kind of kinship.

In any case, one of the most imposing pieces of furniture occupying a portion of space in the room of the person I still call my sister was the *bahut* [round-topped chest, traveling chest], and this *bahut* was related to *Esaü* by the identical hiatus *a-u* in each of them. Another piece of furniture, the mirrored wardrobe in the room she used as a dressing room, was also related to *Esaü* through the interposition of the word *bahut*, which was properly applied to the piece of furniture with full wood paneling in the bedroom but was transferred by me— since I was scarcely very troubled by imprecisions of vocabulary in those days—to this mirrored wardrobe with which, in my mind, the piece of furniture with full wood paneling more or less merged. Already placed, more than a little, in *Esaü*'s orbit because it had insinuated itself into a term actually designating another object, the mirrored wardrobe also entered the biblical character's zone of attraction by way of direct sensory perceptions. When I thought of *Esaü*, what was evoked by the double vowel *a-ü* (whose diaeresis, surmounting the single *u*, seemed graphically sufficient to express the duality) was—much more than the dark trunk in which my sister put her dresses—the delicate smell given off by the pitchpine of the mirrored wardrobe, the slightly sour squeaking (as sour as the smell itself) of its gleaming door when it turned on its hinges, and the brief flash of the mirror produced each time the door pivoted when the wardrobe was opened or closed. What the hiatus *a-ü* seemed to express was essentially the white flash of lightning emanating from the mirror that sent back to me, for an instant, in a harsh reflection that vanished as soon as it appeared, the light that fell through the window. What finally corresponded to the real *bahut*, to the piece of furniture authentically deserving the name, was the mirrored wardrobe rather than the wood-paneled chest. So that, as I recall this today, I would almost be inclined to wonder if—in a more coherent world, one more synonymous with our language and thought (such as the reader of the Scriptures may imagine Eden, that is, the ideal world that existed before the fall)—sisters, if there were any, would tolerate having their mirrored wardrobes designated by any other group of syllables than the *b-a ba*, *h-u*, *hu* that form the word *bahut*.

Associated with furniture—flashing like a mirror or gleaming like old wood saturated with polish—the name *Esaü* is, by nature, also associated with the church, since it comes from the Bible, and (like the name *Isaïe*, its barely transposed homologue) it harbors in its ligneous blondness something of an organ chest. A certain fragrance of incense, also. These smoky redundancies mingle orchestrally with the volutes of the great noisy bookcase overloaded with moldings, each of which, during the Mass, exudes a musical wax when one or another of its many registers is opened.

Also permeated by a smell of incense—or better, the old-fashioned aroma of *papier d'Arménie* [paper which burns slowly, giving off a smell of incense]—is the Feast of the Epiphany. It is hard, certainly, to recognize Twelfth Night in this name whose faded grace is the grace of branches of plants about to fall into dust, like those decorative "money plants," which give off a dry crunching noise if one's fingers happen to brush against them in the chilly setting of the petit bourgeois parlor that it has been their task to ornament almost from time immemorial. At the very most, one would find in the tarnished luxury of these "money plants"—as in the shabby, genteel charm of the name Fanny: a satin blouse that was once brocaded or spangled, a fan trimmed with sequins—a little gold dust, some incense and myrrh, Christmas presents brought to the infant Jesus asleep in the manger by the mannequins representing the Magi.

Another word from the pious books struck me because of its musical tonality: a person's name once again—like *Esaü*, from which it differed very little—*Saül*, the name of the man whom the prophet Samuel crowns king while he is looking for his father's lost jennies. The first time I saw the letters of this name I made the same mistake I had made with *Moïse*: Ignoring the diaeresis, I read it as *Saul* and thought of a *saule* [willow], a *roi Saule* [King Willow], a *roi des Aulnes* [alder king or earl king], as they also say there is a King Candaule and as today I know there exists a *roi Lear* (or perhaps a *roi-lyre* [king-lyre]), the mad old monarch wandering through the wind that transforms his weeping willow beard into an aeolian harp. Falling branches, a storm over the alder groves, thrashing leaves, which is not unrelated to the fate of Saül.

Seized sometimes by prophetic trances during which he is possessed by the Almighty, Saul is unfortunately also possessed by pride. After he has transgressed the will of God by sharing among his troops the booty taken from the Philistines, his violence makes him into one possessed, pure and simple, a characterless instrument through which the "Evil One" blows. Despite the fact that David—like Orpheus subduing the animals by playing to them on his lyre—charmed with his harp the demon that periodically came to inhabit Saul, this method of enchantment soon proved to be as ineffective as the *Romance du Saule* [Willow Song] was in diverting Othello's rage from Desdemona: Saul tries to nail David against the wall with his lance and forces him to flee into the desert. As he falls to the ground, abandoned by God, the Witch of Endor causes the specter of Samuel to appear

before him. Then, defeated by the Philistines, he cuts short any
further sorrow by throwing himself on his sword and dies the lan-
cinating death he had tried to inflict on David.

Saul therefore has a strong exterior, but he is hollow inside, really
no more than a reed, a flute traversed by discordant pulses, one whose
column of air never stops quivering, more often harsh than melodious.
His name, with its measured pace, associated with the chiming of a
clock and appearing to be the result of the same precise quantifying as
the words *scrupule* (etymologically, a "small stone" representing a light
weight) or *calcul* [calculus, calculation] (the allegory for which might
be a player of the triangle, the most geometrical of the musical
instruments, as much because of its sound as because of its shape),
this name, embellished with a diaeresis as though with two silvery
little drops falling at twilight from a mule's bell, designates—
fallaciously—a cruel, irascible character embodying excess rather
than heavenly inspiration.

Much more than to some *Well-Tempered Clavier* or the exact honesty
of a triangle beater, it is a name related to the solar explosion of the
striking of cymbals or to the seismic oscillations of certain instruments meant to be shaken, like the Chinese hat, or the sistrum, which
goes back to ancient Egypt and of which they sing in the second act of
Carmen:

> *Les tringles des sistres tintaient . . .*
>
> The sistrum beaters sounded . . .

words which used to intrigue me very much because I didn't know
what a *sistre* was and tended to think the word was a name for
bohémiens, otherwise known as *gitans*, *tziganes*, *zingari*, *romani*, or
gypsies, the latter name based on the centuries-old belief that a small
tribe of them had come with its tricks and secrets from Egypt.

The steam-driven organ of the merry-go-round (often framed by
two anthropomorphic colored figures, one playing the triangle and
the other the tambourine), the greasy music of the wrestlers' booths
(where a bass drum and battered brass cornet summoned the crowd to
the Goliaths in moustaches and tigerskin shorts), the municipal brass
band or musical society (preceded by a fringed gold banner on which a
lyre is embroidered), the gaily capering orchestras of permanent
circuses (though they are bourgeoisified versions of the orchestras of
the traveling shows) are the only ones that produce strains of music

comparable to the metallic sonority of *buccins* [Roman trumpets], an eminently martial term that, because it is so hard and so male, calls to mind a word that is, if possible, even harder and more male, *butin* [booty, spoils, plunder] (despite the vulgar feminine obtained by slightly altering the initial *b* into a *p* [*putin*, whore]), *butin* in which there is none of the grace attached to the idea of the bee who gathers honey [butine], but whose two syllables fall drily, thick and fast, just as the Philistines must have fallen under the blows of Saul's men.

Showmen, ragmen, and (though to a lesser degree) street hawkers, chimney sweeps, coal merchants: so many groups of professionals who—not counting the mobs of hooligans, who moved around too much—represented peculiar varieties of human beings and tended to establish themselves, in relation to the majority of people, in ethnic groups as properly defined as might have been, in their time, the Amalekites and Philistines in relation to the Hebrews. And I mustn't forget the Vatican Swiss guard, whose padded calves could be taken as a characteristic of the Swiss race as a whole.

Amalécites [Amalekites]: bricks of *terre cuite* [terra-cotta], or the smoke-blackened face of an old servant (of a cook named *Félicité*) baked and wrinkled by the heat of her *marmites* [pots]. *Philistins* [Philistines]: *fil* [thread], *intestins* [intestines], *instincts indistincts* [indistinct instincts]: a ball of thread tangled with greenish intestines or the gurgling of indistinct instincts. In *Amalécites* there is the *tacite* crackling of earthenware jars (porous like the ones in which smoldered the lamps Gideon had hidden, trying to make their walls transparent, as he and the Hebrews slipped by night among the Midianites accompanied by the fragrance of holy water spiced with anise). In *Philistins*, we find the *lest* [weight, bulk, ballast] of an abdomen loaded with serpentine viscera and the fecal bronze color overlaying the statues one used to see in the windows of truss suppliers. The name *Philistins* (which always had something brackish about it for me, like Célestins Vichy water) now seems to me well suited to serve as a label for the lapping, babbling mob, a mob that wails though so flaccid, that swarms though so indeterminate! a mob formed—though it never emerges from the slough of formlessness—of individuals who will never know anything about anything.

I can therefore say of these two peoples—without yielding too much to the mania for half-consciously retouching a person's features until one has found a certain "family resemblance" between him and a relative—that their names resemble each other. This is the case with a lot of names, of groups or individuals, whether it be the *saltimbanques* [showmen] (with the three syllables in bif-boom-bah rhythm) or *Jésus-Christ* (close to *crypte* and *cri*). But it is a very different matter with *Saül*; contrary to what happened with *Esaü* (in which the hiatus plays a large part, reinforced by the preceding saw cut of *za*), in *Saül*— perhaps because of the too soft *sa?*—the *a-ü* does not squeak: it is obliterated, forgotten, drowned, entirely annulled in the limpidity of *ul*. In the same way, the distance from Boaz to the Beauce is the distance from our tranquil wheat-covered plains to the overwhelming spaces in which the heroes of the Bible moved about, torrid fields that needed all the blessings of Yahweh to yield anything but tares and couch grass.

The *z*—all of whose heat is summed up in the word *gaz* [gas] (invented by the old physicist Van Helmont, who imagined it to be something like the Latin *chaos*, that is, a rarefied substance)—plays a part in endowing certain names of places or people, read at one time in the Old Testament, with a strange expansive power, with bluish crests going beyond the norm reasonably accorded to any flame, whether it be the shaggy wicks lit on the skulls of the apostles during Pentecost or the white domesticated fires which, before the time of electricity, used to fill the mantles of incandescent burners, little retorts from which an elixir of light poured out in every home.

Z's slow-burning nature manifests itself especially in *Josué* [Joshua], whose final buzzing contrasts with the regular progress of the sun, just as the sudden emission of a quantity of energy that hadn't existed until then in the created world jams certain predictable motions, introducing into the system of balanced forces a new factor whose intrusion changes the entire equilibrium and is, consequently, a cause of serious trouble for the universe and its correct disposition. *Josué*, his forehead in the clouds: he spurts up, reaches the peak of his ascent, and solidifies in a hard column against which the day-star will come to a stop (like a locomotive that has reached the end of its run and whose piston releases a burst of steam, with the noise of a great sigh or a hissing not very different from this *zwé*). *Josué*, an obstinate character: one could believe the name was derived from the Spanish *José* tortured by the addition (splinter or blade going in straight or at an angle) of the *w* because of which the *zé*, already fairly aggressive, changes into the burning geyser of the *zwé*. *Josué*, brother of *José*: a tiny shift from one name to the other but also the transformation, into a Hebrew prophet, of a schoolmate of mine named José Nahon, a boy with close-cropped, vigorous black hair and features already rough despite his youth and who for a long time wore a white linen bandage on one of his wrists because of a deep cut he showed me one day that awoke an enduring horror in me, because the wound seemed to go so far down that I thought I could see in it something like the beginning of an amputation. Now I connect this boy named José Nahon to *Josué*, and the *ü* inserted in the *zé* has the same effect on me of the granular splitting of a ripe fig that I felt when, sitting on the benches of the little school where we were learning to write, my schoolmate showed me this wound, of which he seemed all the more proud because the cut was so deep.

A succession of other names follows *Josué*: *Suse* [Shushan], the typical oriental city, with a murmuring, as of a canal lock, of crowds eddying around palaces with enameled facades and bazaars giving off floods of smells, symmetrical to the flood of smells emanating from *Ecbatane* [Ecbatana], with its preciosity, as of delicately sculpted tidbits of food, with its three transparent syllables building an airy scaffolding of hanging gardens or a theater play; *Nabuchodonosor* [Nebuchadnezzar], the supremely rich Assyrian potentate, a man wearing a high tiara, large robe all sewn with gold, and a vast crimped beard, whom one can only imagine lying down—excessively stretched out, like his name—in the midst of censers, cassolettes, and cushions; *Balthazar*, three *a*'s whose vigorous framework of consonants causes them to ring out like a gong or a knell, just as the voice of the killjoy and prophet Daniel must have rung out in the very midst of the banquet when he interpreted—schoolboy who really knew his lesson!—the sentence that had appeared on the wall as though on a blackboard: MENE, TEKEL, PERES; *Eléazar*, stabbing the elephant between whose feet he had slipped, an enormous vault, perfect for suggesting the spacious concourse of the Saint-Lazare station, the inevitable echo of his name, which is immediately answered (as though it designated some kettle or other instrument of torture used by Antiochus against the Maccabees) by the Russian word *samovar*.

If I take positive pleasure today in making all these names march past me, making myself a little dizzy from the colliding syllables and yielding, as I do this, to a surface enjoyment somewhat like the enjoyment one derives, for example, from glancing through an album of old-fashioned costumes that has some documentary value but charms us primarily because of what is striking and picturesque about it, I have to admit that this rather empty amusement is quite unlike the profound, ancient game of which I find it very hard now to gauge exactly how much was serious and firmly believed, but whose irides-cent combinations I know appeared to my childish eyes without my embroidering or selecting at all, with the sharp relief of images living their own lives, beyond all argument.

All of this—at a time when I saw no harm in it—was hardly more complicated than the blue sky (which everyone knows is blue) or the grass (which everyone knows is naturally green). The men in the Bible had names, just as all the people I knew had names, and these names depicted them faithfully, just as the skin that clings to our flesh is exactly the same in every photograph of us. *Josué* was what stops the sun, just as night is night (as its name requires, since it is the opposite of day) and just as Judas (despite the appendage *Iscariote* similar to the *bouillottes* [foot-warmers] that used to heat railway cars) is the judas hole, the traitorous aperture that allows one to watch what is happen-ing inside prison cells. Exchanging *Moisse* for *Moïse* gave me a feeling of dizziness, because not only was a word coming undone but a part of the nature of things was metamorphosing; a change of identity was taking place in the very person of the prophet. Thus Jesus, at first *petit Jésus*, turned into *Jésus-Christ* when he became ripe for the suffering of the cross, that is, for the tortures that would actually tear from him *des cris* [cries].

Later, when sacred history became French history, when we moved on from holy prehistory to a properly historical period and when—in an evolution that paralleled this change in temporal perspectives—I had grown considerably bigger, we came to the names of dynasties: Merovingians, Carolingians (called also Carlovingians), Capetians, Valois, Bourbon, Orleans, and Bonaparte. But none of these names, however moving they were (and not even Carolingians, beautiful as a minted coin—like a gold carolus—of which certain collectors might especially prize the variant "carlovingians" like an imperial effigy preferable when its forehead is encircled with a crown worked in gold rather than being bare or simply laureate), none of these ambiguous words that share the characteristics of job titles, names of races or species, and family names (one can be named Bourbon, Valois, Bona-parte at a pinch; Orleans is still acceptable; but what is a Mero-vingian, a Carolingian, a Capetian?), none of these appellations, of which we only know that they are attached to a few special series of individuals, is capable, even if outfitted from head to foot and isolated in space like a figure sculpted in the round, of turning any of the characters clothed in it into a creature of flesh and blood instead of a hazy form wavering in the stage lights of a theater.

Of all the names in Roman history—antechamber of our own and already inserted into the perfectly straight frames of chronology—I will cite here only the name of the emperor *Dioclétien*, more succinctly *Dioclès*, like *Damoclès* and his sword, *Androclès* and his lion, *Coclès* and his hollow eye. *Dioclétien*: I had come upon it in a composition subject or the text of a dictation or a French reading. Up to then—when I had gotten to know the stories about the Christian persecutions that took place during that emperor's reign—what I had always understood was *Dictolétien*, dilating the name slightly and complicating it rather wantonly with a dose of preciosity, whereas it was already pompous enough, apparently, in the same way that a column with its capital has no need of any rostrums, useless extra burdens that add nothing to its grandeur and only break its verticality by encumbering it with tiers of ornamental rams of warships commemorating victories at sea.

The teacher I was indebted to for the text in which this curious stone was set, recut as *Dictolétien*, was Monsieur Roger. He was a man with a completely round head, an authentic instance of brachycephalism. Round glasses, a thick, short but uncared-for moustache, baldness contrasting with the abundant, curly tufts that garnished the sides of his head. His great ambition, as he admitted, was to write a dictionary. As a sample of this work, he would quote to us the entry for *timbre* [fixed bell with striking hammer; snare drum; quality of tone]—the only one, perhaps, that he had begun drafting—with an enumeration of the various phases of the word, which is related to *tympanon* and whose meaning travels from *tambour* [drum] to *timbre-poste* [postage stamp] by way of the bell, the rounded part of a helmet, and the heraldic insignia.

Monsieur Roger—who for us was knowledge incarnate—had dictated the anecdote whose hero, at one point in the story at least, was named *Dioclès*. Did I have such blind confidence in everything my teacher said? In any case, it did not occur to me at first to ask how such an abbreviation could have been derived from the name *Dictolétien*. Thus stripped not only of an ending that connected it to so many kings of France and gave it freedom of city over familiar soil (a normal amputation, since it was a diminutive), but also of the distant and in some way dictatorial nature that my way of treating it, multiplying its consonants, had injected into the beginning of this name, *Dioclétien* changed into *Dictolétien*—which was in keeping with the very high opinion I had formed of the mental capacities of Monsieur Roger, which for me could only be a further reason to introduce into the relatively simple word he had dictated, as I wrote it down and reread it, an additional element suitable to the complexity I attributed to the knowledge enclosed in his large, spherical noggin and to the authority I lent his person itself (which was, to tell the truth, simply pedantic)—*Dioclétien* had now been shortened to *Dioclès*, soft, ochrous clay, mediocrity that was not even gilded.

This name, which I had involuntarily overelaborated—like a baroque artist incapable of contenting himself with a line or a simple volume who turns abstract space into an animated place overpopulated with shapes—had begun to resemble, in the remodeled version I had taken such pains to augment, the sort of sculpted breastplate or shield that a craftsman patronized by the fairies covers with a profusion of mythological scenes. Then the paradoxical simplicity of the diminutive, which acted as a discreet recall to order putting everything back in place and obliterating that phantasmagoria, had no doubt led me to conceive the possibility that some mistake had been made, so that under the chiseled gold of *Dictolétien* I discovered the metal of *Dioclétien* (more resistant, perhaps, but certainly less dazzling), an emperor who would now, because of the ablation of barely one syllable, be gelded of the long train of his purple cloak.

Here the process did not turn on the pure difference in quality between two variants of the same name. Even less did my mistake result in a simplification, since, quite the contrary, what was involved here was a prolongation, an interpolation. Like a copyist anxious to establish at any cost something that is not manifested in his text, I had moved a vowel, constructed a block of two consonants (one of which, the *t*, was added deliberately) in such a way as to obtain a word worthy of being at once applied to a monarch, read in books that impressed me, and spoken by a teacher who enjoyed a reputation among his students for being a fount of knowledge. And this word, which was more substantial, of a design more angular and exact than the name furnished by the real version, could only make the latter seem drab and disappointing to me—because it lacked a nobly articulated structure—when I was finally forced to accept it.

The word *Dictolétien*, stiff as a lictor's fasces, sparkling like the river Pactolus, muscular as the torso of a Roman soldier whose pectorals alone provide him with an efficacious suit of armor, was now reduced to *Dioclétien*. Because he had been renamed, had seen a name torn from him that had the value of an insignia or a title, the emperor

himself lost face. All he could do now was to go off and molder in the
dumping ground for figures that have been withdrawn from circulation. And this was what happened to him almost immediately, during
the posthumous life he led for so short a time in me, for I was quick to
forget someone who was, in effect, content to be the prosaic *Dioclès*
after having been the prestigious *Dictolétien.*

From the time of my remote childhood up to my accession to the
contentious state of adulthood, through the troubled stage of my
adolescence, many notions dried up this way, one word being substituted for another the same way one nail drives out another, and the
baggage of images hanging from the hook of each of these words
yielded its place to a less luxurious (though perhaps more judiciously
comprised) outfit like the elegant and inconvenient leather suitcase,
valuable only as a piece of ostentation, that one exchanges for a small,
lightweight suitcase sparer in form and less rich in material, but
unquestionably more practical.

Still on the subject of my schooldays, at this point I can talk about
the *présidences*, rectangles of tender pink, pistachio green, or bluish
cardboard that we were given to represent good points in the little
coeducational boarding school on Rue Michel-Ange where I studied
sacred history and also learned a little arithmetic, grammar, plain
history, and geography, as well as the *leçons de choses*, indisputably the
most beautiful name one could give to the study of the natural
sciences, a window onto the outside world. By definition, they invested us with the dignity of good children as with a high office. Each
piece of cardboard we were given was a sort of pass admitting us to a
moral and civic empyrean. *Présidences.* Physically, they were thin
leaves of paper like the cylinder- or cornet-shaped wafers sold by the
vendors with revolving stands; symbolically, they were certificates
that genuinely conferred on us a presidency, the presidency of a
studious pupil luxuriously installed in a cloud and contemplating
from the top of this lookout post, where he is as serene as a guardian
angel, his less favored fellow students who continue to wear out the
bottoms of their poor pants on the hard wooden benches.

After the little coeducational boarding school on Rue Michel-
Ange, which was run by a widow, and before the crucial entrance into
the lycée, there was a school for boys situated on Rue Boileau run by a
priest. The poetic regime of the présidences was not in force here, and
at this point I became acquainted with the more rational system of
exemptions.

It may be that I am making a mistake when I say this: either I may be slightly anticipating the memories of my first years as a day student at Janson de Sailly, or I may be confusing the stories told me by my brothers, who were at that time pupils at Jean-Baptiste Say, with things I remember myself. Called familiarly *Jean-Bapt* and on notices *J.-B. Say*, the middle school on Rue Chardon-Lagache* was identified with its street because of their equally morose names. Today these names probably blend more or less in my head with the dilapidated building on Rue Boileau, as they do with the endless row of busts that embellished the facade of Janson, to form one harsh line of high walls the color of brick or plaster.

Compared to the présidences, which were solely qualitative, elementary distinctions merely intended to situate you in some way rather than weigh or measure you, the exemptions represented a perfected instrument corresponding to precise quantitative laws, since some bookkeeping was involved in this system. Not only did a prescribed number of these recompenses give one the right to have one's name written on the honors board, but there was a balance between good marks and penalties. In principle, one exemption could redeem you—or more accurately "exempt" you—from one hour of detention when you had been punished for some piece of negligence or some misdeed. Opposite the DEBIT column of the debts to be made good, payments for bad conduct, the exemptions theoretically constituted a CREDIT, the same way indulgences and prayers can shorten the stay of souls in purgatory.

In practice, things weren't always organized in keeping with this rigorous arithmetic, because after a certain number of hours of detention had been accumulated, it was no longer possible to redeem oneself of all of them, no matter how many exemptions one had. Thus, as soon as one had risen even a little on the ladder of quantity, this category became nebulous; the exemptions no longer represented anything more than the guarantee of a vague indulgence, and beyond this stage, which was also not very clearly determined, since no accounting was involved anymore, the one charm of the new system disintegrated along with what differentiated it from the summarily qualitative charm of the présidences.

However mongrel it was, for me the system of exemptions was a sign of progress toward something more structured, more manly, after the era of the coeducational school, which had been totally imbued

---

* *Chardon*: thistle; *gâcher*: spoil, waste.

with the hazy ringlets of little girls (and sometimes even of little boys like me, who would wear their hair in almost the same fashion as the girls for a long time), a phase that was painted in bland colors, like those pieces of cardboard that illustrate it today in the imagery of my memory. From a female world, where all distinctions were only a matter of nuances, I entered a more clearly circumscribed sphere, ruled by the earliest features of a masculine geometry, the same way the circle of a Twelfth-Night cake or a Sunday leg of lamb in a shape that is not as easy to divide up is ruled by the carving knife of the head of the family.

Changes of labels reflecting changes of ideas, archaic names, alphabetical signs that seemed like keys, misshapen words offering their enigmas: doors half-opened by certain elements of language or writing into a space where I was out of my depth. After their long eclipse, these phantasms reappeared when age had begun to ripen me. Then I found myself in a second childhood, under the flag of poetry acknowledged and practiced as such, and, imprisoned at the center of their wheel, I was once again dizzied by the revelation of so many perspectives. But in the end everything died down. The frenzied dance froze in place. As had happened during the period when a few principles were being inculcated in me—soon without the sweetening of présidences and exemptions—intended to make my mind capable of objective knowledge, everything gradually returned to a sculptural immobility, becoming a group of figures polished by wind and rain blending into the substance of a monument or allowing itself to be swallowed up by the emptiness of a museum room. Should the blame for this be laid on my disgust with these too easy miracles, which were neither controlled nor sanctioned, or on a certain weariness? The only obvious thing is that as their function was more clearly delimited and their meaning further refined, letters and words, once cabalistic stimuli to illumination, submissively took their places in line and became very nearly "dead letters."

Persephone

I have just moved. Abandoning the western quartiers where I was born and which, except for a few trips, I had never left until this last month—April 1942—(living on Rue Mignet in Auteuil until I was married; then in Boulogne, right next to the *Air Liquide*; once again in Auteuil: first with my mother, then near the Pont de Grenelle on Rue du Préfet Poubelle, inventor of the garbage can, which bears his name; finally, since September 1940, once again in Boulogne-Billancourt, where the catastrophe that had occurred at the Ripolin factories at an earlier time, making such an impression on me, recurred in the form of an aerial bombing raid), I decided, or rather, the course of events carved out a path for itself in such a way that it caused me to decide, to make a radical break with the unity of place in the theatrical drama I am constantly enacting (like everyone else, though he may not realize it) throughout what I will theatrically call "my life."

Now I live at 53 *bis* Quai des Grands-Augustins, a few steps from the Pont-Neuf and across from the Ile de la Cité. More urban than all my former residences (since this area abounds in people, transport vehicles, public buildings, cafés, restaurants, and shops, and since the moving rumble of the underground trains that go from Austerlitz to Orsay make the windows and floors tremble from time to time) my new residence also has a country feel to it. From my place on the fifth floor one can see some trees and the river—so that one almost has the sense that without taking the trouble to go down to it, one could get wet in it—and one can hear birds and bells ringing from different places until the coming of night, rather late at this time of the year, wraps an insulation of darkness and silence disturbed only at long intervals by the trains around this room where—with a lot of detours, returns, erasures, scratches, and various divagations—I am presently writing.

My change of home not only means I am now in a central quartier and no longer a peripheral one, but also that I am on the Left rather than the Right Bank. Until lately I had always been a tenant of the Right Bank. Preferring Montmartre to Montparnasse as a pleasure district; crossing the water only with the vague sense of taking some kind of trip; never imagining that the heart of Paris, after all, was not Place de l'Opéra or even Place de la Concorde but Notre Dame, hugged by the two banks; appreciating, not without a secret disdain, the beauty of the old neighborhoods situated across the Seine the same way a tourist who loves the picturesque goes into raptures planting himself in front of the artistic riches of the old part of the city though it never occurs to him—other than as an eccentric, even unseemly thing to do—that he might live elsewhere than in a hotel built in the domesticated neighborhoods, whose streets are perfectly straight, roadways wide, and sidewalks clean, and whose constructions are the most comfortable, the most civilized, and also the ugliest.

Yesterday evening, a few storm clouds hovered over the Seine in the glittering moonlight, looking exactly like the worst color prints sold in department stores. The statue of Henri IV, nicknamed the *Vert-Galant**—inscrutable sphinx, *diable Vauvert*,† or effigy of the Commandant—stood there countering with its paradoxical blackness the traditional question: "What color is Henri IV's white horse?" In a small waterside restaurant slightly below the level of the sidewalk (a detail indispensable to the perfection of the setting, to which I attach an importance that is certainly exaggerated, since a setting, whatever it may be, will never be more than make-believe), I was sitting with some friends who, although it was nearly ten at night, hadn't had dinner yet. Watching them eat their poor substitute for boiled chicken (an extra flat omelette and dreadfully anemic spaghetti), I contented myself with drinking muscadet, dreaming of Nantes, of its slave-traders' houses, of the whole romanticism of ports as though I were a traveler avid for exotic sensations rather than an authentic inhabitant of the neighborhood. It's true that I have just become a

* Lusty gentleman of the green woods.
† Devil of the wilds.

native, and I am still living buried up to my neck in the incredible feeling of being out of place inherent in the condition of "someone who has just moved," which is merely a replica of the condition (though this one is tragic) of "someone who has suffered a disaster," though on a comic level, where everything that doesn't contain blood and ruin must inevitably be situated.

When our normal gestures and words go drifting away, when our normal habits are all led astray, the whole of the outdoors seeming to conspire with malicious pleasure in confusing their paths, when all of our movable goods temporarily gather in heteroclite formations (like the preposterous associations of successive pictures in a single rebus, joined despite their disparateness by the link of contiguity), when the complete upheaval of objects that are usually submissive to us, and the imbroglio of relations that results from it, present us with a vaudevillelike image (translated into a language of misunderstandings and coincidences between the bedsheets) of what death may be, now that relations between people are finished, between the world and us: the *tu* is *tué* [the intimate you is killed], the diplomatic *vous* [formal you] keeps losing its way. At the very beginning of this species of catastrophe (which harms not only our relations with things but our bonds with other people, since such a confusion obliterates external reference marks as well as the fixed points in which the agreement between the *I*'s was daily ratified), the *us* melted like snow; confronting the *he* or the *they* of objects that are now menacing—or at least alien—all that is left is the *I*, enclosed in its alveole. But what is an *I*—a single, isolated *I*—without a *you*, without a *we*, without an *it* or *he* gravitating around and providing the material for a hierarchy whose summit he occupies, primary and singular person? Torn from the *I-you-he*, cut off from the *we-you-they* (not to mention the *I-you-SHE*) the *I*, in such obviously absurd conditions, is now scarcely more than a child who, wanting to count out loud to himself, all alone, recites *am-stram-gram pic-et-pic-et-colégram bour-et-bour-et-ratatam mistan-gram* and endlessly circles around in this combination of words and movements that has been reduced to a futile mumbling, since he has no friends there, at once on his side and against him, to justify such an enumeration and, by raising before him the breakwater of another person, to create limits that confer on him an existence as a separate body.

As I see it, then, these are the bases on which one could imagine a "philosophy of moving," dry stone foundations whose constituent parts, taken in their crude state and left autonomous, should (as in all self-respecting constructions of ideas) hold fast by their own gravity and have no need to be joined together by the artifice of any sort of cement. What I don't know, however, is whether the thought I'm describing here will be crushed in the egg by a bear's ill-timed paving stone,* to borrow a metaphor evoking the idea of a permanent foundation, in connection with what is essentially the element of panic contained in the small-scale end of the world of moving house?

So, I am struggling this evening with my pen and paper (the most physical of my writer's instruments, joined to my head by the middle term of my hand) in an apartment I rented more than two months ago now on Quai des Grands-Augustins.

A spacious room, a pretty view, air, calm, walls painted a uniform grayish color—not too light, not too dark—a desk on which I can open my notebook wide, set out matches, books, and an ashtray and plant my elbows firmly, sitting in a comfortable chair—all this is a great deal, but not nearly enough to create a favorable atmosphere. For this is not really an atmosphere. The things of the outside world have very little influence on my work, and it is all too convenient to challenge my surroundings to explain the poor or fruitful results of my efforts, when it appears beyond question that everything happens in my head and it alone is responsible, not only for what I extract from it directly but for what I have the illusion of taking from outside, if it is true that only my own thoughts are reflected back to me from things (in themselves indifferent) even when I believe they have emanated from the "atmosphere."

Whatever I may say about things (moved sometimes by the desire to incriminate them in order to disclaim responsibility myself, sometimes by the opposite desire to pull all the covers over to my side), there still exists a sort of balance between them and me. And it would be a very uncomfortable task to try to apportion what is due to each of these two terms, joined at the same time as they are opposed in the mysterious sequence of mental attitudes that people call "inspiration" as though to stress its analogy with a mechanism of the body that is itself an exchange.

Of the various places that inspire me (by that I mean, the sight of which feeds me, infuses me with invigorating air), among those that contribute to the charm of my new neighborhood, there is one I

* Reference to La Fontaine fable.

haven't yet visited: the Square du Vert-Galant. Beyond the Pont-Neuf, it occupies the whole tip of the Cité, the most fluvial part of the island, whose triangle thins down to the level of the water, bearing a mass of thick trees shading the benches where strollers come and sit. A spur of verdant nature plunging between the dirty waves of urban detritus, as though to quicken their flow or excise their wound. A wedge of paradise that seems to enjoy—in relation to the blocks of old or modern houses rising nearby—a privilege of extraterritoriality favoring the alimentary function of nurses as well as the confabulations of lovers.

So slow is my pedestrian stumble through the underbrush of sentences, where it might seem that I too am walking (but this would be a pure illusion, for I hardly feel I have a free enough hand, here, to abandon myself to the restful pleasure of strolling around), so uncertain is what I am obliged to call *mon travail* [my work]—in the full sense of the word, about which Bréal observes in his *Essai de Sémantique* that it is connected by a common etymological stock to the idea of the *cheval entravé* [hobbled horse]—that in the interval since I put the closing period on the preceding paragraph (a round dot, like the shape of the mouth when it makes the slight whistling sound that is our civilized substitute for a sigh), I have had time to walk around the Square du Vert-Galant once and to learn, during a dinner with a few other people in a building in Neuilly, a curious historiographical detail relating to this spot. Here, it seems, stood the funeral pyre of Jacques de Molay, the last grand master of the order of the Knights Templar, condemned as a relapsed heretic by Philippe le Bel and burned on the so-called Jews' Island, a piece of information I acquired from the MELE-PO volume of the *Nouveau Larousse illustré*, page 149, which I consulted because my faulty memory (or uncertain knowledge of history) made me hesitate between the two spellings *Molé* and *Molay*.

From the Square du Vert-Galant, when one has gone down one of the two symmetrical stairways connecting it to the roadway of the bridge (like the steps of a stairway on stage leading to the proscenium where the most thrilling parts of the action are taking place) one sees a series of grotesque masks, faces that are all quite different: some bearded, others smooth, but all grimacing and arranged in a line all along the bridge, a row of faces that seem to be the constituent parts of a choir about to lend a voice to mineral substance, vital spirits of granite, spontaneous fruits of the stone. All this is just a few steps away from a stout tree that leans to one side, supported by two metal props resting on the bridge, the tree from which Judas hanged himself, according to a tradition widespread in certain Russian circles in Paris, if I am to believe what I was told by a boy—himself a Slav and an actor—whom I met during my first visit to the square, where he sat reading and thinking on one of the benches (my only visit, so far, even though it is so close to my house). The top of the tree extends past the horizontal edge of the bridge, cutting across it obliquely, and one can quite easily imagine Judas or some other criminal discovering a gallows within hand's reach and deciding it was more expeditious to knot a rope around it than to jump over the parapet and throw himself into the river. It is nonetheless true that I don't believe what this boy told me and even wonder if he didn't simply invent the so-called tradition. Why am I so concerned about historical accuracy that I reject the idea that Judas should have hanged himself from a stout tree, though it is not far from the church of Notre Dame and is also already of a venerable age and grows on a piece of earth formerly called the Jews' Island? Such fastidiousness with respect to the conformity between events that must really have taken place in the visible world and what I read or hear about them may seem rather surprising in me, who pride myself on my feeling for poetry and also take an almost obsessive interest in the most trivial facts relating to the most private and least easily verified things that happen inside me. Such fastidious-ness: I write this and immediately see that I haven't even asked myself the question of whether Judas belongs to historicity or is situated on the same level as the characters in fairy tales; so strong, therefore, is the hold on me, still, of what I was taught when I was young, so far beyond any possibility of a critical examination are certain of the fictions represented to me in earlier times as truths, indisputable because of their sacred character!

I derived nothing, finally, from that walk in the Square du Vert-Galant. I continue to string sentences together. I alter them and lengthen them as though capriciously, unable to persuade myself to present the simplest thought without muffling it in useless uphol-stery. After mentioning my partial homonym Michel Bréal, after consulting the Larousse dictionary, after reporting part of what a certain person said to me, I am no farther along than I was before: the same screens separate me from reality, and it is as though these sentences in which I become so entangled—sometimes adding words to them, sometimes replacing one word by another—are the image of the difficult communication with reality into which I try to enter, paralyzed as I am by the most contradictory impulses and lingering in detour after detour, justified only by the irrational repugnance I feel at the idea of going straight to the point, however much I may want to establish the most direct contact between reality and myself. The Square du Vert-Galant still stands at the tip of the Ile de la Cité, with its burden of opaque green foliage, its ground that my feet have trodden. Even though I have seen it from inside, heard it (the rustling of its leaves), touched it, and breathed it, it remains separate and remote, as though I had never gone there. This is understandable where sight is concerned, the most abstract of our senses, the one that constructs all things as things belonging to the outside, projected at our far edges, mounted like a stage set. Up to a point this is understandable where hearing is concerned too, even though what strikes our ears is thereby already penetrating us, insinuating itself smoothly or erupting violently deep inside us. But feeling? smell? What one touches, what one sniffs? It is hardly believable that things experienced in this way should leave so few traces, and that after such a thorough penetration I should now find myself sitting at my desk, glancing from time to time through the panes of my shut window as though to assure myself that nature is still quite alive, that it hasn't vanished or petrified, while I, tied down to my task of writing, slave away at untangling its confused, sandy trails.

If, too often, I have the distressing feeling of being separated from nature by a multiplicity of screens, I think it is possible to see these screens reflected in my way of writing, even without observing what goes on within the four walls in which, geometrically, the secrecy of my study is physically manifested. In almost each sentence I construct, there sooner or later appears (either occurring right away or being introduced afterwards) a variable number of words that play a subsidiary role, whether they answer a need (more overpowering every day) for oratorical precautions or fully detailed reasoning, or simply act as fillers because of what I need for my rhythms (since it turns out that even though I am writing in prose, I can't help expressing my ideas in the form of periods, groups of always more or less cadenced propositions). Correctives to an assertion that seems risky to me even as I formulate it, or vulgar wads of sound with which I stuff my sentence—like a sick horse into which a dishonest dealer insufflates the appearances of health just before he tries to sell it—these words, which I'm determined should justify their existence with respect to both the logic of what is said and its balance (for I can't tolerate the presence of an addition that disturbs the harmony of the sentence any more than that of elements whose function as padding would be too obvious) may be recognized for what they are by anyone who will go to the trouble (or even those who won't) to examine the structure of my sentences a little more closely: recognized for parasitical formations proliferating in everything I write, masking the authentic thought rather than helping to express it more precisely, and revealing themselves to be, in the end, in some sense a series of screens coming between my ideas and me, obliterating them, smothering them under the weight of too great a mass of words, finally making them foreign to me or dissolving them completely, in the same way that too many accumulated sensations, if they remain within the bounds where I can savor them, far from reinforcing each other and representing so many openings on reality, are haloes of light dimming it or membranes separating me from it.

Whereas, despite my efforts to give them more life by plunging them into the flux of language, too many of my recent impressions are merely transient compounds, precipitated without structure and with uncertain color, I find relegated to the dust traps of my distant past certain experiences that nevertheless retain a surprising authority, compared to those completely fresh experiences that one might imagine—quite wrongly—to have a capacity for ascendancy in direct relation to their newness.

Of those experiences which have not been dulled by filth—time merely having covered them with a slight patina, softening their contours a little and completing their fusion in a shared "atmosphere"—a few, perhaps more involved than others in the bushy thickness of nature, seem capable of being brought together under the same heading. And the sign I have chosen to place them under is at once floral and subterranean, the name "Persephone," torn from its black earth and lifted to the sky of a chapter heading.

The acanthus leaf one copies in school when one is first struggling to
  handle a charcoal pencil,
the stem of a convolvulus or other climbing plant,
the helicoid inscribed on a snail shell,
the windings of the small and large intestines,
the sandy coil excreted by an earthworm,
the childish curl of hair enchased onto a medallion,

the foul simulacrum that a slight pressure of the fingers draws from a
    "père-la-colique,"
the marbling on the edges of certain bound books,
the ironwork with "modern-style" curves at the metro entrances,
the intertwining of the embroidered monograms on sheets and pil-
    lowcases,
the spit curl pasted to the grease on the cheekbone of a prostitute in
    the old days at the Casque d'Or,
the thin dark braid of steel rope and the thick blond weave of ship's
    rope,
the circumvolutions of the brain, which can be seen when one sits
    down to eat a sheep's brain,
the corkscrewing of a grapevine, an image of what one will see later,
    after the juice is bottled—the corkscrew (itself prefiguring the
    endless spiral of drunkenness),
the flow of blood,
the conch of an ear,
the windings of a path,
every variety of festoon, volute, scroll, garland, coil, arabesque,
the spur (which for the sake of the argument I will imagine to be
    spiraled) of a two-handed sword,
the twist of a ram's horn,
all of this seems to me latent in the name of "Persephone," awaiting
    only an imperceptible trip to be released, like the ribbon of steel
    tightly doubled over among the cogs of a clockworks or the coil
    spring in the box with the closed lid from which the hairy-bearded
    devil has not yet come out.

Essentially, then, this is a *spiraled* name—or more broadly, a *curved*
name, but one whose gentleness must not be confused with the
inevitably soothing nature of blunt things, since—quite the contrary—its piercing and penetrating quality is attested to by the
comparison one can make between its component syllables and those
that officially identify the insect known as the *perce-oreille*.* For not
only do Persephone and *perce-oreille* both start with the same allusion
to the idea of "piercing" (more doubtful in Persephone, because of the
s, which gives it such an undulating, grassy quality, makes it so
chimerical, so transient, that one would be tempted to effect an easy

* Earwig, lit. "ear-piercer."

metathesis and call her *Fée Personne* [Fairy Person]), but both of them end with a reference to hearing, in the insect expressly through the articulation of the word *oreille* (that is, the organ through which auditory sensations enter us) and, in the goddess, less directly by means of the suffix *-phone*, which we also find in *téléphone* as well as *gramophone*, an instrument for which this very euphonic termination, which defines it marvelously as a musical mechanism, is even more correctly appropriate than for the preceding word.

The insect whose main job is to feed by gnawing the insides of the stones of fruit and who sometimes, they say, also perforates the human tympanum with its pincers, has in common with Demeter's daughter the fact that it, too, plunges into a subterranean kingdom: the deep country of hearing, whose description belongs more in the realm of geology than any other natural science, not only because of the cartilaginous cavern of its organ but because of its relation to grottoes, gulfs, and all other kinds of pockets that form in the earth's crust and because of their emptiness turn into resonating boxes for the slightest noises.

Just as one can become uneasy at the idea of the tympanum, that fragile membrane, in danger of being perforated by the minuscule pincers of an insect—if indeed it hasn't already been broken by an overly violent noise—one can also legitimately fear for the safety of the vocal cords, which can break in a moment when one cries out too loudly, for example, or when, having subjected them to too great a tension (as a result of a fit of anger or sorrow, or simply participation in a game where the main thing was the pure pleasure of bawling), one *casse la voix* [lit. "breaks one's voice"]. An accident against which my mother would sometimes warn me, whether she was really afraid it would happen to me, or—and this seemed more likely to me—she was using this danger to scare me into being quiet for a while. Arising from Persephone and the earwig, who are united by a cement of relations hardened—in full brightness—by their names, a strong suture is thus joined between the throat and the tympanum, both objects of a similar fear of harm, quite outside the fact that they belong to the same cavernous kingdom. And finally, caverns become the geometrical place where they all come together—the chthonian divinity, the stone-piercing insect, the matrix where the voice forms, the drum struck by every noise with its stick of vibrating air; caverns: dark systems of pipes plunging into the most secret parts of our being in order to conduct to the completely bare cavity of our mental space the gusts of wind—of variable temperature, consistency, and pleasantness—propagated in long horizontal waves after having risen straight up from the fermentations of the outside.

So that on the one hand there is the outside; on the other, the inside; between them, the cavern.

These days when people describe a voice as "cavernous," they mean it is low and deep, even a little too much so. For example, a *basse-taille* [basso cantante, singing bass, but *taille*: cut] compared to a *basse chantante* [also basso cantante], with its higher register and more supple song, whereas that of the *basse-taille* would seem more suited in its roughness, shaped as it is with blows from an ax, to the voice of a stone cutter, a carver of funerary marbles, a miner with his pick, a gravedigger, a well sinker and (to refer to a social situation which is not, strictly speaking, a job) to a monk, who with heavy steps pursues his slow journey down the covered arcades and down the years toward his spiritual quarry.

An excellent specimen of this *basse-taille*—with which the idea is associated, like a stone around one's neck, of steps one fashions in the ground, as if going down to the cellar or, one foot at a time, to a level a certain number of yards below sea level—is the dentist whose office was situated on Rue d'Auteuil and who used to come to the house to sing with my father—whereas we went to him not for exercises of the throat but for the care of our teeth—since his voice was so deep and so powerful that it shook the windowpanes (as when a truck went by filled with barrels or paving stones) and every time this phenomenon occurred, the quaking, imitated by my own eardrums, was unfailingly registered in me by the blossoming of a shiver of terror. When he sang, this middle-aged man—very tall, balding, white-haired, with somber eyes and a serious expression whenever I saw him—opened the sort of mouth it is customary to compare in size to an oven. Had he perhaps gotten into the habit of exhibiting such a lair (the den of a primitive man, a troglodyte, or an ogre) because of leaning over the wide open mouths of his clients? Whatever the case, this detail was hardly likely to reassure me. Today, when I can view the thing more lightly, I ask myself whether it would be pleasing or in excessively bad taste to imply that there could exist a relation between the fact that this person concerned himself professionally with *hollow* teeth (which he filled) and the extremely heavy and cavernous nature of certain notes that issued from the vast natural resonating box that served as his *violon d'Ingres* [hobby, lit. "Ingres's violin"].

The song that issues from the mouth after crossing the white barrier of the teeth, though it is born in the throat and follows the same path as speech, is nevertheless different from speech, not only because of its melodious nature but because it seems to us to come from much farther away. In fact, it seems to rise from the very cavity of the chest and often from the nethermost depths of the entrails, charged with vibrations that are merely the exhalations with which it has become impregnated during its latency period in this subterranean world. Whether it is the voice of an Arab singer—or, even better, Andalusian—which seems to clear a passage for itself through the organs by drilling the canal of a narrow wound so penetrating that the deepest muscles are affected; or whether it is the voice of an opera singer, hewn from the middle of a rock or shaped from the most supple steel, in the case of a male singer, or emerging from the warm earth of a greenhouse or drawn out into a brittle filament of glass, in the case of the female. Whether it is the most vulgar voice, issuing from the most ordinary sort of person in the most insipid love song or the most trivial ditty, the singing voice compared to the speaking voice is a mystery.

Mystery—if for the sake of the argument we wish at all costs to give features to what by definition has none—can be represented as a border, a fringe encircling the object, isolating it at the same time as it emphasizes its presence, masking it at the same time as it qualifies it, inserting it into a motley of things without identifiable connections or causes at the same time that the particular color with which it tints the object extracts it from the marshy bottom where most things are jumbled together. Compared with ordinary elocution, musical elocution seems to be endowed with a similar iridescence, a fairy cloak that is the sign of a connivance between what could seem to be merely a human voice and the rhythms of fauna and flora, even those of the mineral kingdom where every impulsive motion is transcribed into a fixed form. And when we move on from spoken language—itself fairly enigmatic, since thought only becomes real the moment it is formulated, whether externally or not—to sung language, we come face to face with an enigma of the second degree, since, although we are closer in one sense to the structures of the body (of which each note emitted seems to be the direct fruit) and, therefore, apparently more sure of standing on firm ground, we find we are grappling with the ineffable, the melodic line presenting itself as the expression, in an idiom of pure sound, of what could not be said in words. So that with greater reason when the source of the song, instead of being a human mouth (that is, an organ we are more or less familiar with), is a mechanical device adding to what is already strange in musical speech the surprise of its being reproduced, one finds oneself confronting an almost pure mystery.

Of the various objects among my parents' possessions when they lived on Rue Michel-Ange, one of the most consistently interesting to me as a child was the cylinder gramophone my father would often use, on Sundays or free evenings, to arrange a concert for himself or record something.

I owned a phonograph too: a machine produced, I think, by Pathé, a company that for a long time—and well before it became primarily a movie company—was the only French manufacturer of any repute of this kind of machine. My modest-sized phonograph, which I must have received on some New Year or other, was much less sophisticated than my father's. Not only was it not equipped to make recordings but it could only be used for small- or medium-sized cylinders, not big ones like the ones that could be heard on the other gramophone, which came with strange accessories that crowded some of the cupboards of the house along with the vast series of rolls (as we called the cylinders) that my father had recorded himself and others of virgin wax that were waiting to be recorded.

When one wanted to listen to a medium-sized roll on the *junior* machine that I was free to use as I liked, one had to increase the gauge of the driving cylinder. This was done with the help of a metal handle fitted over the latter, which could receive only the smallest cylinders so long as its diameters had not been increased in the proper proportions. Connected to the horn by a short rubber tube similar to the joints of gas stoves and whose color verged on brick red, was a sound box of the type commonly called sapphire—a small round box whose bottom, a thin sheet of mica or a similar material, bore the minuscule, hard appendix intended to transmit to this sensitive wall the vibrations inscribed in the wax cylinder—a sound box that, when it was taken off, could be entirely contained in the palm of one hand, and transformed into waves of sound, the oscillations communicated to it by the roll, all of whose surface appeared marked (in a helicoid too tight for one to be able to see it as anything but thin stripes very close to one another) by the furrow of varying depth carved by the original waves when the *Etablissements Pathé Frères* had recorded the tune from a grand opera, comic opera, or operetta or some other piece of music or recitation selected for a commercial recording.

As for the driving cylinder—arranged horizontally, so that if you discounted the scale, it looked like a steamroller immobilized and suspended a few inches above the ground—a small number of very simple visible gears connected it to a clockworks. The uniformity of its speed of rotation, indispensable to correct audition, was ensured by a regulator composed essentially of three or four small lead weights arranged either as the three points of an imaginary equilateral triangle or opposing each other two by two like the ends of the branches of a cross or the cardinal points of a compass—triangle, cross, or compass that would be pierced in the middle by the line shaft on which the device was mounted. Attached by soldering or some other means to the median part of the same number of metal plates a few centimeters long and flexible enough to allow for a spring effect, the lead weights were joined to the line shaft by these plates, whose ends were screwed to two moving rings capable of sliding along the shaft in a double motion that made them come together again (like an object and its reflection, when one moves the object close to a polished surface and the image appears to come closer too, moving through the imaginary space opened behind the mirror), the respective paths of the two rings starting from two points situated symmetrically with relation to the vertical plane in which, when the machine was running, the wheel that was formed of all the weights revolved.

In their resting position, these heavy little weights were quite close to the shaft, the metal plates then lying almost parallel to the latter and the two rings remaining at the farthest point of their separation. But when the mechanism started up, and as the speed increased, one saw the lead weights, subjected to the more and more pronounced action of the centrifugal force, gradually come away from the shaft, while the elastic plates were subjected to the effect of traction in their middles, which distanced them in turn from the shaft over a fairly large portion of their length and at the same time reduced the original separation of the two rings. Seen as a whole, therefore, the system tightened and expanded at the same time, becoming narrower between its poles (represented by the two rings) as it increased at its periphery (the semitransparent grayish band into which the lead weights, at first visible as so many autonomous solids, little by little melted, to the observing eye). A change of appearance that was accompanied by the muffled purring of the functioning of the clockworks, sometimes joined by the nervous noise of a sudden jolt in the action of the spring.

Besides the pleasure I derived from actually listening to the rolls, a very distinct part of my enjoyment, when I operated my phonograph, consisted in watching the visible changes that the regulating system underwent when the mechanism was started up or stopped. To see these weights, which I knew for a fact were isolated individuals, first start to turn, slowly enough, during a very short time, so that my eye could follow their motion, then faster, so that I had the impression, not of three or four but a multiplicity of weights, and finally, the speed having reached its upper limit, to see them change into a sort of single body of circular form and blurred appearance, almost immaterial; to see them, inversely, when I stopped the mechanism, leave this nebulous state and condense after a short time into weights first spinning, then immobile, having recovered their existence as distinctly circumscribed and enumerable objects, to be present, as at a show, at this succession of metamorphoses, was for me as great an entertainment— or nearly as great—as to listen to the sounds that the sound box extracted from the black, more or less scratchy wax of the rolls.

A very different but equally lively pleasure was the one I felt in handling these cylinders. First withdrawing one from the jacket of grayish brown cardboard in which it was put away, plunging my hand inside it and spreading my fingers in such a way as to take it out of its box, holding it only by this pressure against its inner wall, my fingernails and the outer sides of my fingers feeling, then, the contact of the circular ribs, four or five for its whole breadth, with which the inside of the roll was equipped so that it wouldn't slide once it was placed on the driving cylinder, feeling also the delicate plush with which the interior of the box was lined and listening to the very slight squeaking produced by rubbing the striated surface of the roll against this soft padding. Then adjusting it on the driving cylinder, forcing it a little (which was necessary, since the roll was kept in place the cylinder only by the adherence of its inner surface to the latter's outer surface) but not too much (since to push it too far would have been dangerous for the roll, which might have broken to pieces). Finally, examining everything before starting up the machine to see if it was all in order and to enjoy the sight of the coinciding of the outer edge of the roll and the flat side section of the cylinder, or of the slight protuberance of one over the other (because the rolls, theoretically identical within one size, were not all, in fact, of strictly equal dimensions: sometimes a little smaller, so that the driving cylinder would be a few millimeters short; sometimes a little larger, which led to the opposite result and allowed the driving cylinder to reach far enough so that, on its free side—the side on which the adjustment was effected—it protruded slightly).

Even though in principle, the only way to handle the roll without damaging it was to put one's hand inside it or hold it by one's fingertips at the outer edges, using both hands or one hand widely extended, one other attraction was the mild tickling—or caress—of the ridges when one's hand chanced to graze the surface of the roll. I still have such an exact memory of all these joys, which I savored as a connoisseur, that (when I think about it with some attention) the fingers of my right hand, for example, can still feel the precise degree of resistance of the key to the clockworks when I wound it up and the effort they had to make to overcome this resistance, until the impossibility of winding any further told me the spring was as tight as it could be and until the key reached its final stopping point after my attempt—which for a moment might seem to succeed, but in the end proved to be futile—to make the tension of the spring advance one more notch.

The familiar knowledge I had of this phonograph, which I both observed and manipulated, was very different from my relationship with my father's, which was marked by a sense of ceremony. I'm quite sure that never in my whole life, unless it was purely by chance, almost by accident, did I touch that *graphophone*, which for me must have represented the most precious thing in the house, besides the beautifully bound books in the library.

Graphophone was its name. Not a corruption of "gramophone" (the result of its having taken one of those wrong turns that caused certain words to reach me disfigured), but its authentic name, the specific appellation given it by the company that had manufactured it, that is, the Edison Company (if indeed the prestige attached to the figure of the famous American engineer is not tempting me against my will, to adjust the real facts by attributing as eponym to a company that produced appliances which, during the period I'm speaking of, had only half emerged from their heroic age of scientific inventions, the name of the man who was one of the main pioneers in the practical application of electricity). The word *Graphophone* was inscribed, probably along with the name of the firm—decorating the simulated folds of a banderole like an emblematic figure—either directly on the light wood case in which the clockworks of the mechanism was enclosed or on the cover of the same material intended to protect its other organs when it was not in use, the case being a little less high than it was wide, the cover somewhat resembling, because of its volume and its shape, that of a typewriter dating a certain number of years back. Graphophone: a name very distinct from "gramophone" and which I would be inclined to contrast to it as being applied exclusively to the old cylinder players, whereas the words "gramophone" and "phonograph" designated record players with or without horns. Graphophone, which I never pronounced any other way but this— *grafôfône*—with the two *o*'s very closed, as though to associate the musical mechanism my father owned with either the animals of the *faune* [fauna] or the satyrs or goat-footed beings that peopled the woods in ancient times.

I can't really give an exact description of this graphophone. Not because I didn't often study it, but because I never handled it; and also because of the feeling of wonder that befuddled my mind every time my father used it. Believing from the very outset that it was in some sense a miraculous instrument, defying by definition any sort of analysis, I never seriously asked myself exactly how it functioned. What was undoubtedly most remarkable about it was the fact that it assumed two distinct forms, depending on whether one used it to plow the sounds into the depths of the wax or to make them rise up again—ripe grain or resuscitated cadavers—from the long trench that had been thus hollowed.

When my father wanted to record a specimen of the vocal or instrumental talents of some member of the family or friend (sometimes a professional performer, sometimes an amateur musician), he had to take a number of attachments from inside or the top of the cupboards where they were kept.

First of all a large parallelepipedal stand of wood covered with red plush that my father placed on a pedestal table or some other sort of table and on which he set up the graphophone, which was thereby raised to the proper height for the performer (at least in the case of a performance on the violin, or a song for which the singer had to stand up).

Next, a long cone made of hard, shiny cardboard of a slightly greenish gray color, rather like a pointed magician's hat in size and shape, which must have been substituted, during the recording, for the sort of fragment of hunting horn or outsized bugle that usually served as a horn. Near its bell-mouthed orifice, this cone was attached to a strong, partly curved bar of metal that passed above the apparatus as a whole and was fixed to the back side of the case containing the mechanism by two metal brackets placed one above the other about a hand's-length apart, each provided with a large eyelet through which the rectilinear part of the bar was fitted. Suspended thus (in a manner not unlike the way curtains are hung over certain kinds of children's cots, with a bar running from the bottom of the cot and ending in a coil to which the muslin is attached), the cardboard cone—set at a perceptible horizontal for this use—was equipped at the mouth with a special sound box: not the simpleminded looking round box, with a golden rooster stamped on its upper face and bearing a sapphire on its transparent bottom (which would describe the Pathé sound boxes) but a much smaller and flatter capsule almost entirely of metal (whereas except for its sensitive diaphragm, the other sound box was made of a black material similar to ebonite) and also provided with a kind of steel stiletto. The role of this stiletto (nickel plated, I think, like the rest of the capsule, which made the whole thing look like an instrument of a delicate sort of cruelty) was to engrave, in the wax of the rolls that looked like solidified milky coffee (whereas the commercial ones were black), the sound vibrations received by the magician's hat, which was supported—in addition to being suspended—by a device I never really observed in detail and of which I can only say that it ensured the movement of the sound box parallel to the axis of the roll while the latter was turning, a twofold motion whose result was to trace that long, tight helicoid in the wax, transcribing the succession of sounds. During the operation, there formed on the surface of the roll a bit of blond dust that my father would remove afterwards with a chamois or small rag. I loved the smell of that wax dust.

When it was a matter of simply listening to the cylinders, the great magician's hat and its cumbersome suspension system disappeared, replaced by an honest metal horn pointed—for technical reasons I know nothing about—in the opposite direction from the one in which it was proper to point the cardboard cone. Rather like a machine that can be made to run backwards by turning some of its parts around; rather as though, given the ideal couple of opposites formed by, on the one hand, the inscription of the sounds in wax, and on the other, the later restitution of these same sounds from the shallower and deeper marks containing them *in posse*, one only had to reverse the steam to go from one to the other of these two operations.

The reproducing horn, triumphantly open at one end, and whose shining surface (a true cuirassier's cuirasse . . .) seemed, because of its brightness, to be an optical equivalent of the sounds that gushed from it, narrowed little by little until at the other end it was no more than a dark tube, like the tight neck (or bottleneck) that is often the only way a semblance of common measure is established between the open air and the immured atmosphere of an underground cave. This narrow, black part of the horn drew one's attention most of all, as though one's curious gaze had first collected broadly in its bell mouth and then been imperceptibly pooled and guided toward that central well, which, one knew, led into the darkness of the sound box.

For a fairly long time—was it the mark left by an illusion I had believed in as being positively real before I was initiated into the mysteries of recording?—it was impossible for me to listen to a sung tune, such as a duet, reproduced on the phonograph, without immediately picturing to myself the two voices that alternated and sometimes mingled as issuing from two minuscule creatures standing in that dark corridor, small personages who seemed to me as lost in space as real singers observed through the large end of a pair of opera glasses from the very back of a theater in the highest tiers, when they look like automatons who have stepped out of the prompter's box, ridiculously small in relation to the vast architectural setting of the stage. Today, it seems indisputably correct to me to compare the fictional figurines I imagined placed in the dark, constricted part of the horn to flesh-and-blood actors seen from the upper balcony or "gods" of a theater and contrasting, as much by their remoteness as by their absolutely paltry size, to the considerable mass of the great chandelier suspended almost at eye level. I see, in fact, that the bell mouth of the horn can correspond quite well not only to the idea of reversed opera glasses (with the spectator placed, like the auditor, in the spot where the diameter is the greatest and the spectacle, like the music forming in the sound box, in the spot where it is the smallest), but also to the image of a theater hall such as it is inscribed on our eyes in keeping with the rules of perspective, with the stage, because it is so far away, seeming very small compared to the spacious area in which we are sitting. I don't believe, however, that such observations could have played a part in giving birth to this illusion or that they could have occurred except after the fact. I would be much more inclined to think that the cause of this stubborn illusion is the image of the throat, in the bottom of which, when one puts out one's tongue and says *ahhh* . . . (as one is asked to do by the specialist armed with the silver spoon conducting the examination), the uvula can be seen hanging down like a stalactite of flesh whose mobility makes it look like a living animal. The throat: the natural organ of speech, just as that manufactured object—the horn of the phonograph—is the reproducer of human voices and other sounds. The uvula, a little muscular tongue that I find it hard to think of, even now, without those two small personages coming and attaching themselves to it, the two figurines I used to situate in the bottom of the phonograph horn, unable to conceive of the latter in any other way than inhabited by an animate principle. Just as a violin has its *âme* [sound-post, lit. "soul"], a little stick fixed in place between the two walls of the resonating chamber whose exact position, they say, is part of the secret of its quality, the throat possesses its own, which is none other than the uvula; and the phonograph horn has this pair of figurines, the veritable animating soul of the song, whose presence must be invoked, since the action of the sensitive diaphragm of the sound box hardly seems enough to explain the burgeoning of all those vocal notes.

Except for this pair of fictitious homunculi—figures so very daintily fashioned by my mind—the most delicate of all the parts of the machine was obviously the *diaphragme* [sound-box, the *g* being pronounced]. For me, the very name of this part—the gramophone's heart or brain—designate it as fragile in the highest degree and more likely to break into pieces than any other part. I have some trouble, in fact, picturing the word *diaphragme* without conceiving of it as being closely related etymologically to *fragment*, a notion that may seem irrefutably demonstrated by the existence of one and the same compact block of sounds in both these substantives.

Without the cause having anything to do with the well-oiled mechanism that transmitted its more or less silent movement to the roll-bearing cylinder by way of a thin strap, from which the ascending and descending branches passed through two small parallel slits in the upper face of the box in which the clockworks was enclosed, a supple band of tawny copper activating a drum whose diameter was perceptibly less than that of the cylinder and mounted on the same axis, the stream of music that welled up from the scores in the roll was sometimes interrupted by brief cracklings, coming singly or in a series and caused by the sudden jolts imprinted on the point of the sound box by the tiny scratches accidentally marked in the wax after the roll had been repeatedly used.

It wasn't the sizzling noises the telephone sometimes makes; it wasn't the hissing of damp wood as it burns or the crunching of dry leaves trampled underfoot. Because of its slightly fatty quality, it was more like a tongue smacking or perhaps a whip cracking lightly (the sort of whip children use to spin their tops) but distinctly deeper and thicker, and also offering a whole range of variations, in the same way that when one weapon is fired, with theoretically identical projectiles, not all the detonations are the same, some sharper or louder, others slower or more muffled, because of small differences either in loading or in the caliber by which one cartridge is distinguished from another, however homogeneous their series may be, or for any other reason that could be classified under the negative label of the unforeseen—as though under the heading MISCELLANEOUS in a daily accounts notebook.

This noise—which truly gave the impression of a fracture or the fragmentation of some kind of mineral substance—interrupted the tranquil flow of time. If it had been more violent, it would have caused the start of surprise provoked by a gunshot. Too weak to make one start, it was nevertheless perceived with enough intensity so that the flow of things seemed suspended by it, as was that of the melody. It was an authentic explosion (though on a reduced scale), since this gap tore from the steady guideline that was the uniform ribbon of duration the thing that struck one's hearing in this way and for a split second shattered the temporal framework that usually surrounded it, while one's awareness of the song one was following within oneself volatilized, melted by this untimely noise or breach of continuity. One was astonished, listening to it, that the sound box didn't break into pieces or at the very least atrophy. In the same way, it might seem strange that the disturbing pulsions of air did not eventually burst the windowpanes in all the confined places where the dentist with the cavernous voice chanced to appear, that giant whose size so exactly matched the volume of his singing.

A tempest in a teapot (or even in a cup for mixing watercolors), a seismic tremor racking the thickness of a crystal lens, that pocket-sized end of the world was entirely expressed by the syllable *fragm*, identical in both *diaphragme* and *fragment*, like a flake of rock that one can rediscover in exactly the same form in rocks whose structures are different but whose main elements remain constant from one to the next. This isn't true of all sequences of words interconnected in this way: *austère*, for example, whose austerity seems so obvious that one can also see it, in part, in a word like *stère de bois* [stere, or cubic meter, of wood], no longer has anything austere about it in the Battle of Austerlitz or Austerlitz station. The same is true of the word used vulgarly for a man's sex, which no one would think of seeing either in *épine* [thorn] or in the Latin equivalent of Persephone, *Proserpine.*

Having nothing in common with the stream of harmony that the sound box and horn helped propagate by digging a bed reaching from the acoustic layers hidden in the depths of the wax all the way to the great sea of the ear, these unexpected cracklings, though their origins were known and ascribed to the physical condition of the rolls, were quite disconcerting. Due to shocks whose immediate receiver was the sapphire (as it was the receiver of the smaller and more orderly tremors that gave rise to the current of sound) they certainly were to me; but they tended to seem like sudden starts of surprise for which the body of the sound box itself had become the theater, drawing them from its bowels rather than receiving them from outside, thus acting as a separate cause of disturbance rather than as a passive instrument, amenable to solicitations from outside. What exploded in the sound box and seemed bound to split its transparent wall was therefore an autochthonous thunder, not simply an echo; a din that was the interior fulguration of a fragment of matter here present, not a rumbling sound reverberating from cloud to cloud and coming to us from a distant place; a molecular sort of fire from heaven, unlike a noise occurring somewhere offstage, very different from the thunder about which my nurse, trying to soothe me in my fright, said to me—at a time too distant for me to have any other access to it except by way of the stories that were told me about it—that its great voice was only the racket of the "little angels bowling," making the celestial vault tremble the way children playing shake the ceiling of the apartment immediately below the one where they live.

If I try to think which word might best sum up the convergence I see between what certain sounds meant to me and the idea that I have today about mineral matter as the concrete representation of what is most inexorably closed in the external world, the first word that comes to mind is "anfractuosity."

This word conveys all the roughness, or all the nicks, that not only affected the surface of the wax when the rolls had deteriorated but destroyed the integrity of that emanation so difficult to describe, that emanation which was, as it happened, music, whose amphibian nature could be compared to that attributed for so many centuries to waves or corpuscles of light, conceived as intermediaries between matter and spirit. Above all, "anfractuosity" conveys the idea of a fault or crack in a rock or boulder, and this idea takes us back to the image of lightning, since bolts of lightning often appear in the same form, as cracks, not to mention the fact that when they descend on an object they are capable of splitting or cracking it. Lastly, in "anfractuosity" we hear a little of the unpleasant noise that had nothing in common with the noises normally reproduced, but exploded like the cry of the wax or the sound box itself. The word "anfractuosity"—as it is situated in my vocabulary—therefore contains a paradox, since here I am using it to describe not only the roughness and impenetrable hardness of rock but also the auricular breach through which, I would now like to think, I was penetrated by the mineral world, that is, by what seems to me most irreducible and alien.

Apart from the wax of the rolls, apart from the wood of the machine's cover and the chest containing the bottom (or the simple rectangular piece of wood, in the case of my phonograph), apart from the special materials of the components of the sound box (the sapphire of the point, the translucent mica—or other substance—of the diaphragm, the black material of the casing), the many parts so skilfully coordinated to produce those complex machines—my own phonograph and my father's graphophone—were made of metal. Exactly what kind of metal I don't know; but I do know they were made of *metal*, an inanimate substance different enough from everything to do with stone that I'm quite sure I never clearly realized that metals, like pebbles, millstone grit, plaster, rocks and crystals, belonged to the mineral kingdom.

Just as the word *bristol*—which seems to me typically British, perhaps because I connect it, wrongly or rightly, with the city of Bristol—seems so synonymous with the flexible cardboard it designates that as one pronounces it one seems to hear the very special noise made, for example, by a postcard when, holding it between the fingers of both hands, one bends it alternately in one direction and then in the other so that the air is suddenly whipped at the moment when the bending changes direction, the word *métal*, articulated over three consonants supported by two very clear vowels stripped of every trace of gangue as if they had just an instant before been purified by fusion in a crucible, seem to me completely suitable for signifying these special substances which, along with gems, constitute a sort of aristocracy in the mass of the inorganic.

The things in the New Year's Day catalogues that my brothers and I leafed through so feverishly as soon as they arrived in the house— examining, comparing, noting, checking off in blue and red pencil the toys that were not too expensive and seemed the most enticing from their brief descriptions—were often made of metal. That was all it said. No indication of exactly which metal. The reference to metal, however vague it might have been, was enough for me, since at that time I wasn't at all concerned about scientific precision. Besides, it didn't occur to me that the generic word metal could include gold, silver, platinum, iron, and all the many other common or precious elements distinguished in mineral chemistry from the so-called met-alloid substances (a deceptive appellation, as it happens, since they haven't the remotest resemblance to metals). For me, metal was just as particular a substance as, for instance, zinc or tin, and I would have been very surprised to learn that this word applied to a family that is actually quite varied, capable of being separated into many different species whose shared characteristics are not always clearly apparent. Metal was something white and shiny like silver, though it wasn't silver; something fixed, defined once and for all, certainly related to other similarly colorless and glimmering metals, but with no more relation to gold or copper (too red and too yellow) than to the dull gray substance known as lead.

Besides metal as such, there was, of course, Britannia metal. But even though the addition of a qualifier might rather naturally lead me to think that metal was capable of offering some variety at least—the sort of variety defined by this precise designation, which was attribu-table to the need to show that here was a substance different from the first, if only because of its origin—even though I could have guessed that this metal, capable of such variation, was not, as I had believed, a specific substance, what was probably needed to dissipate this false notion by making me see certain complications in the world of metals was a word more suited than Britannia metal to expressing the hybrid nature of alloys.

It wasn't bronze, or brass (both rigid in a way that was too ancient), or the mixture curiously known as *maillechort* [German silver] (in which there was a slight taste of metal, due perhaps to the fact that a hissing immediately followed the palatalization, forcing the tongue to contort somewhat?). It wasn't silver-gilt either (the result of the strictly logical marriage of gold and silver, nobler metals than all the others and occupying a hierarchical position intermediate between the latter two: "silver-gilt metal" coming below "gold medal" but above "silver medal," just as a lieutenant colonel, with his mixture of gold and silver stripes, is inferior to a colonel but superior to a major).

It wasn't any of those words, not even the last, though I had no doubt it was a mixture, that gave me access to what was disturbing in the idea of an alloy, that intimate union of two or more solids that must have been previously fused in such a way that they could penetrate each other completely, each irradiate the other until they were one, as would seem possible only for liquids such as water and wine or milk and coffee. I am tempted to decide that what allowed me to accept such an idea—at first rather bewildering—was the word *laiton* [brass], precisely because it contains an image, wrapped in a sound at once heavy and light, of a kind of *lait* [milk] (almost *laitance* [grout]) that seems to be of a metallic nature rather than of animal origin.

If in *bronze* I always hear bells tolling and in *airain* [brass] helmets and weapons clashing, I immediately see in *laiton* a poor, shabby substance like the *fer-blanc du ferblantier* [tinsmith's tinplate] or the kind of metal *bidons de laitier* [milk cans] are made of. The mediocre result of an organic casting that promised better when it began and whose constituent parts, it seemed fair to anticipate, would want to solidify into a richer alloy (worthy of the living alchemical treasures implied by the fact that the word *lait* was attached to a subject of the metal kingdom).

Yet it is true that in *laiton*, a bastard name, the monosyllable *lait* is depreciated by an ending that gives it the prosaic quality inherent in a number of other things whose names end in *ton*. Even without drawing on the vocabulary of colloquial language, such as *miroton* [beef hash with onions] and *capiston* [captain], we have only to leaf through a rhyming dictionary to find many examples of words that end on that miserable note: the *béton* [concrete] used to build shelters, the *bouton* [button] for doing up one's trousers, the *coton* from which caps are woven, the *molleton* [soft, thick flannel] of clothes worn around the house, the *ponton* [pontoon] tied up at water's edge by damp-rotted ropes, the *toton* [teetotum, a small top inscribed with letters] that is the very image of the characterless person at the mercy of every external impetus and turning, like a weathervane except that he doesn't creak, before every passing breeze.

But now, suddenly—and I'm not even talking about the indecisive, malleable quality pervasive in me (whence, perhaps, my fascination, most of the time, with words that have two aspects)—I realize that in one specific respect I am somewhat like that sort of person. I, too, revolve like a weathervane, or rather like a maddened compass whose needle is attracted by the changing north of all kinds of words one after another, words that guide me (or lead me astray) in this interior journey whose milestones are childhood memories. Then why do I always hesitate at the idea of diving straight in, why have I continued to spin around this way, instead of hurling myself unequivocably into the lake whose stagnant waters attract me so, which would be the only way of escaping the sterile contemplation of a motionless Narcissus assuming different poses as he watches things come toward him, watching himself assume poses? A contemplation that will only end when I make a single bound into the midst of the waters and merge at once with the image that earlier I insisted on observing curiously, rejecting a healthy, virile plunge in favor of aesthetic daydreaming scarcely interrupted by distracted meanderings whose only result was to lead me from one spot to another on the bank.

But I have to admit that this is a bad metaphor. Sometimes a compass, sometimes a Narcissus, in the end I don't know which subterfuge to use to get myself out of this, having first compared myself to something essentially uncertain and mobile, then to a character so immobilized in his contemplation of himself that he looks almost petrified. At that point it occurred to me to introduce the meandering, calling to the rescue the idea of wandering about in the vicinity of the lake as an intermission—or a form of recreation— between two long sessions of contemplation. Thus, rather laboriously, I succeeded in reconciling the two contradictory terms that I had posited in the first place: wandering (as a compass needle moves in all directions when it has lost its bearings), and fixity (like the immutability of someone who, no matter what he is talking about, always comes back to the subject of himself). By doing this, I have performed the trick without too much trouble: here I am, then, Narcissus running through the woods and always returning to the lake where his childhood memories lie sleeping, at first simple markers (mirages, perhaps, arising at intervals along his walks?), now pure water reflecting back to him the slightly murky but wet and tender image of himself. What still remains to be done, however, is to dive in, to make the liberating jump that will let him immerse himself in these childish waters, waters that become real at that instant (more real, in any case—the logic of the development requires this—than they were in their primitive state as markers or as mirages serving as markers). But here things get complicated, and the comparison turns out to be decidedly mongrel. For the least one can say about it is that

Narcissus's leap is a "death leap" which, if it frees him, only frees him by annihilating him. . . . Whereas I?

Well, I should stop this fooling around. And I should address these childhood memories straightforwardly, since I am *dying* to do it.

Nevertheless, it isn't so easy to wash the dust of words off oneself even by diving. And if I now leave metals behind and go on to talk about mines, I am immediately stopped short by *mine de plomb* [pencil lead].

Sharpening the lead of a pencil. First removing a few shavings of wood with a penknife (rather thick shavings, because one likes to feel the blade bite frankly into the ligneous fibers). Then, resting the now exposed end of the narrow cylinder of graphite either on the tip of one's left index finger or some other resistant surface, and holding the penknife so that its blade lies at an oblique angle to the column of carbon, carefully giving that column a pointed tip by means of a series of tiny scratchings that extract from it, with a small noise, slightly irritating to the teeth (though rather pleasant), a little gray powder that darkens the tip of one's index finger (if one is using it for the operation) or is simply deposited in a minuscule ash heap that one will later clear—blowing on it quickly—from the surface used as a support (if one has chosen the latter method in order to eliminate the risk of cutting oneself or the small inconvenience of dirtying a fingertip). Thus shaping the blackish pencil end into an infinitesimal cone as pointed as possible; listening to the squeaking of the steel edge against the ferruginous substance of the lead; feeling, through one's perception of this squeaking, how hard both these two solids are, which are being rubbed against each other: more effectively than any experiment elaborately prepared by a physics teacher and either successful or unsuccessful, these acts of an elementary simplicity bring us into contact with mineral matter, here entirely comprised within the ridiculously narrow limits of this dark, gleaming body, close to the precious stones because of its exactitude and its delicacy, even closer to coal because of its opacity and color.

Here I am talking about the traditional pencil leads, the ones made of graphite, the spinal columns of present day pencils. But there are also the leads of colored pencils, softer and greasier, of an almost claylike compound; those of Conté pencils, rough, noisy on paper, made of authentic charcoal; and, lastly, those of the repugnant invention known as the ink-pencil, which has to be moistened before being used and leaves on the tongue a faint, bitter taste, on the lips traces of purplish-blue, a most chemical sort of color and one emblematic of bishops, perhaps because of the strange reactions effected between earth and sky by the great princes of the church, heads of those immense stone laboratories in which the miracle of transsubstantiation is supposedly accomplished every day.

Nor should we forget the foresty smell or the fragrance of varnish given off by the pencil when it is still new, making one want to bite it. In the center of this wooden envelope, itself surrounded by emanations of stimulating perfume, is buried the carboniferous seam of the pencil lead, of which the slender, rigid shaft with a round or polygonal section enclosing it seems to be not only the protective sheath but the nourishing environment. Thus, in true coalmines worked deep in the earth are vegetable humus and geological sediments heaped up above the coveted substance, like piles of provisions that allow it to batten secretly and keep forming itself anew.

Between the lead of a pencil and the lead in a mine lies all the difference separating convex from concave and positive from negative. If a pencil lead is essentially a seam, a dense, substantial cord running through the thickness of the wood, the seam in my idea of a subterranean mine—though it is the very reason for the latter's existence—is so obliterated that it all but disappears: the mine is no longer more than a passageway, a more or less ramified tube piercing the opacity of the beds of minerals, perforating it with its emptiness the way the cellular bole of wood is braced through its entire length by the pencil lead and perforated by its fullness. The same word, then, has changed signs, though without the slightest external mark to reveal such a radical mutation. Whereas originally it designated a tangible body filling a clearly defined portion of space, which it rendered palpable, now the sound *mine*—an unusable rag signaling demolition work—is attached only to the nullity of empty space, to a hollow trench crawling like a kind of death through the compact reality of the earth's crust. Now, insinuated into the heart of the almost impervious wall that this crust interposes between the relatively peaceful air we breathe and the ceaseless effervescence of the hypothetical central hearth that fills the earth with fire the way a living animal is filled with blood, is the inanity of an endless finger of a glove. More effectively than the drainage of sewer mains or all the pipes and fittings that run from top to bottom of a building, the substanceless finger—or bundle of fingers, in other words the hand—of the mine becomes the optimum receptacle, whatever direction it is aimed in, for the most dreadful noises.

Gnomes' rumblings is the phrase that tends to agitate my lips before passing through my pen when I think of the ill-defined murmurs associated with the word *mine*, once it is freed of the spindle of wood that weighed it down and domesticated it. Gnomes' rumblings: the sound of picks echoing from gallery to gallery, the clanking of the little carts loaded with large pieces of coal detached from the seam, the stumbling (not pawing or whinnying) of the old blind horse over each wood tie of the narrow gage railway, the sigh of the elevator that goes down so quickly that one's stomach leaps, the tread of heavy boots, the brief calls, the muffled panting, the rattling of lamps and tools. Gnomes' rumblings: bubbles of confused sounds one could swear one heard bursting at the mention of words such as *ressources minières* [mineral resources], *bassin houiller* [coal bed], or *entrailles de la terre* [bowels of the earth].

Elves more than sylphs, and gnomes, the spirits of the earth, more than nixies (of whom one will dream later, when the first shoots of desire begin to sprout) are childhood's allies. Perhaps because of their pygmy size, which makes them like children despite their long beards, or, more specifically, because of the relationship between their small size and the objects that surround them. They take shelter under mushrooms as under umbrellas the way children hide under tables. They move about at the level of the roots of immense trees like very little children for whom a crowd of adults consists above all of a forest of legs through which, without too much trouble, they have to thread their way. There are all kinds of objects belonging to humans which, given the difference in scale, would be rather dangerous for the gnome to use, just as there are objects meant for adults that a child, because of his size or for quite different reasons, is not in a position or is not allowed to use. Sharing with the gnome, because they are about the same size, the same *angle of vision* (which is as much as to say, if one can allow that in this case the physical determines the shape of the mental, that they share a common *point of view*), the child recognizes in the gnome what he himself would be if he could become old without leaving the frame of his childhood, and everything he is told about the gnomes' doings and observes about them as they are depicted in drawings—their manners and customs, pranks, misadventures, tribulations—will enter a sympathetic ear or eye.

"I am a little g-nome," I declared once in some situation that made me aware of being little, without my wanting to confess this in any way except by insinuating that if I was a "little person," I was one of a certain species, a "little person" comparable to those mischievous creatures who, because they belong to the fairy world, are situated beyond the jurisdiction of bigger people, compensating, in this completely ideal way, for their physical insignificance.

I did not at any time suspect that gnomes were endowed with the power of the spirits of the earth, a bookish notion (and one that came to me belatedly when, as an adult, I was attracted by the picturesqueness of magic). But I have no trouble seeing that power in all its fullness in what I knew about pit gas when I was a child.

Pit gas, of course, had nothing to do with gnomes, who were light, fantastic creatures (and, what was more, creatures of fiction), capable of playing bad tricks, whose jokes, however, remained innocent, whereas the pranks of the pit gas were much more dramatic affairs. Nevertheless, this gas, which is blamed for so many accidents in the mines, had one thing in common with the gnomes: like them, it was a spirit. I have never thought of pit gas as an inert body whose pernicious effects can be explained by a purely natural action. Veritable presiding genius of the mine, pit gas is a maleficent personality, in every respect similar to a gas but only in external ways, because it is endowed with a will and acts according to its own whims. Besides being wicked, it comes from the family of the will-o'-the-wisps, which are gases, or breaths, at the same time as they are igneous spirits.

The attraction I have always felt to what lies beyond appearances means that for me the words "marvelous" and "nature" are almost synonymous. Wasn't it true, then, that the same inclination drew me toward fairy tales and later toward what may at first seem as different as possible—so-called science books? The books that explain, for example, how lighting gas is made (by distillation from coal, the gaseous mixture being collected under a large bell whose lower edges rest on a sheet of liquid and which is like a diving bell at the exact moment one begins immersing it); the books that talk about calcareous substances such as plaster or plaster of Paris, materials defined by the experiment in which one pours a few drops of vinegar on a piece of chalk (producing a characteristic boiling due to the release of the carbonic acid that has instantly formed); the books embellished with illustrations depicting lime kilns, archaic quarrymen's wheels (such as there used to be in the quarries of Chelles?), cross sections of blast furnaces (enormous fiery urns with masonry walls, filled to bursting with fusible or combustible substances); the books that offer a range of colorful concrete facts rather than the boring gymnastics of numbers, a working knowledge of which arithmetic books set out to teach, always gloomy despite efforts to make them attractive using pictures of, for example, larger or smaller flocks of sheep and longer or shorter rows, in greater or smaller quantity, of soldiers, training the pupil to count by asking him to enumerate human or animal units (with the tip of his index finger, touching each isolated sheep or soldier shape in succession while making the count, figure by figure, barely moving his lips, or silently, in his head).

Among all these items of heteroclite information—concise sketches of special details for a panorama of the world—a choice place was allotted to those having to do with human industries. Before my interest fixed on nature itself and became what it is today, a sort of openness or expectation akin to sexual excitement, I seemed to be drawn by the power that man could have over it. Very naively, because I wasn't yet in a position to distinguish between raw nature (which is given to us without having been shaped in any way, like a desert or a virgin forest) and the kind of humanized nature represented, for example, by a cultivated field (fairly similar to a mine, in fact, except that one derives edible plants from the first whereas from the second one extracts useful mineral products). During this indecisive period, which lasted from earliest childhood to adolescence, I was probably mainly attracted to everything that gave me an image of my own searching, my own attempts—which were not well thought out, moreover—to put myself on the same level as my environment, or even, tentatively, to dominate it.

Love of nature is the sentiment of an adult city dweller, profoundly experienced in the artful dodges of civilized life and wearied by them. For the child, not sophisticated enough to experience such a nostalgia for what is "natural" and to divide up what is around him into clearcut categories according to whether there is artifice in it or not, everything that is distinct from him is "nature," whether it be animal, plant, rock, person, or manufactured object, even including his own body when he is still at the point of exploring it. A quarry, a mine— excavations dug with human hands—are to be placed, for him, in the same family as a cave, and he scarcely notices that the last is a geological formation whereas the first two, works of art, are, in the end, caves whose essential particularity resides in the fact that their origin is factitious and not natural. If, among the external objects I experienced directly or discovered in books (a source almost as natural when one is a schoolchild), those for which I showed a preference, as my curiosity asserted itself, quite often bore the lovely name of "inventions," one could find the main reason for this in the fact that perhaps they seemed to me imprinted with the same character of autonomous formations presented by, for example, things that grow in the earth; at the same time that, since they were inventions, they seemed to me pieces of nature that man had been allowed to fabricate instead of receiving them already made, a sort of magic coming into play, but a purely human magic whose technique I could, with the help of time and work, one day understand, which would admit me to the secret of the gods. When I had disassembled the mechanism of these inventions—which did not exceed the limits of the possible, seeing that they were, precisely, "inventions"—I would, in fact, have understood the workings of nature, because there was no reason to suppose that comprehension of the whole would be denied me once I had comprehended certain of its parts. Only later did I appreciate the enormity of such an illusion (if indeed I am not the victim of an illusion today, in thus explaining my old taste for "inventions"). This occurred when I realized that in the end I was always running up against this underlying "natural" foundation, of which one could only know that it was there, whatever form it might assume and however deeply one might imprint changes on it.

Starting from the elegant Fusée, the first locomotive for which the Englishman Stephenson was responsible (a tall machine on legs, with a slender and elongated chimney, rather like an insect), it was easy for me to go back, in order to understand the action of the steam on the piston, to Papin's "digester" (an object all the more integrated into my familiar world because it was a domestic utensil and because one of the other students in my school on Rue Boileau had the same name as the famous inventor, which provided my friends and me with material for frequent jokes about the Papin in question, a sickly boy who looked a bit like a street urchin, with his pale, pockmarked face). If the functioning of the slide valve that regulates the admission of vaporized water into the cylinder where the piston goes up and down remained a fine point among the various points that had to be elucidated if one wanted, as I did, to possess the complete theory of the steam engine, the few notions I acquired about suction pumps and force pumps (which require the use of valves or clappers) enabled me quickly to grasp—even though the device was, in this case, more complicated—what I read on the subject of the slide valve in the *Nouveau Larousse illustré* because I had already had a glimpse, in very simple examples, of the action of those mechanisms whose essential property was to open and close alternately. When at last I understood—or thought I understood—the mechanical workings of the main parts of this machinery (including the rods and eccentric gear that transmit the stroke of the piston to the wheels and also govern the movement of the slide valve), I reached the Q.E.D. and felt satisfied. I would never have suspected, then, that the mystery begins the moment one imagines that everything has been explained. The real problem in the steam engine is not how one contrives to make the axle turn or the vehicle move by using the pressure exerted by a mass of steam against the disk of a piston. The question is rather to find out how this steam forms and by what strange perversion of natural qualities water, once it exceeds a certain degree of temperature, ceases to be a liquid and passes into a gaseous state. And if theories of physics themselves account for the modalities by which this change is brought about, one can always wonder why a substance, whatever it may be, is thus transformable, subject to such vicissitudes, instead of remaining forever what, observing it at any one instant of time (and under whatever avatar it may present itself then), one is justified in believing it to be, once and for all.

It has seemed to me for a long time that the very model of invention was the discovery Archimedes made, illuminated by his famous principle—"Any body immersed in a fluid . . ."—when he was lying lazily in his bathtub and crying out "Εὕρηχα!" as he struck himself on the forehead. We must be careful, though, for there is invention and there is invention. The fact of being suddenly illuminated by what is colloquially called a "brilliant idea" is very different from the object invented, the Concours Lépine inventions, like Eureka pistols and rifles, whose arrows are an undeniable brainwave (as their name indicates). That is, because of a piece of slightly concave rubber that swells out at their tips, they adhere by suction to the wall or any other sort of vertical surface they are fired at. At the age when I owned a few of these arrows with suction cups, propelled by a spring, for shooting at a target, naturally I always viewed the "invention" under its most immediately material aspect. If I concerned myself about any mechanism at that time, it was exclusively about the functioning of the device I saw before my eyes (either as an image or in reality) and not about the successive collusions of thoughts that, finally assuming a form, had resulted in the device making its appearance in the world. In this I was like most people, for whom the "inventor" is essentially a craftsman, an astute assembler of apparatuses, almost a street hawker, unless he is an innocent maniac, incapable of imagining anything effective and wasting his time and money in useless research. I only understood the importance of invention relatively recently, when the word became synonymous with discovery for me, and, even more, when I was capable of understanding the famous anecdote about Christopher Columbus and his egg: "One had to think of it"—a remark more loaded with meaning, in truth, than the proud Εὕρηχα and more apt to show that authentic invention is not so much the accomplishment of a tortuously clever intelligence as it is rather like the bread and water on which every truly free human act is nourished.

Standing outside the three natural kingdoms (animal, vegetable, and mineral—a primary classification, like the first question you ask when you play "portrait": "Is it a man or a woman?"), the world of inventions represented a group of species a little apart, in a region endowed with its own sun, as was the marvelous world of toys, for me, at first. Inanimate—even more, perhaps, than the kingdom of minerals and, because of this, even farther removed from man, if that was possible—this kingdom of inventions nevertheless affected man very closely. Because it was his creation, his appendage, I would almost say his annex, taking pleasure in giving a sparkle to this word, which I used to mutilate when I was taken to a department store and we had to go to what I imagined was called *la nexe*, in other words the supplement (the sort that every fat dictionary has), the dependency, the satellite, the suboffice, even less separated by the street from the store itself than one house is from another by a party wall.

Closely akin to "inventions"—like a snowplow on a locomotive, which I knew only from pictures and would so have loved to see in real life (it was disappointing to me not to see one anywhere in Switzerland when my parents took me there to spend our first vacation abroad, because I had imagined that in such a country, a country with glaciers, therefore a cold country, the trains could not fail to be equipped with them); also like a wind-cutter which I had the opposite pleasure of recognizing in a dictionary illustration after having seen examples of it with my own eyes on locomotives of the P.L.M. during one of the many short visits my family made to Nemours after my sister married someone from there—closely akin to "inventions" and with their roots (like most of the latter) in the mineral world, were *expériences* [experiments], strange productions by means of which certain portions of nature turned into a sort of theater where objects—those lifeless characters—or other elements conventionally confronted emerged with a magical power almost as great as if they had been mythological or human heroes.

An *expérience*—if, to begin with, I perform an experiment on this word without trying to penetrate the thing more deeply—sprawls, spreads, stretches out like a liquid contained in a vat, a tank, or a test tube. Whatever tilt the receptacle might have, the liquid is a horizontal surface scarcely disturbed by the bursting of a few bubbles. Patient and serious, the physiognomy of this word adapts perfectly to the experiments described in the physics or chemistry textbooks used in school, the ones whose impersonal and voiceless actors are not only the real things set in motion but also the expert hands that perform the manipulations; it is just as well suited to the sort of *expérience* [experience] that mature people generally pride themselves on having, contrasting it to the *espérances* [hopes] of the young, as though the lessons taught by the truly crucial experiment which is the conduct of one's life only resulted in narrowing the range of these hopes of which people like to speak in the plural, until they come to that greedy singular, expurgated of all excess: "experience," which is extenuated, almost expiring, and from which nothing emerges but the excremental.

Of course an experiment implies the idea of something elaborate, if not artificial (and in the latter sense it differs very little from "expedient"); but it also involves something hieratic, solemn, not simply sophisticated or pedantic. Instead of being taken as they are, things have been carefully selected, elaborately prepared, stripped of the patina of randomness that had been deposited on them over the years by a motley contact with too many circumstances, and they are now brought together, as in an airtight chamber, on the floor of the stage where they confront each other in their eternal being as "things" harshly exposed to our gaze, draped in robes with long, stony folds like tragedians whose action consists not in a succession of gestures but a series of attitudes, and whose motions consist of variations of their immobility as time—the only real action—passes. Thus, Foucault's pendulum, suspended from the vault of the great central hall of the Conservatoire des Arts et Métiers like a symbolic figure in a sacred enclosure, an installation intended to demonstrate the earth's rotation while also marking the rhythm of time; thus, in a more natural realm, the taper or candle in the Dog's Grotto that burns when it is held at the height of a man but goes out as soon as it is put on the ground, proving that the carbonic gas filling the grotto, a denser fluid than air, accumulates in the lower layers of the atmosphere, so much so that human visitors to the underground cave are in no way inconvenienced whereas a creature of smaller stature—an animal on all fours like a dog—has a very good chance of suffocating there after just a few minutes.

In the first of these two experiments, the interaction takes place entirely between the metallic mass of the pendulum and the superhuman, invisible power of gravity. In the second, it takes place between the flame rising from the candle and the impalpable environment in which the lungs, at each intake of breath, draw in a noxious influence. In the first case, a chapel, in the second, a cavern illustrate this ideal "airtight chamber" which is the place of choice for experiments, an abstract space whence all foreign interference has been carefully eliminated and which is made as dry as possible by the need for complete integrity.

If I see a very large dog—a Saint Bernard or a mastiff, for example—that is out of breath, panting, letting its tongue hang out, I will probably, for the space of at least a second, have a fleeting vision of that large dog suffocating in the cave they used to tell me about, illuminated, as by the scanty glimmer of a miner's lamp, by the candle of white wax around which the guide's fingers are folded. If, finding myself in the nave of a church, I lift my gaze to the lights hanging from its vault, it is hard for me not to think of that pendulum, revealed to me later, which—like the one that at this very minute I assume is hanging from my brainpan—continues a silent soliloquy that can't be interrupted by any physical catastrophe, not by the suffocating of the dog, slow to vomit, or by the rapid extinguishing of the flame that crowned the candle. Only here do I approach (or imagine I am approaching) the true experiment, the one whose function—in a close or distant way—is to reveal to me the inexorable features of destiny, and the only one, it seems to me now, to deserve the name "experiment," which used to be primarily suited to designating those obscure dramas whose protagonists were forces and objects and whose scenarios were reproduced in books of "science at home" with engravings to illustrate them.

A very large dog out of breath, a tiny, weakly lit underground cave reached by way of a slope of rocks or a mountain path, a slightly stinging smell or flavor—these are the most picturesque of the images evoked in me by the idea of carbonic gas. These same piquant effluvia, this same tininess of a place whose lack of light is a second source of uneasiness, this same difficult respiration, which could be the result or the cause of the largeness of an animal, the expression of its obesity or the origin of that swelling, related—in such a plausible way—to the unilateral blockage of the breath: all these various products issuing from a single mine I rediscover in an almost identical form in another fold of my inner earth, the fold that would be known, in the nomenclature, as CHRONIC (illness) or ILLNESS (chronic) if I were to create an atlas of my subterranean thoughts.

This notion of "chronic illness," which seems to me (perhaps because I recast it involuntarily as I exhume it?) to have been closely related linguistically to "carbonic gas" and also to "bichromate batteries" (which I had known about earlier because of the New Year's gift catalogues, where I had often read descriptions of electric toys equipped with such batteries), this notion of an ailment that would be differentiated by the fact of being "chronic"—a quality I imagined belonging to the world of smell rather than to the category of time and which I was inclined to look upon as kin to the smell, pernicious in itself, that I attributed to carbonic gas—this notion of a thing at least as noxious as the bad air (putrid matter at the bottom of a trough) deposited in the Dog's Grotto had a flesh-and-blood manifestation that, although it didn't affect me very closely, was nevertheless part of the circle of realities that comprised the setting of my daily life. This immediately perceptible manifestation—whose existence was impressed on me, naturally, more directly than that of the people and things approached only by hearsay or through their likenesses—was a pseudo-uncle of mine who lived in Montrouge with his wife and whose chronic disability consisted of attacks of asthma, while his better half was, according to her, inclined to be "hysterical."

Whatever may be the mistaken ideas I risk espousing by the use of such an irrational subterfuge, here I will once again make use of a method I am not likely to abandon because it represents the best, if not the only, reagent available to me for isolating certain memories of my childhood and restoring at least an appearance of freshness to what, in many cases, would remain a dead abstraction if I scorned such a process. Only by repeating certain words to myself, certain locutions, combining them, making them work together, do I manage to resuscitate the scenes associated with these placards, crudely charcoaled more often than calligraphed; only by arranging these scattered signs, this faded jetsam, side by side in a row (as though I were trying to tidy them up) do I manage to derive memories from their immateriality as phantoms (in which I scarcely believed anymore), memories without any shared characteristics except their capacity to be thus resuscitated, like dead men standing up when their names are called or when a formula is spoken that has no rational meaning but by whose magical whip they are reinvigorated.

In *Montrouge* [lit. red mountain] like a red fire, like a suspect star on the back of the last car of a train, on *Avenue de Chatillon*, like a *jupon* [petticoat], like a *cotillon* [cotillion] hat or novelty made of pale, crumpled paper, lived Aunt and Uncle *Firmin*.

Firmin gives off a smell, a sharp, stale smell or the smell of chronic disease, and is their comfortless apartment, up several flights of hard, wooden stairs, the apartment where, in the evenings, the man and wife played Pope Joan, jackstraws, tiddlywinks—I don't know what else—unless they actually only played these things when children like my brothers and me came to visit, determined as they were to entertain us. *Firmin*, a woolly, greasy name, was this large, sloppy, purple-faced man with his *"étouffements"* [fits of breathlessness] (as his wife called them) and his arteriosclerosis, the latter due to the excessive number of glasses of wine he liked to empty (though he wasn't a drunk, the dear man!) all the blessed day long. *Firmin*, a ropy, syrupy name, was also the black currant liqueur, itself purplish-blue with a slightly sharp flavor (or the very dark tea with a lot of rum in it?) that we were given to drink, along with, I think, small dry cakes placed, once they had been taken out of their paper wrapping or their metal box, in a suitable bowl, either provided with an embroidered doily or not. *Firmin*, a pale, slender name, is, in a parallel way, the spouse of the above-named, in other words our almost-aunt, regarded as family because she was the daughter of someone who for years had served as a domestic in the home of my mother's father, the grandfather who had not only been a true *Républicain*—a title one was proud to be able to bestow on both grandfathers—but also an important civil servant in the municipality of Paris. *Firmin* is this dry, yellow woman with a frail, birdlike voice, darkened eyelids, a black fichu? sometimes indulging in lamentations about her husband's pains and her own, sometimes in the idle chatter of a little girl, impelled to dress everyone up in a special nickname, as though she had to rebaptize the world in her own way, speaking of "dear Mimi" who was suffering from his asthma again that night, telling the latest about "old Umbrella," the shopowner on the ground floor or next door (whose trade actually might have been selling umbrellas), asking after *Galurin* [boater], my father's brother, whom she had called by this name for a reason no one was ever able to explain. On her wedding night, she had refused to share "dear Mimi's" bed, either too modest or perhaps feeling that her condition in life was too superior to his. . . . Very early on, she had started having "her pains," which were being treated by a specialist in the nervous system—without great success—using hypnotic suggestion and electrotherapy. When "dear Mimi" died, she exchanged the reddish housedress in which up to then I had always seen her snugly wrapped for a mourning dress. Then she retired to the Saint-Périne old people's home, in our neighborhood of Auteuil, and lived there for another few years, sometimes seeing "dear Mimi" in a dream sitting at the right hand of the Good Lord, deluding herself almost every night with the idea that she would be visited by the deceased, and, I'm convinced, having given up her former mindless amusements in order to turn tables, for—like every self-respecting serious nervous case—she was gifted with remarkable powers as a medium. . . . *Firmin* was this good man with his clumsy, common appearance, whom my father had brought into his office as an employee and who showed the devotion of a good dog; *Firmin* was this thin woman with bloodless lips, an ecstatic smile and, apparently, eyes that rolled up when she was having one of her "attacks," this armchair pythoness or inmate of Salpêtrière hospital ("*salle Pêtri-ère*," as I called it), this woman soaked in melissa cordial who almost never left her home, having trouble even getting out of her armchair, to which her pains—real, imaginary, or simulated?—kept her riveted. *Firmin*, a soured name, was this gloomy stale smell of a modest, upholstered apartment inhabited by people who no doubt did not wash very carefully and who were associated, on the one hand, with the chronic ailment that makes you suffocate—despite your strength, which people around you call herculean—like the large dog plunged in the carbonic gas, and on the other, with electricity, a fluid whose flavor is necessarily sharp, not only because of the bichromate but because one of the most easily verified effects of an electric current is to cause a rather unpleasant prickling sensation on the skin that I, for my part, have never been able to tolerate. Eugène and Gabrielle Firmin, Avenue de Chatillon, Montrouge—this childless and servantless household, this badly painted diptych reduces the secular couple of man and woman to the dimensions of vaudeville characters, a couple whose union, necessarily followed by disunion (when death comes, after illness), represents the most constant and simplest instance of the human tragedy.

Montrouge—with coarse suburban coloring, with the disquieting glow of the lime kiln on a winter's night—is the first setting of the drama whose last act took place at Saint-Périne, an old people's home built in an airy neighborhood surrounded by vast, peaceful gardens. At Saint-Périne as in Montrouge, however different the sites may have been, the same stingily closed room was the one laboratory in which everything happened, as though the only possible theater for the disease of old age—an actual chronic disease, in the sense that the irreversible wearing down of one's forces is well and truly an ailment of time—was a space irrevocably limited by four walls, the tangible expression of the laws from which, whatever happens, one can't escape.

Was it because the first people I learned to treat the way one treats the elderly were these people, to whose house I was taken on visits and whose main function seemed to be to receive guests sitting by their fireside? Was it because, for a city dweller like me, the norm for my oldest and strongest memories was not an outdoor scene but an interior tableau? Was it, more generally, because the social world is a creation of "big people" (who impose their ways and customs on the occupants of the lower steps of the ladder of ages) and because this older world, which one would only enter when it was agreed that one had become big, crystallized in the form of houses, furniture, household utensils, or knickknacks, diverse products of the industry of men and women living in society? Was it—more simply and to the exclusion of all other motives—because it was a sort of rule of nature that if they owned one, old people tended to dig themselves down into their armchair? I don't know. But the image I formed of old age when I was a child seems almost completely identical with confined places, closed rooms burdened with slipcovers, wall hangings, curtains, and rugs.

In contrast to these narrowly circumscribed places, to these objects which seemed steeped in the vapor of the ever more tired breathing of the people who lived with them, in contrast to this miserable rubble of time measured behind closed doors by marriages, funerals, birthdays, and special occasions, to the dust of all these structures the color of calendar pages, there is the unblemished space of the *open sky*, like the lively, free period of "summer vacation" that interrupts the daily routines of the rest of the year.

One of the strangest of the phenomena that occur outside houses and can be described as "natural" to the extent that they are not part of domestic life, is the eclipse, which it is customary to observe through a piece of smoked glass to protect one's eyes from being dazzled. At Viroflay (which I am tempted to write *Viroflé-é-é*, in imitation of a Viroflay railway station employee who, when a train arrived, announced the name of the station that way, as though it were a flower related to the *giroflée* [stock]), at Viroflay one summer morning a very long time ago, I chanced to see an eclipse. My father, my brothers, and I, along with my sister and even—who knows?—my mother, were standing in the garden of the Villa Suzanne, rented for the whole season, and watching the sun through pieces of smoked glass. I'm not sure exactly what there was to watch. The important thing was not so much what might happen in the sky—though I was surprised that it wasn't blacker—but this business of the smoked glass. Since one of my father's great pastimes during those idle days was to take photographs, I had a vague idea what a sensitive plate was and knew that on that rectangle of glass, coated as it was with a certain substance, the sun would imprint the image of all the real things upon which, complying with all the required conditions, the operator had turned his camera. What interested me about the eclipse was the manipulation of the smoked glass, which was interposed between my eye and the sun (or its reflection in a bucket of water?) as a sensitive plate might have been. It hardly mattered what there was to see; all that counted was the way one went about looking at it. The darkness I expected to follow from the total or partial obturation of the sun's disk being carried over onto the glass in the form of smoky black, the true eclipse was, for me, this layer of shadow spread over the transparent rectangle so close to my eye, like a second eye, like an eyeglass lens, in the intimacy of which the mysterious phenomenon—affecting, actually, the course of the sun—was mysteriously localized. Even the word itself (a rapid sliding, a blink, or the release of a trip lever) contributed to reducing the "eclipse"—the temporary occultation of one celestial body by another—to the proportions of a physical phenomenon on the same scale as the one that seemed essential to me in the manipulation of a camera: the momentary opening of the shutter which, for a lapse of time of variable duration (according to whether one took a "pose" or a "snapshot"), opened a passage for the rays of light, which, after crossing the lens, entered and made an impression on the plate concealed inside the body of the camera. If the cinematic brand name *Eclair* [lightning]—whose age I may be confusing with that of the old company called *Lumière* [light]—always makes me think of the eclipse observed from our house in Viroflay sometime around 1906, I'm quite convinced that the basis for this is not only the similarity of the names and the appearance itself of lightning (a sort of negative of an eclipse, since here it is the illumination and not the darkness that is momentary) but the way this eclipse assumed the quality of a photographic manipulation in my eyes, being truly not cosmic, so that I could not affirm (other than by deduction) that it was an eclipse of the sun rather than the moon, since I had—in truth—directed my attention not so much to it, as a reality external to contemplation, or to what was told me about it, to the smoked glass that allowed me to observe it.

Lightning illuminating a whole section of the sky without taking form, remaining pure color or luminosity. Or the opposite—lightning standing out as a precise jagged line, single or branching, whose path one can follow despite its instantaneousness. Harmful lightning, capable (they say) of blinding you if you try to look at it without blinking. The magnesium flash in the photographer's studio, under the filtered glass roof, that suddenly petrifies and transforms, for a fraction of a second, the subject already turned into a statue by the customary "let's keep very still, now" and then frozen to the bone by the abrupt jolt into this fixed image he will be, without density or life, in the two dimensions of the photograph. The flash itself being a photographer or magician who (as it was told in a news item or summary of scientific miscellanea in the biweekly *Nos Loisirs*) sometimes performs rather curious tricks of physics, such as inscribing on the retina of a dead man struck by lightning the image of the tree under which he was taking shelter at the moment the celestial discharge had electrocuted him. The word *éclair*, meaning pure speed, used—according to what one of my cousins said—to describe certain trains that were more rapid than the rapid trains and even the extrarapid trains, the ones that (he swore) were called *trains-éclairs* [lightning trains]. The pastry variety of *éclair*, paradoxically soft and benign, called, according to the greater or lesser density of color and taste, coffee or chocolate. *Eclair*, the nickname of a young German or Swiss maid who only worked at the house for a little while but long enough for us, my brothers and me, to give her this name, inspired either simply by the liveliness of her gait or, equally possibly, by her real name, deliberately transformed to make it more similar. *Eclair*, which seemed to me like a typical thoroughbred name (the same way a dog is *Médor* and a cat *Minou*) when my brother Pierre and I conceived a passion for everything to do with racing and formed a quasi religious notion of the life of the trainer-breeders, modern patriarchs of a sort, leading a life of strict discipline surrounded by their vast family of jockeys, lads, and racehorses. *Eclair*, which *éclat* [explodes] or *éclôt* [blooms] in a sheet, a zigzag, a tuft, or bouquet of light, then immediately *s'éclipse* [is eclipsed], an *éclaboussement* [splintering] as pure as that of a windowpane that breaks and is replaced by the glazier. The heavy or light *éclair* of the Simplon express or of the town name *Vitry-le-François*, according to whether one has in mind the railway thunderbolt or the meteor, a fleeting *éblouissement* [dazzle] like that caused by the cunning manipulation of a pocket mirror reflecting the sun or by the chance pivoting of a window's transparent panel, which for an instant foments a fire as piercing as it is condensed, quickly resolved into a simple shimmer of silk, without the noise of an explosion or an express train galloping over a turntable before rattling the station's smoky windows. Just as there was this multiform lightning in the sky (seen either nakedly or through the barely fissured or uniformly diaphanous screen of a venetian blind or window) it would sometimes happen that on the earth there would be a glaze of black ice.

As I go from lightning to black ice, from the irremovable pane of the sky suddenly flaming to the temporary glazing of a piece of the earth's surface, I now feel a slight disquiet due partly to the touch of depression one always has when examining something experienced many years before (as it forces one to face the fact of growing old) and partly, too, to a somewhat uneasy conscience. All these things I rearrange, all these ideas I hook onto one another, relying on my words to make them follow from one another, as though I had nothing left in my heart or head but a certain specious capacity to talk—in the end, I'm not sure they aren't the products of a most useless literary artifice even more than of a kind of logorrhea. Tottering between present and past, between imagination and memory, between poetry and reality, I hesitate, I waver, I stagger, I oscillate, and at times I feel I'm very close to losing my footing. . . . What is there to say? In itself, my aim is to rediscover the curious circumstances in which all things were suddenly unstable and in which I felt I was on the point of losing my footing. Is the anguish I experience therefore simply a result of the nature of what I am trying to rediscover? Or is it reinforced by a feeling of dishonesty due to the fact that the rather confused method by which I am conducting my research, the object itself of that research, and the emotion aroused in me from the outset by such an attempt tend constantly to mingle, even to melt into a compound so ambiguous that I can, wrongly, allow into the field where I am letting my pen wander, in this so-called research, every circumstance I can manage to show as being at all unstable; more specifically, to the fact that I am perhaps the submissive victim of a tautological sort of delusion consisting of defining past states—which my research tries to isolate in order to discover a method of reaching similar states at will—by what is triggered in me in the present by the use of a method that can't be discovered, since it has been acquired here and now, and is itself definable simply as something that puts me in a fit state to conduct research into my past? A quagmire where I risk losing my footing in a different way, or a sheet of black ice on which I slip, or a lightning bolt that illuminates me only in order to blind me more certainly.

One day when my second brother came home from school, he said to me: "This morning, there was black ice [verglas]." I was very familiar with winter, frost, hoarfrost, and snow, but exactly what was *verglas*? It contained the idea of *verre* [glass]—as the name showed— and wasn't everything associated with ice by nature glass? The *glâ* ending implied something a bit sinister because of its heaviness, and didn't I already know that it was a sign of death when the *glas* [knell] was rung? There were also the *Jougla* photographic plates.

The shards of a broken bottle, *verre* of a *vert bouteille* [bottle green] (darker than the *vert-de-gris* visible on the faucets of the kitchen sink when the cook had let days go by without doing the brass). Today there is also *boire un glass*, a slang expression for *boire un verre* [have a drink] (and more specifically, if I follow the anglicizing bent to which I am led by the word "glass," a glass of Bass stout). All this makes me think of *verglas*.

One morning, on a day of frost and wintry weather, something formed on the ground, an unknown substance, and my brother told me it was *verglas*. Did I immediately understand that *verglas* was the thin sheet of solidified rain on which one could slip so dangerously? Did I immediately understand the entire lesson about things contained in the word *verglas*? Or did my brother explain it to me after I asked him a question? Or did I say nothing, pretending to know (so as not to seem naive) and only later, when I experienced it myself, learn what black ice was?

Verglas: unquestionably a thing belonging to the city, a secretion of asphalt and pavement; in a sense, it isn't a natural formation. Even though I can describe it as an efflorescence without faking too much, it remains—definitely—poles apart from plants. Certainly it has nothing to do with the *liseron* [bindweed], a summer flower that blooms and sounds its note as true as a *clairon* [bugle]; nothing to do with *géraniums, bégonias, dahlias*, with their painted cheeks, whose names, painted in *minium* [red oxide], ring of decorative metalwork even more than artistic flowerbeds; nothing to do, even, with the *perce-neige* [snowdrop, lit. "snow-piercer"], though it is a creature of the cold, nor with *menthe* [mint], which is never a plant for me but rather a translucid substance verging slightly on the gray of a winter sky, the substance of the little wafers made of icing sugar which were probably the only candies I didn't like. If I deliberately make the word *fleur* deviate—letting it leave behind all it might still contain of mold or soil—and if I say *fleur de trottoir* [sidewalk flower], then *verglas* reappears for me: a sickly florescence born of the city's sudden atmospheric changes, an icy sweat spotting the too tightly drawn sheets of the streets, a breath cooled into a solid mist, marvelously smooth and polished but having nothing in common with what the harsh season might lay down in the open country. White frost, a carpet of snow, mounds of crystals on branches, blocks of ice on the surface of pools, swamps whose stagnation reaches its extreme when it hardens, all this can be found—it goes without saying—in woods, meadows, and fields. But I will never believe that one could go outside the vistas constructed by man and find that specifically city product known as "black ice," that chilly, chlorotic replica of tar, though tar is like a beautiful burning stream of licorice paste (only slightly excremental) spreading in great sheets encrusted with little pebbles like a stick of hard nougat speckled with tiny pieces of almonds, whereas black ice (if it is possible for one to imagine it as edible) would be more like the light glaze of sugar covering the upper face of certain cakes.

Among the mineral substances good to eat—or those one could easily believe to be so—there is not only snow (the most delectable sort of sherbet, even though one knows it has no flavor), and its opposite, asphalt (black, hot, sticking to one's teeth instead of melting instantly), and a normal food ingredient like salt (which, except in the case of salt works, one never has an opportunity to see exposed to the winds in the vast display area of an arranged or natural site); but also clay—a compact mass of pudding or mocha cake—*lait de chaux* [whitewash, lit. "lime milk"]—whose name, in fact, is more starched than creamy—and the coarse porridges of mortars and cements. Also lava flows, which are hard to imagine as different from the foam that forms in great copper basins on the surface of jams as they are being made, without much color but succulent to the point of nausea, which one then tastes, spoonful after spoonful, once the jam has been put into pots and it is time for the basin to be cleaned. Also certain very white, very fine sands like the kind I knew in Nemours— entertaining myself for long periods of time by letting it run through my fingers, though I never went so far as to taste it—rock dust like powdered sugar, the kind of sugar that actually looks just like a mineral, even though it is derived by human industry from the vegetable kingdom and is conventionally included among the substances dealt with in organic chemistry.

The *verglas* in the streets, the *vert-de-gris* deposited on the brass faucets, the rustic nickname of *Vert-Galant* borne—gallantly—by the good King Henry, *Véronique*, not the saint (who gave her name to one of the most classic passes in bullfighting) but the character in the operetta (who joins Estelle for picnic lunches, swinging parties, and other jades' games), these four words—despite their common denominators *verre*, *vert*, or *ver*—divide up into two clearly distinct categories: the first two belonging to the inanimate world of minerals, even when one may believe they are edible and however soft their colors may be; the other two belonging to the world of vegetation, which is always alive, even in the numerous cases where it is neither green nor good to eat. If we add the *ver de terre* [earthworm] (also known as a *lombric* [lumbricus], perhaps because of a certain resemblance between this invertebrate and the *ombilic* [umbilicus], the navel looking more like its hole than the mark of its absence, hollowed out in the form of a scar), if we increase my string of words by this new one— like a necklace of horse chestnuts, so fresh, so glossy, so hard, so pleasing to the sight as well as to the touch—at last, leaping in a single bound the peripheral grass borders of nature, we arrive at the veritable quintessence of life, which is the animal kingdom.

Mineral kingdom, vegetable kingdom, animal kingdom. The marvelous notion of these "kingdoms," as though nature really comprised three realms (such as France, Germania, and Lotharingia), each placed under the particular jurisdiction of a sovereign, a king, or queen similar to the ones in fairytales, whose essential function seems to be to sit enthroned with crown and scepter surrounded by a whole court of nobles, ministers, and counselors.

Precious metals and gems could well be the treasure of the sovereign of the minerals. It would be easy for me to see mistletoe—which the druids cut with their golden sickles, and gathered up in white sheets, loudly celebrating the new year in its honor—as a sign of the royalty of the oak, companion of Saint Louis and almost the only tree I was able to name of all the ones I encountered in the woods of Viroflay (no doubt because of the easily identified appearance of its leaves, which I knew could also be found arranged in a crown around the sun curtain of the kepis worn by French generals). In conformance with the traditional expression, I could see the lion—a quadruped with an abundant mane like the druids with their beards and the Brunhilds with their hair—as the "king of beasts," consequently almost on a level with man, at the very top of the hierarchy of animate beings. But metals and rarest gems, mistletoe, and even big game remain cold allegories, though scarcely paler, it is true, than the completely abstract idea I might form of the sovereignty peculiar to each of the three kingdoms, separate in theory but in fact having imprecise boundaries, as shown by the tangle of forest where birds mingle with trees, insects like ants run about on the ground, and mosses seem to have oozed out of the rocks they grow on.

The anthill. A hillock of earth, twigs, debris striped by the many flowing lines of small living creatures blindly (it seems) pursuing their activities in all directions, hurriedly crisscrossing, laboriously transporting often enormous pieces of material, heteroclite burdens they carry or drag along for some reason that is quite specific but remains unintelligible. Ants are the life of the earth. Animate particles adhering closely to the humus or sand, even animate parcels of some mineral substance, if not the earth itself. I remember one anthill, among others, that lay on a slope and that I imagined extended very far down—even reaching, perhaps, what they called the bowels of the earth, a mysterious place described by certain fabulous tales (I read one, in particular, in the illustrated *Les Belles Images*, where it appeared a few years after those summers at Viroflay, continuing through several issues in the form of small blocks of text accompanying a series of drawings arranged in regular rows of squares, as is the rule in children's newspapers), a dubious place, perhaps also associated with the huts of coalmen, who are ogres of a sort, destitute or half savage creatures who become confused with woodcutters even though they are really creatures of the night, heavy Vulcans in clothes soiled with the mottling of plant or earth, rustics in hobnailed shoes partaking of the subterranean fire. I remember that anthill. I remember the sandy place close to it, a spot my brothers and I called the *sablière* [sand pit], as opposed to the *sablonnière* [sand pit] (unless it was the reverse and the great nest of ants was, rather, close to the *sablonnière*), another place of the same kind as its synonym but not as vast, where the sand was not as white, a difference that for us justified the distinction implied, logically, by the two different names. I remember that commotion a few steps away from another sort of swarming (the minuscule, hard grains into which one plunged one's shovel or one's hands). But having pointed out this association, I can hardly say any more about it. I only know that every time we went to play in that area, my brothers and I watched the anthill. We liked to look at the crowd of moving insects. Flat on the earth and frequently entering it. On the border between life underground and life on the surface. On the boundary between raw material and living matter.

There were also the two hedgehogs in the garden of our dry millstone house. Little balls—like chestnuts, though much bigger, of course—spiked with innumerable bristles. Captured in the woods, they had been brought back each wrapped in the customary handkerchief. Left in peace, they unrolled themselves and trotted here and there with their little muzzles visible, and their little clawed feet, which tickled when we chanced to hold them in our hands, when our palms also sensed the heat of their bellies. We were always afraid they would leave the garden. So as to be able to tell them apart, my father had taken a brush and painted a large spot of red Ripolin enamel or minium on the back of one of them, as though he were touching up a piece of pine furniture or preparing an iron gate before giving it its final coat. Sometimes we would look for the two hedgehogs in every corner of the garden. It was a joy to discover them where they had ensconced themselves, under the low branches—it seems to me—of shrubs with very dark green, glossy leaves, where there was loose earth that they could dig around in, shade in which they were half hidden. To some extent these hedgehogs acted as spirits of the earth, pieces of living nature that had turned into companions of ours, somewhat strange to us but nevertheless familiar.

The earliest impression I had that there was such a thing as animal life, the sense I first had of flesh that seemed endowed with its own peculiar palpitation—a sort of life *in itself*, as distinct from the drowsy or petrified life of things that formed nature's background, as from the almost human quality (that could already be connected to the presence of a soul) of dogs, horses, and other higher animals—the earliest contact I knowingly had with an external body endowed with this sensitivity in its pure state, recognized as such, a mass separate from me as from every intelligence, yet capable of having sensations related to those I knew my own body could have (unlike the total stranger represented by an earthworm, for example, whose death throes, when one crushed it, appeared to have nothing in common with what a human body could feel), what revealed *flesh* to me—to say it all in one word—a substance endowed, pure and simple, with its own independent resiliency (for isn't it true that one of the most obvious properties of the substance called "flesh" is precisely its elasticity?), were neither the ants (too remote, too different from me for this, and also too hostile, because they might bite us) nor even the hedgehogs, animals more on my scale.

If I dig down into my memories, it seems to me I can bring up— with difficulty, and into a very uncertain, perhaps artificial light, whose feebly asserted brightness may result from the fact that the scene it is supposed to inundate is only an imaginary construction—it seems to me I can see a crude form of drama whose theater is the garden at Viroflay, whose actor is a creature very different from the hedgehogs and the ants; a brief tableau whose moral lesson—if indeed it has to have one!—would be this discovery of living flesh, a discovery that today assumes the appearance, for me, of a crucial experience, in the long road I followed through the diversity of nature, a child zigzagging back and forth at the whim of the images that called out to him.

I think I remember, simply, that once, standing in a garden path, I was shown a very young bird, still without feathers, that had fallen from its nest.

A little mass of flagrant nakedness, almost without form, pinkish in color (probably covered with down too thin and impalpable for me to notice it right away, much less retain the vaguest trace of it in my memory). Scarcely even the embryo of a head, seen in profile, lying to one side, with what one could suppose to be an eye and a semblance of a beak. This whole thing moving slightly, just enough for one to know it was alive. Nothing, absolutely nothing in this bit of still almost unorganized matter in distress on the ground, to give any indication of the future motions whose conjugation nevertheless would one day have resulted in flight if the accident whose pitiful outcome we now saw had not chanced to cut short the natural destiny of a creature who we knew was a bird and whose essential characteristic, consequently, would be to fly.

As I looked at this thing, I experienced a great perturbation that I'm not certain was exclusively *pity*. It seems to me that with a feeling of horror, but also as though the very fact of imagining it revealed a very obscure desire, I imagined I could have held this little miserable mass in the palm of one hand. My first sight—and a confused one—of flesh, here in the guise of a suffering that seemed to sum up the entire sensibility of a creature still half in *les limbes* [limbo], the indeterminate place whose existence—or nothingness, if you like—I learned about later, and which seemed to me to be the special domain of creatures not yet formed, when I was told that the souls of children who died at an early age or before birth resided *"dans les limbes"*; *les limbes*, in connection with which I noted—later still, and as though such a homonymy must have a hidden meaning?—that one could also speak of the *limbe* [lamina] of a leaf, a word also very close to *lymphe* [lymph] (itself almost *nymphe* [nymph]), which flows like a kind of sap through our tissues. But confronting the fallen bird, I, who was almost as young as that bird and didn't have a wide enough range of words and ideas to indulge, as I am doing now, in sophisticated games, simply sensed what an overwhelming and incomprehensible thing flesh was, that substratum of sentient life or—to put it better, perhaps—that bundle of sensations unified and rendered material.

Poles apart from this fantastic limbo peopled for me by dead children (who, I was told, had become "little angels," winged creatures I did not distinguish from little cupids, imagining them completely naked, not wearing long nightshirts like their adult brothers), poles apart from the whole fairy world constructed from the beliefs that had been inculcated in me, the fictions I was told, the images born of what I gleaned from the things I saw, the conversations I heard, and later, the alluvial repositories of the books I read, was this object, this bird whose value, no doubt, lay more than anything else in its raw reality: a tiny, quivering pill of feverish life sweating its anguish on the ground or gravel path. Such an encounter, in its rawness, had the feel of a *fait divers* [miscellaneous news item] and was colored with the same terrible luster as those incidents, more "real" than all the others, no doubt, simply because they are more horrible— depicted every week on the cover pages of the illustrated supplements of dailies like the *Petit Journal* and the *Petit Parisien*, harshly colored pictures in which red blood often appeared, as though the emergence into full daylight of the liquid by which the insides of our flesh is bathed more or less obligatorily had to be shown so that the event thus portrayed would be marked with the stamp of ultimate truth. *Faits divers*: a verbal mixture in which the element *divers* [various] becomes the symbol of a crime or a bloody accident. One of many "various" events, that is to say, one of many daily events, of course, and stinking of banality, but lit by a flame of tragedy so that it becomes the most intense, the most vividly perceived event, the choice item, the most substantial of all the "slices of life" or fragments of reality.

Almost contemporaneous, I think, with the baby bird's accident, was an authentic *fait divers*. During the vacation, one of my boarding school friends (as I was told) had thought it would be fun to climb around on the roof of his parents' country house and had fallen, seriously injuring himself by this imprudence. Was this event true or not? All that matters here is the impression the story made on me.

Had my young friend—and maybe even the bird too?—defiantly exposed himself to a danger his father and mother had surely warned him of? Had he been a victim, as he fell, not of an unfortunate mishap but of his own disobedience? At different times in my life—which wends its way across time the way my sentences wend their way from page to page in a time, it is true, that is more limited—I have chanced to think of these two accidents again; but they have never seriously assumed the moral guise of just punishments. What lingers is the idea of bruised flesh, acutely vivid even though I only saw the bird and didn't touch it, and only heard the story of my friend's fall. What lingers is the physical aspect, a memory as persistent as, for example, my memory of a harvester spider (with a body of small volume and long, threadlike legs) that walked over the back of my hand one day when I was picking flowers or playing at planting seeds in the Viroflay garden, tickling me in a hideous way.

My hand, of course, didn't feel the bird; it feared that contact for a moment but it quite definitely desired it too. What was involved was literally a handhold on life. The distressing, exalting kingdom of the mythical Persephone; a kingdom with disquieting means of access, as the hollows in the trunks of dead trees used to be for me, and also everything I associated with spiders and snakes, from bunches of half-unearthed roots to the black holes bored in the ground by rodents, narrow bowels that I took for dens of vipers or snakes; a shadowy and tortuous kingdom whose mystery I think I approach when I recall a dream I had, now many years ago, in which a similar sensation of a small animal mass tightly enclosed between the living walls of two hands raised the curtain on a human scene of opprobrium and suffering.

The setting for this was a synagogue, and the time was the present; in a sunny country in the summer, to judge from the impression I have retained of hard light and heat somewhere offstage during the last part of the dream. As for the structure inside which I found myself, I had pertinent knowledge of its identity as a synagogue, even though no particularly judaic detail, no definite local color at all characterized the setting precisely. A sort of church, but whose altar I did not see; rather small, admitting only a filtered light (in those of its parts, at least, that framed the beginning of the action); without a prayer stool, which differentiated it from a Catholic church; its walls lined with wood paneling; the whole rather reminiscent—if this retrospective comparison deserves any credit—of an orthodox chapel such as I saw, have seen before and since, in Athens or even, in fact, an authentic synagogue, such as I visited in the Comtat Venaissin. As for the time in which the thing was taking place, I knew that it was the present, despite the sort of climate of antiquity that fills most religious buildings (except, in my opinion, Protestant churches, where one never feels steeped in incense as in the musty smells of antiquity or in an ambient holiness).

In this church, which I will call a synagogue once and for all, I am standing surrounded by other people attending a religious service. As a tourist, perhaps; even as an ethnologist (since that is my profession). Anxious, whatever may be the case, to follow the ritual scrupulously and furthermore, not asking myself the question that my inherent rationalism now makes me ask: that is, whether or not I believe in this ritual as I participate in it. I am part of a group of spectators who had agreed to behave acording to a certain preestablished scenario and perform certain gestures: one item, that's all. Nothing, here, that goes beyond the immediate, and it is perhaps because of this that the dream now seems to me a sort of model for what a sacred ceremony should always be.

Just as in a Catholic church the members of the congregation give their contributions to the man taking the collection, here each person has to give the rabbi a sacrificial offering. To this end, I am holding— a light, quivering mass in the enclosure of my two hands—a little gray kitten (with smooth, soft fur) and six little mice. I enjoy the feel of them, a living clump between my palms, and I am touched with pity at the idea of what awaits them: having their throats cut by the rabbi. I ask myself if I should hand them over or let them go.

Then, at the back of another part of the synagogue—a quite vast central (or lateral?) nave with flagstones unencumbered by any seats or furniture of any sort—appeared the actors in the scene which, it turned out, was the high point of the religious service (a little like the elevation of the host in the Catholic Mass). From left to right, advancing abreast toward me in a slow procession: a rabbi—a kind of filthy Arab, his face consumed by a black beard under a veil that covered his head and, bound around his forehead by a braid of wool or silk as was the bedouin custom, fell on his shoulders on either side of his brown, emaciated face—a rabbi who brandished above his gnarled arm a rope with which he threatened, with invectives, another rabbi with a filthy Arab face representing Christ; to the far right, a little behind that second character, an angular, wrinkled old woman—also with a filthy Eastern face (in a squalid white dress gathered by a belt just above her hips and revealing thin bare feet, and in a veil similar to those worn by the two men but that stayed in place without the help of any braid)—an old woman dressed in Ethiopian style and with the swarthy skin of a gypsy, representing the Virgin. In an extraordinarily piercing, choked voice, she lamented, singing like a Spaniard, flamenco style. This was the end of the dream, and I knew—before I woke up—that it was none other than the scene known as the Mocking of Christ.

O Persephone, you artesian well driven into the thickness of nature, revealing subterranean secrets in the form of a shrill or murmuring fountain, are you really this welling forth—or are you merely transformed into it by the play of a random metaphor?

"Once Upon a Time…"

In Revoil Beni-Ounif, on the border between Morocco and southern Oran, during what historians have chosen to call the phoney war, I learned the value of the phrase *Il était une fois* . . . "once upon a time."

Jadis [formerly, once, of old, long ago] is legendary gold, like the treasures of the city of Ys. *Naguère* [not long ago, a short time ago, lately] is tinged with regret, but almost cheerful, like something that might as well be forgotten. *Autrefois* [formerly, in the past, at one time] is more affectionate, old and familiar, like *Il était une fois*, like *la foi du charbonnier* [simple faith, lit. "a coalman's faith"]. None of these adverbs—which signal a more or less detached attitude toward elapsed time—opens a parenthesis in which reverie comes to ensconce itself, as does "Once upon a time" (actually the vaguest of all these locutions, not even referring to any specific past)—a traditional phrase describing periods in the margin of history, a phrase that itself has been around for a long time, as we know because when we were children we so often read it or heard it at the opening of a story.

It was at Revoil Beni-Ounif—a meager oasis where an insignificant native village had sprouted up and next to it a small garrison town—that I was able to evaluate how full of rich perspectives were the words *Il était une fois*, hanging at the beginning of a story they were meant to introduce like the panels of an arras, drawn back by curtain loops, revealing to the person with his foot on the doorsill a succession of marvelous, decrepit drawing rooms. For me to experience so fully the content of this magical little phrase which, by immediately establishing a great distance between us and the action, causes us to drop back through time in a dizzying way, no doubt I needed to be in this rather sinister dump, this breeding ground of melancholy, where I could cultivate at my leisure the classical theme of nostalgia, created here by my distance in space from the life I had left behind me when I traveled away from Paris, so that that life seemed to me scarcely different from a chimerical past, gilded, in any case, with the same emotional glimmers.

Once upon a time ("once" was, in this case, September 29, 1939, a day sacred, like every September 29, to the archangel Michael, my patron saint), there was, in the least shabby of Revoil Beni-Ounif's shops (the stationery store-cum-haberdashery of the Mimosa pension, a small hotel-restaurant run by a prim old lady who was thought by us servicemen to have been, in her heyday, the mistress of the late Lyautey, with his marshal's baton then in his knapsack, and who now managed this place where the officers—and the rare noncommissioned officer who had a delicate stomach or liked to play at being distinguished—were accustomed to take their meals), there was, standing in front of the counter of this store, which was not very hospitable to lower ranking soldiers but was incontestably clean and neat, there was myself, then a sergeant in a unit of artillery workers and at that moment the imminent purchaser of a box of letter paper. The old woman with her smooth-spoken manner (though not without some disdain for this individual who hadn't many stripes and wasn't even a customer of her pension) showed me some boxes, and I quickly and indifferently chose one. There was a picture of a feudal castle on the cover of this box, a reproduction of an old type of engraving blocked in black against the sky-blue or mauve background of the cover (for such was the color of this letter paper). Beneath the medieval structure one could read, printed in archaic characters, the phrase: *Il était une fois* . . .

"Once upon a time": a drawbridge suddenly lowered to allow legendary processions to pass above the moats of time, which suddenly melt into the night. In this particular case, lying beyond the expanse of water I had recently crossed in a convoy escorted by planes and warships, there was the memory, as of a happy childhood, of the civilian life I had left back there at a clearly defined point in space and time; and the blossoming, in a fog of history, of vague ideas of chivalry, as though to induce me to play, with scarcely a hint of ironic complicity between myself and myself, the role (in such a spot, very easy to play) of the character in uniform that I was; and above all else, the sudden revelation of a maxim that ratified the state of exile in which I found myself, paradoxically hurled as I was, by the very fact of having been mobilized, to the edge of the Sahara. Quite frankly, I was delighted by this exile, prided myself on it, and did not feel constricted by it as by a trap (that would come later, but only as an afterthought.) Far from cursing my fate, I actually regarded the happenstance that had placed me there as curiously in keeping with what for a long time had seemed to me to be my destiny: the condition of not fitting in, a condition that had already driven me to travel in Africa a few years earlier, and that explains, in a general way, the taste I have for fiction, for memories of periods from which I am separated by time, and for countries other than my own.

"Once upon a time . . ." Being thus left in suspense—like the very index finger of the storyteller itself, supposing it had been petrified by some sudden external or internal cataclysm at the very moment it was raised to capture the attention of the young listeners—the opening phrase, cut off from any story that might follow and itself interrupted in its flight, raises in the air its useless portal, an entrance to a ruin standing alone, without any other upright remains, a doorframe open on a nonexistent vestibule that ushers one into nothing. All that is left, having been stopped short on the threshold, is the expectation of the person who is now all ears because of this preamble reduced to nothing more than this reference to time that isn't really a reference to time since, of all possible times, it expresses the most ordinary one.

No doubt the primary thing was not that one's mind had been alerted to the fact that something *was*; this simple statement that something existed, not even referring to a subject other than the most abstract grammatical tool, and situated in a totally imprecise past, would be a grayness too neutral to arouse one's attention, if "once" didn't come before. Here, even though nothing is happening yet, at least we have the beginning of a situation; before the backdrops are put in place, creating the setting, the space of the stage is built by that little word which, without going so far as to describe a day, a season or an epoch, nevertheless isolates a certain moment of duration, grasped in its pure state, whose only differentiating quality is to have been thus set apart, put to one side, away from all those other moments from which it wouldn't be distinguishable if not for this very act of separating it from them.

Thus alerted by the announcement that something will be coming on stage any moment now—a thing described as having *once* existed without its emerging from namelessness yet—the mind prepares itself to receive all things, it opens wide, becomes as vacant as possible. But the phrase, though it has barely begun, closes, and the mind finds itself suddenly loosed in this emptiness created inside it, with only one idea, that this thing which was all ready to come and lodge in the framework established by "once . . ." but which, at the last second, failed to show up, was a thing from the past, a gray, cloudy thing, not so much because it had not yet been defined as because it belonged to the realm of fable, which excludes all possibility of temporal specification, except perhaps for a complete return to a period that one imagines to be very old, close to the indeterminacy of origins themselves (given the unreal and *a fortiori* out-of-date aspect of the events that take place there), whereas in reality this period eludes all chronological frames of reference.

I have put the phrase in front of me. I have dissected it unemotionally, like a lover of theater noting everything from behind his opera glasses or seeing everything through his monocle, which signifies his desire to be merely a chilly eye, like the glass disk with which his eye socket is equipped. I have studied its different facets, like an expert examining a diamond to see whether or not it is of a beautiful water. But I forgot that a stage is not merely a medium for the picture created by the costumes and sets, but the site of an action; that a diamond is not merely a lifeless stone, but a crystal that makes bare skin seem more sensual. Now, for the spectator without malice (one who is a member of the ordinary public) as for the dazzled suitor or the woman friend jealous of the rich jewel, it is very different, as it is for the naive witness I feel I become as soon as these words enter me, words which, introducing a story that harks back to a mythical past, transport me instantly into that other past, also mythical, the time when I was a child. What I see then (what is revealed, in fact, by the words "Once upon a time") is neither a theatrical perspective, appropriate to a lover of games of deception and illusion, nor the more or less rare brilliance of a solitaire or a drop of water, but the fairyland of my childhood itself. What there was once was myself as a child, to whom people told stories beginning with "Once upon a time."

To the soldier I was, when my eyes fell so unexpectedly upon this phrase, what appeared was not only the child of before another war nor even the recent civilian. Rather, I also felt that the oddly outfitted and situated character I was at that moment—a soldier wearing a kepi on his head under the African sun (viewed today: a sort of "funny man" under the harsh lights of a circus)—became the subject of a legend, the possible hero of a story that my memory would later have all the freedom to create and in which something of this kind would perhaps be said: "Once upon a time there was a soldier wearing a kepi under the African sun, and the name of this soldier was Julien-Michel Leiris. He owned a box of letter paper on which was written: Once upon a time . . ." So great was the power of this ordinary bit of phrase impregnated simply in the strong smell of childhood and terror when I read it at the edge of the Sahara in the new condition in which I found myself, that as I uttered it I saw myself, without leaving the present, transformed into a creature belonging to the realm of mythology or to the no less marvelous, though real, realm of history. A figure projected outside myself, as though it were the rough model of a future statue. A portrait that had prematurely stepped down from its frame; yet not at all spectral! On the contrary, wide awake and completely alive.

The costume that is more "historic" than any other, the one that, as soon as it is put on, gives its wearer some of the coarse colors of a cartoon strip and simplifies him greatly like a museum mannequin (pure support for an ornament or a costume) is obviously the uniform, clothing worn by those who, from one century to the next, play the part of the chorus singers of history as it is told to children, history as a long succession of opera scenes in which the gestures of generals and heads of state are recreated against background canvases representing palace interiors, public places, or battlefields.

To be outfitted as a soldier is already to be included, as a possible walk-on, in this opera history. If one also finds oneself hurled out to the edge of a desert, the peculiar figure one had already become seems all the more so, standing thus uselessly in the center of the least familiar set. But now the phrase "Once upon a time" is articulated, a stereotyped formula covered with a patina of tradition, on top of the fact that its actual meaning is a signpost pointing to a past of the strangest kind. The resonance of this phrase proves to be so private, so interior, that there is hardly any need to force circumstances to apply it to oneself. Everything conspires, therefore, to introduce into one's mind a distance, a recess, such that one sees oneself metamorphosed—watching this as though from outside oneself—into a character at once remote, imposing (in that it belongs to history) and fraternal (since it is another oneself). A solitary figure appearing to be of the same kind as those characters of high epic poetry that delighted me when I was a child, at that time manifested under the crude features of Vercingetorix, for example, or the less real and also more emaciated features of the Chevalier Belle-Etoile referred to in a love song my sister knew, a wandering champion all of whose nights were spent dreaming as he looked at the stars, since he didn't have a roof over his head, and who symbolized for me, for a time, the notion of giving one's whole life to the pursuit of an ideal; figures rediscovered later, with less rudimentary masks and dressed in modern clothes, in the persons of certain adventurers in the movies. On this jumble of feelings that had gradually accumulated, a little dusting of mockery, when one coolly considered just what this trooper really was, absurdly encamped in an overheated countryside three-quarters empty, enjoying what was known as a cushy job and having nothing in common with a hero except for solitude and remoteness, which favored the morose delectation and abstract exaltations of nostalgia.

A mannequin standing in the midst of a landscape that was only prevented from being nonexistent by—along with a few sordid houses, the cardboard of official buildings, and the neutral material of barracks—the slender, shabbily plumed stalks of the palm grove, the bed of a dry torrential stream, and the nearby wall of mountains on the Moroccan frontier that closed off one whole side. A mannequin capable of assuming the disguises of many different daydreams, embellishing himself with many psychological cast-offs—this is what I had become. Sometimes dressed in khaki, sometimes in lighter cloth, sometimes wearing a colonial helmet on my head (when I was on "town" duty) but most often a kepi, as though to remind myself of the changeable characters in a picture book my older brother owned, a collection of carefully drawn and colored plates showing materials which, used patiently, were supposed to yield, once one had extracted them from those pages piece by piece, soldiers from the Revolution and the Empire armed from head to foot (including Napoleon himself and some of his marshals) as well as other, older kinds of soldiers: a member of the Garde-Française, a musketeer, an *arque-busier* from the time of the religious wars, a knight with a large shield and an almost cylindrical helmet from the battle of Bouvines, even a man-at-arms of the Carolingian era, with a broigne made of metal squares—all this sold by the Hachette publishing company, I'm pretty sure, under a cardboard cover, and it was the work of the black-and-white artist Job, also the illustrator of several impressively designed books, gilt-edged like prize or gift books, in which certain great phases of France's history were described for the entertainment of children; all this to be cut out part by part and glued together, a few human figurines serving as mannequins whose costumes one could vary as one liked, the way one dresses dolls, alternately slipping them, as though inserting them into a case, into the accessories of "full dress" and "undress," for example, constructed with scissors and a glue brush.

An authentic storefront dummy (though, true, I was the only customer who could be affected by this advertising), during my stay at Beni-Ounif I owned some pieces of equipment that formed part of my person and were objects of pride as though they were the consecrating instruments, even the significant attributes, of my divinity.

I'm not talking about the knapsack known as an "ace of diamonds" in military slang. Still less my bayonet and rifle; nor even my gun belt, though I wore it every day, except when I was in duck trousers, and have kept it up to now, appreciating its quality as a beautiful piece of leather equipment (for which, above all, I continue to hold onto it, the only physical vestige I still have of that whole period, except for the gaiters of coarse holland I later wore in Paris, then in the Landes when I was assigned to a munitions depot, and also the Basque beret I bought during the first stage of my return to civilian dress on the eve of my departure for the small region of Lot-et-Garonne, where my final demobilization was supposed to take place). I'm not talking about those anonymous items, which were simply part of the outfit that was included in my condition as soldier and had no true connection to me.

But how very different were my shoes, for example, thick, square-toed regulation ankle boots of raw leather, with nails in the soles, chosen for their old trooper look and their tawny color, which I never sullied with polish, chosen over other lighter and more supple requisition boots when we were given our clothes before leaving, in the Palace of the Mutuality, our company's depot. Though I greased the boots again and again, one of my feet always hurt, but I loved those shoes because of their robust look and also because when they were brand new I had read the phrase "Prison de Clairvaux" on the bottom of them between the heel and the wide part of the sole, a magical sign of origin that made me feel, when I had them on, a little as though I were one of the young criminals serving in the bataillon d'Afrique or a convict. How different also were the sandals I had acquired for the price of seven francs from a native cobbler in Beni-Ounif. Its soles were made from old pieces of Dunlop tire, as one could read before the abrasion of the rubble and dust in the roads had worn them down too much. With these, I saw myself in another way, disguised as a fallen colonial, one reduced to the state of a pariah and living as miserably as a native. For I was very familiar with this kind of sandal, made of a few thongs of leather attached to pieces of scrap rubber and sold in many open air markets of tropical Africa for the exclusive use of the blacks.

There was also my broad Zouave belt, of red muslin or percale, obtained at our unit's store in exchange for the vulgar flannel belt I had gotten in Paris. When we left our base in Beni-Ounif to go about 60 miles into the unbroken desert region, the site of the experiments with toxic gas (using guns, planes, and other sorts of devices) which we had been assigned to carry out, I would carefully wrap that cloth around my hips under my pyjama pants every night—for at that time of year, the nights are cold in the Sahara. In the shabby little quarters I occupied with a few colleagues in the reserve and in active service— two or three of whom were half Spanish natives of the Oran, another a Jew (the aviator who took me on my first flight, a member of the group of people the local anti-Semites, even before the persecutions began, were already calling by the ignoble name of soldering-irons)— there was something intriguing about sleeping thus strapped up in a digger's belt. When I took it off in the morning to get dressed, it inevitably reminded me of the red cloth of a matador's *muleta*, and this reminder of bullfights, which I loved so much—on top of the memory of silky skin that haunted me, of delicate tissue irrigated with blood and quivering like the piece of sheet that brings the bull into subjection—was rather moving next to the photos of naked women one of my companions (a Parisian, a young aviation mechanic) had tacked to the wall for aesthetic more than pornographic purposes.

Last, there was the gray sweater with the rolled collar I had been sent from home, which I put on in the evening to go have dinner at the mess when it was cold, throwing back my shoulders and composing my face so that my forehead was sometimes hard, sometimes more relaxed, but always Olympian, below my close-cropped hair. If it hadn't been a gift, I would certainly have exchanged this sweater for a khaki pullover like those worn by the French or Belgian legionnaires of the radio station. I would have been even more pleased, in fact, to look like a guy from the Legion than to look like a boxer, so powerfully was I influenced, at that time—the desert having destroyed my usual frames of reference—by a certain low-grade romanticism. A prisoner condemned by common law, an adventurer ravaged by alco-

hol and fever, a beefy daredevil, a mercenary of the Legion—such
were the figures with which I childishly played at identifying myself,
the literary models for which had been originally supplied me by the
Emigrant from Landor Road, the "incorrigible convict on whom the
prison doors always close," and many other characters created by poets
and novelists and embodying the incapacity of a man truly worthy of
the name to accommodate himself to our modern life.

A narrow column of sensations planted vertically on the horizontal
plane of an unfertile land, I was alone and resembled, because of that
isolation and my upright position, the schoolboy in the small geography books who, wrapped tightly in his black smock, points out the
placement of the four compass directions, orienting himself by the
position of the sun, which begins its journey in the east and punc-
tually ends it in the west. The north was the Mediterranean coast and
the boats that left from it, connecting us with the mother country.
The south was this desert behind us, the notion of which was a source
of nourishment for me, a symbol of the dryness, the emptiness I so
often feel I have been driven back against and from which I can
sometimes only be delivered by one of those gusts of heat that run
through me like a torrid wind that is itself of the order of the desert
and is brother to that dryness, that emptiness from which it has the
power—without there being any betrayal in this—to help me escape,
because it is (perhaps) only its affirmative aspect, like the flame that
attacks a mineral in order to release a metal from it, as opposed to the
purely feverish and destructive flame that makes people cry out:
"Fire!"

A character whose uniform painted him, superficially, in patriotic
colors, I remained—this is certain—much less focused on the general
commotion in which, not even as a combatant but an innocuous
serviceman, I had my very modest part to play, as on the contribution
made to the imagery of my person by this heavy fragment of history
weighing in the scales of destiny only, it seemed, in order to drive me
to Africa once again and thus add a decisive pencil stroke to the
picture of my life.

For a picture was certainly involved. Not of my life as a life I was
living, but as a form drawn with a line whose adventurous meandering I could have followed with my eye, whose appearance I could have
evaluated with a certain detachment, the way an archeologist studies
the appearance of the tool he has just unearthed or a statistician the
shape of a curve expressing facts to be interpreted.

When I scrutinize this piece of the past, already four years behind me, I see, drawn against the remote background of history, this outline of myself or rather this diagram of at least a part of my life: myself-as-soldier-in-the-desert. An outline in which I recognize myself as I was then, with more certainty, perhaps, as far as the likeness of a portrait goes, than I have in any other, an outline that, thus highlighted in front of the fog of history, takes on some of the firmness of contour with which the great figures of sovereigns or heroes stood out in the sort of history taught me when I was small, dominated by the very lofty individual destinies of great stars like Vercingetorix-who-surrendered, Charlemagne-founder-of-schools, Joan-of-Arc-burned-alive, Louis-XV-killer-of-does or Louis-XVI-locksmith, and Napoleon-who-died-at-Saint-Helena (as the song goes). A version of history in which one could not perceive anything of the agitation of the masses that really constitutes "History" and in which the only things presented for my childish allurement, besides a collection of illustrious personalities, were certain well-defined and labeled events such as wars, battles, peace treaties, and other incidents summed up in pithy phrases that called our attention to them and brought them to life, as though bearing such a name made them almost as alive as people.

Next to the Battle of Waterloo (a rainy gray like the famous gray frock coat or the color the sky might have been that day), and the Battle of Agincourt (painted on an azure field after the fashion of a shield), and that of Marengo (brown, like a sauce, obviously because of "veal Marengo"), and that of Marignan (most like a dish of glazed carrots, of which the *-gnan* seems to me to be the melting quality, or like an edible mushroom whose stem is topped by a vast lansquenet hat with its edges oddly notched and pleated), I discover—if I try to make a list of historic events with promotional subtitles—for instance, the Day of Dupes, a palace comedy accompanied by the rustling of court dresses and the undulation of the cardinal's *jupes* [skirts], so that one wants to note it down, on some social calendar, next to the *bal des Petits Lits blancs* or the *Journée des Drags*.

More clearly connected with my childhood was the *Colloque de Poissy*, remarkable because of the oddness of the word *colloque* [discussion], which can be found in the colloquial expression *colloquer*, used in the sense of "fling" or "pitch" (*Je vais te colloquer une paire de gifles* [I'm going to send a couple of punches your way]) and can be seen as a variant of *collation* [snack], which might have been confirmed for me by an actual meal eaten one day with my parents during an outing in a river boat organized by a certain artistic circle my father belonged to. The destination of the outing was specifically Poissy. After having lunch, I believe, then tea and dinner, we came back up the Seine, and the evening's entertainment had been a few numbers played by amateurs; one gentleman in particular, assuming a discreetly ribald air, had produced a comic song whose refrain was

Y a pas d'mal à ça, Colinette,
Y a pas d'mal à ça!

There's nothing wrong with that, Colinette,
There's nothing wrong with that!

an allusion—meant to be mockingly indulgent—to some liberty or other whose object the said Colinette was supposed to have been during some amorous *colloque.*

Associated with the *Colloque de Poissy* and under the same rubric, that of the Wars of Religion, is the *Massacre de Wassy* [Wassy Massacre]. But if once again food is involved, in this case it is because of the town of Wassy itself, the source of the meringues known as *caisses de Wassy*, though I didn't know whether the word *caisse* should be understood as actually designating them (they were light, porous and almost hollow, being so crumbly under the teeth) or whether it applied, more simply, to the thin cardboard box in which they were placed. Thus linked to the pastry, the Wassy Massacre remained in my eyes something relatively cheerful, without any hint, in any case, of the sound of alarms, the stunning hammer blows, and the stale night smells of blood associated with that other carnage of Huguenots, the Saint Bartholomew's Day Massacre.

Last, many years back—if one adopts the point of view of that History with a capital H that maintains such fragile relations with my own—the Battle of Jemmapes appears, which always made me think of *jaune de Naples* [Naples yellow], a color I had in my box of watercolors (glowing with vermilion) and which always seemed to me one of the most precious and delicate, after the day my brother Pierre and I both at once recognized the same color in the coat of a little monkey working for the Corvi circus, an itinerant company that gave shows in Versailles during one of our summers at Viroflay. The action took place, I think, not in a ring, but on a stage or on boards. The only attractions I remember were the Monkeys' Meal (in which a chimpanzee cook officiated and the "little Naples yellow monkey," smaller than his comrades, was either the last one served or robbed of his food by the bigger ones, which aroused our amused pity), then a pantomime called "The Deserter," enacted exclusively by dogs, at the end of which the poodle who had the part of the unworthy soldier played dead after being shot by another species of canine. "In the days when animals could talk": a formula as marvelous as "Once upon a time," indicating a time that was even more fantastic, if possible, a world within which fairy creatures and intelligent animals mingled, though without merging—creatures capable of talking, perhaps, because they exist only in a world that is itself no more than a tale or a maxim, animals who know how to perform tricks that can be seen, but on the level of pure appearance where the other type of fiction, the show, is situated.

"In the days when animals could talk" is clearly not the time of La Fontaine's fables. Those animals are not true animals, and those fables are also not real stories. A fable is a short text one learns by heart, whose form, stipulated once and for all, is clearly defined: a thing in verse that one recites without thinking about it too much and that sometimes one only manages to stumble through. A fable isn't History, and it isn't fairyland either. What happens in it is without importance; the only thing that counts is the text, those immutably fixed words, none of which can be changed without inviting reproach. In a fable there is also no room for daydreaming, no mist like the mist surrounding the past, nothing about it to make one stand gaping as before a supernatural being. Whatever they may do in them, here the animals are conventional creations from whom, it is understood, one can expect anything and who never become a source of marvel, since in a fable everything is meticulously calculated and foreseen, "ruled like music paper," according to the whim of its author.

Things are quite different in the fairy tale and also in History. Here, the actual words of the story hardly matter: one only pays attention to the characters and the events. Even though they may not be real (even those of History, lost in a murky past) one can at least develop them, feed them from one's own resources, give them substance—no excessively strict form being interposed between us and their existence, though they have the fragility of beings that are nothing beyond the account we are given of them. In the fairy tale, a talking animal is, if not visible and palpable, in any case portrayed, given a piped white bonnet with strings like the wolf disguised as Grandmother, or stout boots and a plumed hat like the cat belonging to the Marquis de Carabas, and this ability to assume a form is due not only to the fact that certain specific details of these odd costumes are given in the text itself or its illustration (if we are reading the tale ourselves and not simply having it told to us), but also to the fact that we participate very closely in the story; it is not an immutable thing we must fix in our minds exactly the way it is but rather a canvas given us for our amusement, with all the colored wools available to our imaginations.

"In the days when animals could talk," an even more perfect Open Sesame than "Once upon a time." The time involved here being by definition a time when another sort of speech was dominant (since man was not yet the only one to possess it), this fragment of a sentence opens the door on a world one has reason to believe is entirely governed by a different syntax. Language, the very medium of the story, is from the very outset pushed back somewhere short of human language, put on the level of the animals. And it isn't simply the thing that is being told, but the act of speaking or telling, and even the storyteller himself, that withdraws this way to an infinite distance. For we don't know if the formula that thus establishes a connection between time and speech is solely intended to announce that the story will talk about the time when speaking animals existed or if, rather, the story is supposed to talk about one of these animals attributed with the gift of speech. "In the days when animals could talk," a way of immersing in the mythic past the speech of which the present story is created, and this at the cost of a very gentle slide back from the present speaker to those legendary speaking animals whose ability to talk is understood to be a symbol of the remoteness of their time.

No doubt it is quite natural that a circus show intended for a public most of whom are still in the earliest years of their lives, be a thing close to childhood. For the adult in the audience, its meaning is ambiguous, oriented as it is toward the past on the one hand (because it reminds the elderly child watching it of his earlier life, and also because of its traditional side), and on the other hand taking place in a most insistent present: the present of the laughter it sets off; and of the tremulous anxiety with which one witnesses a feat of strength *at the very moment* it is being performed, a feat that may end in failure at any moment; the present—of a decidedly "modernist" sort—expressed by the Anglo-French pidgin of the clowns and, more generally, the cosmopolitanism of a program in which all nations appear together as

in an Exposition representing the evaluation that takes place at the
end of an era. Such spectacles have an immediate charm resulting
most of all from a play of contrasts: the brilliant, restless fantasy of the
costumes against the austerity of the setting (the ring with pure light
falling on it from the electric lamps and a sharp smell of dung rising
from it), the alternation of broadly comical scenes with dangerous
acrobatics, the exceptional nature of what is shown contrasting with
the ordinariness of the public assembled there in the round to admire
other human beings whom everything contributes to turning into
fantastic creatures. But the adult who goes to the circus experiences
something more than this superficial seductiveness: the power of a
deep poetry, one of whose primary stimuli should be looked for—
beneath the picturesqueness of these contrasts—in the fact that
within the magical circle of this place, *right here* coincides with *over
there*: the sharpness of the event that is taking place right here before
our eyes and that we live through in its own moment; and the mist of
strangeness that gathers over this event as soon as the disjuncture
appears by which it is sent back there, toward a past that belongs to
the nursery and to folklore.

The circus is, of course, very different for the child from what it is
for the adult; it is simply a special world where people who seem
deliberately odd and animals that are much more accomplished than
the sort one would see in the street are able to do tricks that people
and animals of the everyday world would be quite at a loss to perform.
For the child, there can be no question, here, of a withdrawal into
legend (such as that introduced by "Once upon a time") nor of poetry
(for poetry implies at least a trace of lucidity and irony). The child is a
loyal partisan of everything he sees at the circus, though sometimes
afraid (for instance, by the grimacing, painted faces of the clowns,
who are always preparing to set off various explosive devices, as in my
military experiences in the Sahara) or amazed (at the acrobats, for
example, or the horses, so elegantly adorned and so well trained). The
circus show, an uninterrupted succession of strange and admirable
things, is, properly speaking, a wonder; unlike the fairy tale, in any
case—which is also wonderful, but whose radical falsity one is quite
aware of—here the child is given a guarantee of the truth of what is
happening in front of him: the self-importance of Monsieur Loyal in
his suit, with his long whip in his hand, the fact that the members of
the public are constantly challenged, induced to become involved in
the action (whether the circus people deliberately mystify them or

appear to treat them like associates to whom one reveals one's cards)
are simply intended, in fact, to create a parity between the scenes in
the ring and the undeniable reality of the spectators crowding the
tiers. Thus, everything that happens in the circle of sand, at whose
edge the child is allowed to sit, will seem to him at once really
miraculous and miraculously real. And he will barely be able to stop
himself from thinking that they are trying to fool him when they
swear to him—in an attempt to reassure him if he becomes afraid—
that all this is not serious but only for laughs.

If—fleeing the desert I was standing in just a moment ago,
disguised as a soldier—I now pretend to transport myself to that
other sandy space, a circus ring (which is perhaps simply the *color* of
sand, its floor being not true sand but some sort of flat surface covered
with a coconut fiber mat) I won't see an earlier version of myself with
childish features, dressed in a suit with short pants and sitting next to
my mother on a bench or a chair in a hall like that of the Nouveau
Cirque or the Médrano. I won't feel against my neck the large
starched white collar I wore for so long with a Lavallière tie knotted
under it. Unable to remember a character whom I did not take any
trouble at that time to play well or badly and who was not the object
of any particular attention on my part, I will see, instead, this
fragment of what I devoured with my eyes during those performances,
each of which had the look of a gala, in particular the maneuvers—
first along an inclined plane? then on a rectangular board previously
arranged in the center of the ring?—of a Mystery Ball, a fat blue
sphere, perhaps spangled with gold stars, which, as it went from one
spot to another, seemed to roll around all by itself. At the end of the
act, the ball opened and a pretty gymnast in a bathing suit emerged
to take a bow. This happened at the Cirque Rancy, when we were at
Viroflay. During the same matinee, an acrobat—whose act consisted,
I think, of balancing on a pole—was the victim of a minor accident—
an awkward movement or a fall?—that caused him to dislocate or
sprain something, or perhaps suffer some quite different injury, one of
those I have never been able to define clearly or differentiate (having
thought, up to now, for example, that to dislocate something implied
that something had been torn). This caused a moment of confusion
among the circus personnel, was the occasion (it seems to me) of an
announcement to the public and rather frightened me, this abrupt
intrusion of a *fait divers* into a world which, though it was real, had
been no less, until then, a pure marvel. As for the Mystery Ball—

which for a long time I thought of as a thing that was actually as tightly sealed as a normal ball and as mysterious—I rediscovered it a little later, in the form of a mechanical toy. The sphere descended along a ribbon of metal arranged in a helicoid, but I don't know if, once it reached the end of its path, it opened, to the appearance of some simulacrum of the pretty gymnast, whom I picture to myself in a tightly-fitting blue outfit, her forehead almost entirely hidden by a black bouffant hairdo.

Many years after that, I am in a hall of antiquated architecture with gilt moldings, where the velvet-covered seats are occupied by people in evening dress, very different from the easygoing folk sitting under the canvas structure of a traveling circus. We are at the Théâtre de la Gaîté, where the Ballets Russes are performing this season, in the year 1923 or 1924, and where I am attending a performance of *Parade*, rediscovering, in the presence of this spectacle (which is not a circus but a transposition of what one sees at the circus, or in the most dusty music halls, or on the boards at fairs), the freshness of vision one generally loses as soon as one's first youth is past. On the curtain that Picasso painted for the ballet—whose sets and costumes he also made—a circus scene is represented: a female dancer balancing on the back of a big, white, winged horse resting its neck on the withers of a smaller horse. Now one soon recognizes this Pegasus—who disappeared when the curtain was raised—among the figures in the ballet, in the sordid guise of a caricatured quadruped: a shabby pelt concealing two dancers. Then, at the end of the show, when the curtain comes down again, there is the big horse again. From the old nag that makes us laugh, then, we have in the end returned to the courser that makes us dream, so that everything has really taken place in the gap separating these two figures, each of which is a portrait of what the mythmakers, on the one hand, and the buffoons, on the other, have imagined a HORSE to be. As it comes in the wake of the unreal Pegasus painted on the curtain that is the physical manifestation of our expectation, one would think the picador's old horse (covered with patches though it was never torn), gamboling grotesquely across the empty space of the stage, has absorbed all the reality comprised within its three dimensions and attained the condition of being "realer than real," one of the great goals that modern art is so anxious to pursue. The fall of the curtain afterward returns everything to the dream that this "realer than real" could not, finally, do without. For everything insists on oscillating between two poles: one, a reality as bare and present as possible; the other a mythology, here a fabulous mythology, in the strict sense, as Pegasus is fabulous, whereas else-where it can take the form of a nostalgic reconstruction of the past created by memory and answering an obsession with what is *over there* or *beyond*, similar to the obsession that is likely to be satisfied by the exercise of the imagination.

What I experienced as I looked at the curtain was above all a sense that there was a resemblance between me and the little horse. At that time I had no inclination to play the part of the *maudit*, the adven-turer, or the bad boy. I hadn't yet acquired that almost mystical notion of the African sun that tormented me for such a long time, starting when I happened to travel south; earlier I had been much more attracted by the north, whose hardness and cold enchanted me by contrast to the idea I had formed of the south, where one dissolved in sweat. If I dreamed of distant countries, they weren't countries full of snow, still less countries full of fever, but simply the sort of fictional Edens that poetry seemed able to offer me. I envied the great Pegasus, whose tracks I would have liked to be able to follow—I, the stum-bling colt whose first attempts at lyrics had been mere half-formed stammerings. Of course I was no longer the naive child one took to the circus, but I wasn't the aging intellectual, either, who little by little fashions a tragic clown's mask for himself, if indeed he does not pose for his bust in an attitude of completely "historic" gravity. Capable of confronting dream and reality without irony and without any attempt at compromise, and of experiencing their difference as a gaping wound, I did not yet ratiocinate on the motives one might have for writing and only wished to become a poet, to cure myself of reality through dream, or to adorn myself in the eyes of others with the prestige I thought permeated those who suffered from such a wound. Comparing the big horse I saw on the curtain with its ridiculous double moving about on stage, I thought of this dream and this reality as two opposed worlds separated by a terrible gap and was engulfed by the painful desire for an impossible identification with the big horse. Faced with that beautiful white animal, I was as moved as though I had transformed it—the image of what I despaired of being—into a symbol of the man of genius who, using the dream in any way he likes (at least it seems so), is in some sense its very incarnation.

However unsatisfying my life as a whole may appear to me, from the point of view of this fusion of dream and reality, I must neverthe-less recognize that I have sometimes thought I saw the two terms unite—and this was when I was quite lucid, not in any sort of "waking dream"—in spectacles offered me by life itself which I could accept as they were, without submitting them to any poetic maceration.

During the summer of 1933 (I had returned from a long trip to tropical Africa a few months earlier and was getting back in touch with France again, somewhat as though this were a new country that would provide me with ample material for "exotic sensations") I went to Lannion one day from the beach in Brittany where my wife and I had settled for the vacation. In a square of this little town, whose name I relish (because it has a real country ring to it, and when you hear it you seem to see the peasants going to market with their arms through the handles of baskets filled with game birds, chunks of butter, or fresh eggs), we saw some mountebanks dancing on stilts. Two adults and two children, in all likelihood from the same family, including, besides the father and mother (who could both have been about thirty) a little boy and a little girl. All four were dressed in dazzling colors with espadrilles on their feet. The father, clean-shaven, wore a top hat and an ample gray-blue clown costume with a repeating pattern of two monkeys. He blew into a cornet as he moved around on his stilts, and also played an accordion. Pretty and quite brown, the mother had on a red pullover, and her yellow skirt was covered with an apron whose red verged on violet. As she danced, she accompanied herself with castanets and sometimes twirled rapidly around, her skirt lifting and belling out and revealing little, old-fashioned white pantaloons that came down to her knees, ending just above coarse stockings of cotton fabric or brown lisle. After twirling, she would lift her left leg until it was horizontal and arc it with its stilt over the heads of the closest onlookers. The little girl (very tanned, with a sky-blue bow in her hair) and the little boy (in a Zouave costume, with wide, dark red pants) both played tambourines. When the dance was over, they took up a collection, the children holding out their tambourines to receive the money and the mother collecting it directly, hand to hand, from the windows of the second floors of the houses. Then, their ritual concluded, the whole family went off with vast strides to give their performance in another spot, and one watched them for a few minutes longer, very tall, gliding Indian file through the narrow streets. I was so charmed by the scene that I noted it down in detail as soon as I returned from Lannion, and until now it has slept in my notebook, like a few other scenes that (without always knowing exactly what they meant) I felt—and this is why I noted them down—would one day assume some kind of significance.

Such an explosion of freshness, the dapper quality, despite everything, of these poor people's music, stood out against the routine
bustle of the busy market town like a bed of flowers at the back of an
old provincial courtyard. One couldn't imagine there being the least
discord within that family, that the father might drink, for instance,
and once he had drunk, beat the mother; nor that the mother could be
a shrew or run after other men (whether the father, in his own interest,
encouraged her to be a gutter prostitute or more or less closed his eyes
to his wife's escapades, or whether she herself was crafty enough so
that her husband didn't notice anything, or whether she didn't care a
damn about his protests and his threats). Nor could one even begin to
imagine that the children might be thrashed when the earnings were
too small, and the prospect of being put on short allowance caused a
fit of temper on the part of the authors of their being. Even less could
one conceive of this little company as a troupe that had happened to
fall in together, the man having one day picked the woman up God
knows where, with her two children, or maybe only one, unless the
dashing patriarch himself had already engendered, in another bed, or
in two other beds, the pair of little tots he was now dragging around
behind him, in the expectation (who knows?) of a third, after which,
one fine night, he would go off bag and baggage, his stilts on his feet
like seven league boots, so that he would already be loitering about
under different skies at the hour when his little family, just waking
up, had scarcely finished rubbing their eyes. A touching quartet,
whatever the case might be, and a true fairy-tale family: not so much
of human beings as of sprites or sylphs, living on next to nothing and
hugging the airy element so closely that they had nothing whatever to
do with our heavy terrestrial habits.

That same day, in Lannion, like anyone else on a trip to town, I
made a few purchases. Since the leather belt that held up my pants
had broken (a real piece of junk, bought in Paris in some department
store I can't remember any more), I went into a harness maker's shop,
and then and there the good man made me a belt of the very best
quality, cutting the thin strap before my eyes from a large piece of
cowhide, then piercing holes in it with a punch and attaching it to a
steel mounting after decorating it with a stippled line about one
millimeter from each edge, using a serrated wheel. I was to wear this
belt for several years, and every morning when I put it on and every
night when I took it off it gave me the feeling of euphoria that comes
from any contact with something solid and beautiful.

In the course of the same walk, I happened to notice in a shop window a book that a friend had mentioned to me a short time before, Michelet's *Sorcière*, and I went in and bought it. Although it will soon be ten years since I bought it, I haven't finished reading it yet. Not that it doesn't interest me in principle or (this goes without saying) that I read so little and with such difficulty that I can't get to the end of a book within a period of ten years, which would be more typical of a mental defective, which I really am not. But it often happens that I get bogged down in my reading this way (as I perhaps get bogged down in my current work of writing). It is not necessarily because the thing I am reading positively bores me, but rather because very few books manage to hold my attention for very long. I take up one that responds to my preoccupations of the moment, and I read a certain number of pages in it. Then something new comes along in my preoccupations that attracts me to another book, and I generally drop the first one, too anxious to go on to the second and, in truth, reading so slowly that whatever interest I might have in finishing the book I am reading, once and for all, it is incapable of overcoming my impatience to begin the one that happens to respond to my new preoccupations. Partly out of laziness, partly out of instability, this is how I end up allowing unfinished reading to accumulate, though periodically I liquidate my accounts by systematically resuming the books I have abandoned, several at once, if need be, when I know— from what I've read of them so far or from what I've heard or read about them—that they deserve to be absorbed to the very end. Michelet's *Sorcière*, however, has so far eluded all these attempts to go back upstream and make sure the works I turn away from without any valid reason as I go along shall have been reduced to as few as possible by the time I die.

I have lost all memory of what first, and finally, distracted me from my reading of *Sorcière* and made me break it off. The strange thing is not that I was distracted that one time. Since I have so much trouble avoiding this wavering of attention that makes me flutter from one spot to another, always fully alert, of course, to what I am experiencing but incapable of maintaining this level of alertness for very long, it is not surprising that the very real fervor with which I approached Michelet's work did not last very long, despite what I might have gained from those pages, in which a vast section of history is organized into a masterful picture articulated on the basis of what it means rather than being presented as a pointless accumulation of details collected as the hazards of erudition dictate. Michelet's *Sorcière*, a brilliant view of what witchcraft must have represented in feudal Europe: a way for the little people to find some compensation in an imaginary world for the life of humiliation the big people made them suffer. A view all the more apt to touch me since in Abyssinia, where I had been shortly before acquiring the book, I myself had observed at close hand instances of peasant women being "possessed" that seemed to respond in large part to a desire for revenge on their parts, a desire that was satisfied on an imaginary level, where they avoided the domination of their husbands, who were exalted and powerful lords to them. It is a fact, however, that one day I simply stopped reading *Sorcière* and never went back to it. What could be the reason for this?

Most likely it is pointless to look for a real reason here. The first interruption was probably caused by my return to Paris at the end of the vacation and, perhaps, my resumption of other reading I had abandoned when I left for Brittany. For a while, *Sorcière* must have stayed on a corner of my table, unless, in my passion for tidying things up, which I have always had (here I remember the project I would embark upon from time to time when I was a child and which I called the "great tidying," which consisted of counting and classifying all the soldiers I owned, lead or tin, drawing up statistical lists in which all these precisely enumerated soldiers were divided into categories according to weapon, rank, size, and the substance of which they were made), I put this rather thick book (an unmatched volume from the complete works, which may have caused me to have a certain antipathy toward it, for my love of order is too maniacal for me not to have a horror of unmatched things) on a shelf in my library, probably rather high up, where there was a collection of books I owned that did not properly speaking belong to literature. Thus exiled to an inaccessible spot (whether I put it there right away or on some other occasion decided to clear a place on my table and rid it of the books I knew I wouldn't go on reading for some time, or at least not in a sustained way), thus placed on a shelf high enough so that I couldn't reach it except by climbing a ladder, I purely and simply abandoned this book, often thinking of taking it up again, but without this thought seeming urgent enough to me for me to make the small effort to go get the ladder and, even more importantly, to overcome the absurd uneasiness caused in me by the fact that *Sorcière* (combined in one volume with the *Légendes démocratiques du Nord*, another work by Michelet) was an isolated element of a series. There was also something vaguely irritating about combining under one cover a work about medieval witchcraft and a collection, not of legends taken from Nordic folklore (as the title might have implied, if it weren't for the word *démocratiques*, though that was printed in small characters as though trying to escape notice), but texts relating mainly to the history of Poland and its national heroes, with mention (obviously) of the famous Adam Mickiewicz. Ever since I became a sort of specialist, even a professional, where poetry is concerned, I have so detested these national poets—who are too much the celebrators of the nation to be true poets—that the very fact of *Sorcière*'s being paired, united in a single volume, with a text haunted by the literary ghost of Mickiewicz could have been quite enough to lower its value for me. If one adds to that the complete lack of interest that had long ago succeeded the adolescent fervor I felt (like quite a few boys of the time before the Versailles Treaty, I believe) for subjugated Poland, one will perhaps understand that in the final analysis the slight annoyance this book caused me—not only because it was an unmatched book but because of the arbitrariness of its composition—overshadowed the attraction I felt to one of the two works thus yoked together either by their chronological proximity or the whims of publishing. In the end, it was as though one of these works had in some way contaminated the other, and as though the repugnance I felt for the *Légendes démocratiques* had slipped over onto *Sorcière*, making me forget it was not an academic work presenting a piece of official history but an ambitious attempt to revive certain aspects of an ancient time that had to be reconstructed from within and revealed by plunging the reader into the very heart of a mentality and thereby revealing its perspectives, rather than by confronting him with a dead mass of material facts.

One thing that delighted me when I entered the sixth class and embarked, with the study of ancient history, upon the first cycle of the secondary school education's program of history studies, was that in addition to the history of reigns, battles, and events, we were also given a little history of civilizations. To know how the Egyptians made use of the flooding of the Nile, to see a cross section of the great pyramid showing it was a tomb, to learn that the Egyptians embalmed the dead by stuffing them with aromatics and that they were the inventors of those peculiar signs known as hieroglyphics—this interested me much more than all I had been taught up to then about the same region: the successes and failures of a certain sovereign, his good or bad behavior toward his people, the reforms he had carried out, the alliances he had signed. A resurrection of ancient times, not just a story about things that had happened—this was how I regarded history during this sixth-year program in which Eastern nations, Greece, or Rome, showed the human species living in different conditions from the ones we knew. Conditions whose most attractive aspect was probably that they were "ancient," as though a certain distance in time was enough to make an epoch interesting, either because of that separation in time itself or because the fact of being remembered despite such a separation seemed an undeniable mark of greatness.

When I was little (I mean well before I was old enough for the sixth class), "ancient times" referred to something rather different from the period described by "Once upon a time." Almost as nebulous, even though it was understood that the epoch of ancient times had really existed. It was the time of thatched cottages, candles, and liards (such poor coins, of such a parsimonious thinness, compared to the opulence of crowns, doubloons, and pistoles, the oriental picturesqueness of piastres and sequins). It was the time of the little chimneysweeps who ran along the roads with their headscarves tied over their foreheads, the good old days of old wives' tales and people carrying baskets full of wood on their backs, the time of the town of Montbéliard whose string of syllables, like a hurdy-gurdy tune, always gave me such an extraordinary impression of a sleepy old market town far off in the mountains. In ancient times there were also knights' tournaments, war-horses, secret dungeons, various forms of torture, such as water torture, people wearing doublets and jerkins, courtiers, lovers of madrigals, cotillion dances, coaches, and shepherds and shepherdesses with crooks.

Ancient times corresponded roughly to the period of the monarchy. The sack of Rome by "our ancestors the Gauls," Vercingetorix's surrender to Julius Caesar and even the Gallo-Roman era (so pale and empty, after episodes like that of the *Vae victis!* and the siege of Alésia) were not yet ancient times. Inversely, and almost at the other end of history, no longer ancient times, were the taking of the Bastille at the time of the first July 14, Rouget de l'Isle singing the "Marseillaise," and Napoleon and his mameluke Roustan.

The ancient times continued, of course, to exist in the depths of the countryside, more faithful than the towns to the old ways; it had deserted the towns and cities and now snugly warmed itself at the hearths of smoke-filled hovels, confined in the out-of-the-way places where in the old days it must have been born, somewhere in Romanized Gaul, in the vicinity of the first small Frankish kings. In the city, the "excesses" of the Revolution following upon the "abuses" of the ancien régime had marked, not only the advent of the modern era but also the end of the ancient times: a profound upheaval in people's way of life even more than a political storm bringing about the royalty's downfall.

The time of the kings (those kings belonging to the time when the life one led was really not at all different from the life people lead in the country these days), the ancient times were measured fairly precisely in the chronology by the uninterrupted series of reigns that followed one another, in France, from the coronation of Clovis to the death of Louis XVI. If, in my first years in the lycée, after a brief phase of Bonapartist enthusiasm during which my brother and I read the newspaper *L'Autorité*, I prided myself on being a royalist—at first a partisan of the Duc d'Orléans, Philippe VII, then of Don Jaime de Bourbon when I became a legitimist—this was not only for reasons of snobbery. A restoration of the monarchy not only seemed to me fair (since the power would be returned to those who had once exercised it for the greater glory of the country or at least for that of their descendants, which for me was the same thing) and necessary for a healthy organization of France (so that the management of the State would pass into the hands of men who had been brought up to do this, and so that, in addition, the "workers" would be kept in their place— for at that time I regarded them with the mixture of fear and antipathy that badly dressed people inspire in bourgeois children even of modest means), but it also seemed to me that—since what was involved was, precisely, a "restoration"—it would be a return to the ancient times. Later, when I began to care about justifying what I referred to—in keeping with the common practice—as my "ideas," this last reason actually seemed the most valid to me: one had to be a royalist because it was the only way of going *against the current*, going back up the natural slope of history, which was the most noble political ideal and the only one that truly represented an "ideal," not only in that it opposed the established order but that it went against the motion of reality itself. I was almost certainly fooling myself, however, when I put forward such a reason; what must have been at work in me, primarily, was—a result of pure anguish about the future, which for an adolescent merges with his future maturity—a sort of stiffening against the thrust of time, a rejection masked under the gentleness of a nostalgic impulse in the direction of the past as though, in the end, the ancient times—a time well before my birth or a kind of hazy childhood of the centuries, preceding the mechanism of the modern era in all its precision—had come to mean an imaginary refuge where I could timorously go to ground in my retreat before the looming of age and, in the end, death. To be a partisan of a king: a way of turning away from reality, of fleeing what I found overwhelming about the course of events, by keeping my eyes fixed on a calm and ancient horizon, as reassuring as a fairy tale. And no doubt even here, harking back over these memories, I am merely clinging to my childhood, as to a place of asylum from which I will never be torn again.

A place where ancient times persisted more than anywhere else and that, furthermore, shared some of the qualities of both the countryside and a museum—both conservatories of the marvels of the past, one open-air, the other enclosed—was the park at the Trianon. Queen Marie Antoinette, with a crowd of ladies of her court and noblemen from her entourage, had come here once dressed as though for a masked ball, to play at being shepherds and shepherdesses, taking delight in immersing themselves in something archaic and apparently trying to live the sort of artificial life peculiar to certain knickknacks depicting old-fashioned characters and also to museum dolls. During the time when I was taken to Trianon, I had not reached the age when one begins worrying about creating a political facade; not even knowing what it was to have an opinion, I was at that time quite far from espousing royalist convictions. At the very most (in the very hypothetical case in which someone had taken it into his head to question me about this) I would have said I was a Republican, being aware that my country was France and that France was a republic; republican in the same way that because of my first name I was *Michel* and because of my family name, *Leiris*. But without this question of partisan color being in the least involved, since it didn't exist for me at that time, I had been touched by the memory of those dead and gone pleasures of the court, with their feigned simplicity and all the supposedly tender and naive things that could be embellished upon the theme "It is raining, shepherdess . . ." I felt pity for that dead, decapitated queen, and I was especially surprised that in spite of the failings, however serious they were, that the people had wrongly or rightly reproached her with, her proclivity for rustic freshness and sheep had not testified convincingly to the candor that lay concealed in her soul despite everything, enough, at least, so that she would be spared her tragic end on the scaffold. I myself loved sheep, and I couldn't imagine that any person who devoted herself to the care of animals, whatever she was like, could have a bad heart (except for the drunken carter who treated his horse so brutally, a sort of helot whom I was to discover a little later). Not for one second did I dream that those sheep, so gentle, raised so gently, were raised to be eaten one day and that, even if one was content to care for them just for their own sakes, tying ribbons around their necks, such sensitivity could go hand in hand with a complete lack of understanding of the misery of human beings.

Associated with ancient times—however diverse, contrasting they may have been—were overriding notions of order, calm, happiness, goodness. The unfortunate creatures living in ancient times, and even the wicked, were unfortunate and wicked in a certain way that didn't leave a stain, didn't break the thread, didn't seem to be responding to any injection of mysterious venom into the nature of things. Did these benign views simply arise from the fact that in one's imagination things of the past have very vague outlines and are thus transformed into phantoms whose very unreality allows their bones to drop away? Or did they arise from the vapor of piety which, for most children and many adults, surrounds everything ancestral, a mist comparable to the patina of plant life which, as the years go by, softens tombstones and transforms those angular blocks into restful objects of worship? Had what had been revealed to me of it by the traditional stories and museum relics already been idealized, as happens little by little to the figure of a dead person, for most of the people close to him, whatever the faults and idiosyncrasies might have been that made them turn on him every day when he was alive? Or, by the very fact of being ancient times, that is, something beyond reach that I hadn't even known directly, did this confused succession of eras long past—and yet close to me, since I was shown traces of them everywhere—assume in my eyes a value unattainable by things that were simply *here?*

In the realm of music and imagery (realms, among others, that offer a possibility of *elsewhere* to my increasing reclusiveness as a grown man) there are a few things that seem quite different from one another but touch me in very similar ways because the quality they share is, I believe, that they take me back to the time when I believed in ancient times. For example: certain passages in the orchestral works of Stravinsky closest to the humus of the people, like the dance of the Moor in the third scene of the ballet *Petrushka*, a rhythmic gesticulation performed like a solitary rite in the chamber with rich oriental decor in which he has been locked, this automaton with the face of a black man, at once innocent and terrible, who had to be, it seems, part of the author's original idea, a hybrid creature, half man and half wild animal. Certain of the engravings, too, in old books on witchcraft, notably R. P. Gauccius's *Compendium maleficarum*, which appeared in Milan in 1626, a reference I take from *Le Musée des sorciers* by the occultist Grillot de Givry, a popular modern work I acquired about fifteen years ago and in which I have found several reproductions of these figures. In the engravings, there are sabbat scenes taking place in the open country, in almost bare, slightly undulating places, under skies also full of folds and without any indication of whether it is day or night. Perhaps because of the fact that this is a picture (even better—a black and white engraving) everything seems to be taking place in the most orderly way and the greatest silence, unlike what one might imagine from the current use of an expression like *mener un vrai sabbat* [make an awful racket, lit. "hold a real sabbat"]. No orgiastic outbursts in the gatherings depicted in these engravings. The men and women who take part in the sacrilegious ceremonies, dressed (to all appearances) like people of quality, have a formal demeanor. The expressions on the faces of the women, marked by a mixture of boredom and submission to fate, are touching. The devil, sometimes standing and sometimes sitting on a throne, is rarely shown full face, and it is as though his deceitful character is indicated by the fact that he only appears in profile and all one can perceive of that profile is its arrogant jagged lines. These two things—the music that accompanies the Moor's dance and seems to have been flattened and scratched by time, and the line drawings of sabbats the color of dusk or dawn over ruins—arouse in me the same very distant melancholy, as though they reached down to one of the most primitive and deepest layers of my innermost being. When I listen to or look at them, I have something of the same feeling as when I write; what would most accurately describe it would be the trite phrase *ça me serre le coeur* [it gives me a pang, lit. "squeezes my heart"], which should perhaps be corrected to frame the truth less crudely, to *ça me tire le coeur* [it tugs at my heart] (downward, I will add, meaning that when I am seized by that kind of slightly bitter enchantment, my whole heart takes a kind of plunge, drawn toward an ancient depth of fantasy).

Other pictures of the sabbat show girls dancing circle dances, slowly, it would seem, and with their backs turned to the middle of the circle. Like convicts chained around the same pillory post, each one isolated in her own suffering; like caryatids on the merry-go-round of a traveling fair imperturbably making their periodic circuit.

A circle dance whose accursedness is symbolized by those hands grasping one another without their owners being able to look at one another and by those backs diametrically opposed to one another; a circle dance that is the opposite of the beneficent dance in which the union of the dancers is shown by the convergence of all their eyes on one center. Here, there is a pervasive idea of something fixed, something desolate possessing each person, so that she can't communicate with the others. Here, like the black man in *Petrushka*, with his scimitar and turban, or the figure in an old town clock that strikes the hours with its single gesture, the characters are unchangeable, diligently (it seems) executing, each for herself, an infinitely repeated pantomime, whose meaning escapes them.

The same sadness associated with a music box tune, a barrel organ, a cracked carillon or the extinguishing of flames—sometimes more muffled, sometimes drier, sometimes more tender, sometimes more depressing—clings to certain names of streets or other places lying deep in my childhood.

At Viroflay, there was Avenue Gaucher (where we lived) and Rue de la Saussaie (a street with a laundry, and the one we had to walk down to get to the Louvre-Versailles tramway). Names belonging to early autumn rather than summer, associated with days of bad weather when one got one's shoes muddy rather than sunny days when all one brought back on one's shoes from a walk in the woods was a fine dust. Warm, damp names, the second smelling frankly of dishwater or the laundry room, whereas the dampness of the first was more the dampness of leaves weighed down by the rains of a storm, heavy showers with fat, tightly packed drops that swelled the streams and sometimes made them overflow.

In Auteuil itself, there was Avenue Mozart, which I would perhaps place under the sign of gaiety if it weren't for the sadness that is almost necessarily sprinkled over the things one remembers by the very fact that they are *things remembered*. Avenue Mozart, which I never actually realized was named after the musician I liked better than any other; Avenue Mozart, whose name describes, instead, the noise and the high body of the compressed-air Boulogne-Madeleine tramway that ran along it, especially the species of polished brass boiler in front, gleaming like a caldron or the brass hanging lamp we had in our dining room on Rue Michel-Ange, in those days, when many buildings weren't yet lit by electricity. This tramway, which some called a *"tramouay"* and others *"tramvay,"* just as certain people

(mainly ladies trying to seem distinguished) said *"vi"* instead of *"oui."*
The hanging lamp, called a *suspension*, whose name and shape made
me think of Murillo's painting *The Assumption*, which I saw reproduced in some pious image or on a page of some prayer book, a wonder
that was quite different from the *ascension* that Christ performed by his
own means, without having to be supported (like the Virgin surrounded by clouds and angels) or suspended (like our lighting fixture
above the steaming soup tureen). This tramway which I would sometimes see returning to the depot, situated at the corner of Avenue
Mozart and the street that was in fact called Rue de l'Assomption, a
tramway so tall with its upper deck that, seen face on under its
carapace of metal, it assumed the majestic look of a helmet. This
suspension, attached at one end to the tramway and at the other to the
Assumption, and this because of the voluminous brass organ behind
which one could make out the bust of the moustachioed motorman,
who surely did not say *"vi"* but *"oui"* and maybe even *"voui."*

All of this (well before the subterranean bowel of the *métro* and the
rubber wheels of the bus reached us) was in the Auteuil district.
Auteuil: the special sonority of this name, because it is the name of the
neighborhood where I was born. I didn't discover it: it was always
there, for me, like my own name. Sometimes when I hear it, I try to
imagine I am hearing the name—new to me—of a village I am just
entering that I don't know yet. Strange feeling I have, laboriously
trying to remove this pair of syllables from its natural element, to hear
the *au* and the *teuil* as though they were the physical media of some
other signification.

I know both the name and the physical form of Auteuil, since I
lived there so much of my life, only moving to a different neighborhood after the occupation began. The name and form of this place,
more special than any other in my emotional landscape, seemed to me
to be joined together by a sort of necessity. In the same way, if I have
known someone for a long time, his name eventually forms an undeniable portrait of him. But other place names have left deep impressions on my memory even though they weren't connected to a clear
form. *Montmorency* is one of them, designating a region I saw when I
was too young to be able to retain the least memory of it, but it was an
area my mother talked to me about often and starting a long time
back, as one of the places she remained most attached to, having gone
there for the holidays with her own mother shortly before the latter's
death, when I was still—or almost—in swaddling clothes, symbols

of the frailty of the newborn child. Until the last few years, the only thing I saw when I thought of this region was the following, no doubt constructed out of what I had heard about it: small houses buried in greenery, an ivy-covered wall, a garden with my mother sitting in a wicker armchair along with, perhaps, my grandmother (whose image I can only remember from photographs I was shown later); enveloping everything, a veil of musty old age, and I don't know if that veil *already*, in their time, lay over this group of things (as they really were or as I imagined them from the faded tones of the old family photos) or whether my memory hasn't, rather, interposed it *now*, in the process of remembering, in the sort of camera obscura of my head.

As for the name *Montmorency*, in *montmo-* (so close to *maman*) there is something of the murmuring of a baby looking for its mother's breast or lap. Yet this repetition, at the beginning of the first two syllables, of the same movement of the lips, reminiscent of a kiss or a suck, may have another meaning. Looking at it differently, in fact, I can see this redoubling as an onomatopoesis capable of transcribing—just as much as *teuf-teuf*, which is the way the noise of a locomotive is usually reproduced—the puffing and blowing of two trains that were as familiar to me as mechanical toys: the Ceinture and the Auteuil–Saint-Lazare train. What I see in my memory as the basis of this metamorphosis (a radical alteration, even though the structure of the word is not at all changed) is the fact that the two railway lines I have just mentioned shared a section of their routes that actually ran along Boulevard Montmorency before reaching Boulevard Beauséjour. For in the old days, when I was taken for a walk in that direction, I keenly enjoyed watching, every time a train passed, the thick, white smoke of the locomotive rise in fat puffs from the bottom of the sunken railbed, the walls of which resounded with its animal *teuf-teuf* that seemed to be imitated by the word *Montmorency*.

A few years ago, however, when because of a dinner with friends I happened to go to a certain spot in the suburbs to the north of the city, which, at least in its name, still bears a trace of the period when it was under the rule of the dukes of Montmorency, I wasn't thinking about that *teuf-teuf* but about everything old and maternal associated in my mind with this famous name, now merely a place name, though it once also applied to people. An impression of *déjà vu* that I had twice that day though without recognizing anything specific: once near the station, in front of some houses built of white stone and red brick in a fake seventeenth century style; and then at the end of a grassy avenue bordered by gardens full of thick vegetation, the avenue leading to the poky little house where my friends and I were going to have dinner. An impression of decay having to do with me directly, comprised within the framework of my own life, since it was connected to things that had been close to me once and that I almost might have believed I remembered; another kind of decay, too, one beyond the limits of my own life, one that belonged in the general framework of time long before my birth. A doubled old age, in which the historic past converged with my own and in which Louis XIII musketeers mingled with the ghosts of my own early childhood.

In Montmorency, as in Auteuil, the locomotives are fat, good-natured animals with a leisurely gait and cowlike breath, for here only slow trains go by. At Nemours, express trains speeding along below the bottom of the garden of the house my sister and brother-in-law lived in resembled riotous knights with their wind-cutters like the lowered visors of helmets. I always made this comparison more or less explicitly, and it was actually because of the fact that they looked both ultramodern and medieval that these locomotives with wind-cutters used to enchant me so. I would feel the greatest satisfaction when I saw one of them go through a level crossing at top speed: for example the train that went to Dordives, a name in which it seemed to me I could hear the whistling of steam, the seething of the boiler, the whole racket a locomotive makes.

Nemours itself was calm, suiting the claylike color of its name, suiting the gray stones of the church as well as the gray tint of the rocks scattered through the surrounding countryside. Still calmer was the neighborhood of Saint-Pierre-lès-Nemours (where there was a house we went to in the summer, a few years before my sister's marriage), a neighborhood with an even more archaic name than that of Nemours, because of the curious *lès*, which resembled *les* without being quite the same, thus slightly feudalized by the addition of a grave accent.

At Saint-Pierre-lès-Nemours, the house we lived in was called the Villa les Roses, and it was in the garden of this house that I took my first steps; one of my favorite companions was the owners' dog, an old white poodle named Bouquet. Also at Saint-Pierre-lès-Nemours, but a few years later, the house my brother-in-law had inherited from his mother was called the Villa les Gaules, and I was never able to find out if the word *gaules* meant the country of the Gauls or the poles of the line fishermen one came upon in such great numbers by the banks of the Loing, sitting in flat-bottomed boats. The dog belonging to this house—as though there has to be a dog attached to every house—was a comical sort of mutt, but sturdy under his close-cropped hair, black and white with a little red thrown in. A rover and a fighter, he was the terror of the other dogs in the area. An excellent friend to me, but one I also found disturbing because he sometimes indulged in a certain kind of behavior against my body whose meaning I did not understand for quite a long while. Standing up on his two hind legs and hugging one of my legs with his two front legs, he would gradually begin moving the way the piston of a locomotive moves and would achieve a semblance of coition with the part of my flesh that lay between the top of my sock and the bottom of my shorts. I was horrified by this contact, especially the moment the dog wet me (with a liquid that I thought for a long time was urine) after a few minutes of feverish agitation during which he looked completely crazed. Nevertheless, I was flattered too, as though the dog loved me in particular and was not simply suffering from a general pruritus that could have been appeased on any object. But the worst thing, perhaps, was that the dog's expression tended to become human at the very moment he was behaving in a peculiarly animal fashion. A faun without malice, a goat with fleshy, benign paws, who, however, unfailingly upset me when he threw himself into his wild dance. For then I was touching on something as fundamental as what I thought I saw a few years later in the dance of the thick-lipped automaton of the Ballets Russes and the silent, still dance of the fiends in the illustrations of those ancient books of demonology.

The memory of this old disturbance at Nemours, caused by an animal (not quite so elegant, surely, as his fellow dogs of the "days when animals could talk"), is not entirely unlike, I think, something that happened in the same area much later.

Having returned as an adult to Saint-Pierre-lès-Nemours for a very short stay and gone for a walk by myself one morning away from the houses, I entered a quarry that was deserted, because this was Sunday; but it was clear from the presence of a narrow-gauge railway line and a few tipcarts that it was still being worked, and on weekdays no doubt workers came here. Moved by my isolation, by the air of abandonment of the place, by its almost exclusively mineral nature, and the leaden sun reflected on all sides by the walls of that spacious matrix fashioned by the efforts of human industry in the depths of the earth with picks, shovels, and cartridges of dynamite, I stopped for a moment and, standing in the rays of the sun, yielded without shame to the so-called solitary vice. An homage not only to the elemental earth but also to my childhood itself, reflected back to me by every spot to which I can attach the name "Nemours."

A harsh sun striking my bare head, a great heat filling an enclosure with dazzling clouds of dust, and this infinite desire that it seemed only the partnerless love of Onan could offer even a simulacrum of satisfaction—didn't all this prefigure, within the frame of a day of boredom and heat spent at Saint-Pierre-lès-Nemours, the long months I lived in the desert during the first year of the war? In the Seine-et-Marne as in the Sahara, within the space of a few hours almost as much as during an accumulation of weeks, I sensed—as though I had touched it with my finger—what it was to be *alone*. I was prompted to seek some result by making an illusory agreement with the outdoors around me: a carnal agreement that for a moment connected me symbolically to the quarry, widowed of its workers; a more cerebral agreement that united me with the desert landscape, conceived as the image of my condition or the outside world's specific answer to what my fate, that inexorable figure, was waiting for to complete itself. In both cases, I obscurely appealed to a magic which, whether crude or subtle, was at least a link, an immediate way of attaching myself to the outdoors. In both cases, behind this magic, there was the phrase "Once upon a time," a piercing memory of a close or distant past that consumed me at the same time that it exalted me. In both cases, I was dominated by the need for a fusion or identification with what surrounded me, a need that arose from the fact that, separated by a gap in years or space from the creature I had been, if I wanted to find my feet again and feel intensely myself I had to find some support in the intangibility of things, derive from the apparent complicity of this motionless outside world the sense of a sort of eternity. At Nemours, not far from the old castle (where there was a deserted museum that I would visit later still, discovering iron rings in the walls of a dungeon now empty of prisoners, then, high up in another small room, an ancient velocipede? Worthy counterpart to the large, quite rusted tricycle I used to mount in the attic of the Villa les Gaules) at Béni-Ounif, where I imagined (given the combination of war-related circumstances that had sent me there) I had to some extent become part of history—what counted more than universal and historical time was lived time: the child I had been and never would be again (whence, I think, the melancholy that had driven me to take that solitary walk), the civilian that I had ceased to be, that I was not certain I would ever be again.

The atmosphere of that small old town left behind by the man out for a walk from Saint-Pierre-lès-Nemours, then the silence of the quarry he walked into, where the suspended work and the abandoned tipcarts seemed to describe a break in the flow of time, a halt to the glide of life similar to that which petrified the guests at Sleeping Beauty's palace; the vision of a fortified castle flanked by pepper-pot turrets as on that box of letter paper bought by the serviceman in the South Oran who was girded round with a whole apparatus of both noble and commonplace traditions because of his military clothes (a pretext, above all, for a coquetry as vain as the childish pleasure in costumes); the presence, in the background of the stage illuminated by the solar projector, of an irreducible mass of past, despite the lightning quick flow of seed through the man in the quarry and the corrosive exaltation that ravished the soldier in Africa, in his proud isolation; here, the Loing canal (which my sister's brother-in-law, the one who went mad during the 1914 war, had painted in a rainy watercolor that hung from one of the dining room walls), a rectilinear road of dead water bordered on either side by a long row of trees all the same and sometimes enlivened by barges towed by mules who were unhitched when they came to the lock; there, the immense expanse of rubble that was the Saharan plain unfolding its gentle, worn land-scape between my eyes and the horizon—when I open myself to such images and articulate them in words, I give them a meaning such that I more or less expressly recognize that rooted far behind me, there is such a thing as time. A time I have to accommodate as best I can; a time—past and, theoretically, still to come—to which I apply a good part of my efforts, trying to find a common denominator between this time and my life. Whether I have recourse to my memory, collecting what I feel are the most meaningful of the vestiges of moments I have lived through and trying to draw a picture of myself less ephemeral than I actually am; or whether, more ambitiously projecting my person fictively into a kind of timelessness, I set about transforming the trivial and serious things that happen to me and the great human events I may have brushed up against into so many features giving specificity to my form as mythical hero or great leading role; or whether, renouncing this self-contemplation, which is too much like the sensual complacency of an adolescent touching himself, I at last come to the point of *taking action* and try to change what happens in other people's time by what I deliberately do in my own time.

Like the mountebanks in Lannion blossoming in their paper-flower grace in the midst of the folk from the market, a merry fireworks can sometimes explode and give me the illusion, for a moment, of being outside myself and outside time. But immediately those old family stories come back to rivet me, through my own past, to the thickness of the entire impersonal and anonymous past in which they themselves are embedded.

The great floods of 1910, the overflowing of the Seine where normally there was a steady traffic of *bateaux-mouches*, which I was often taken on, embarking at the landing stage called La Galiote [canal barge] (a wet word, like *les Gaules*, and one that also smelled of the *bouillottes* [footwarmers] that heated railway cars, even the boat itself when it started up and the motion of the engine, with large roilings near the screws, made the whole hull vibrate): a public calamity, which for me—as for many people of all ages—was most of all a great spectacle. The rebellion of the water, which I cannot dissociate from my sister's marriage, since when her suitor first started visiting us, my brothers and I were told that this provincial with his glasses and his goatee—of whom I was jealous the entire time the engagement lasted—was a "flood victim" from Nemours coming to talk business, to discuss the compensation that he (supposedly) had a right to demand as one who had suffered from the overflowing of the Loing. A Boulangist crisis, which I wasn't aware of but which my mother told me caused my father great concern, since he was an upper level civil servant in the police opposed to the dictatorship and worried at seeing how, even among his subordinates, the General's cause spread like oil on water. The famous winter of 1871, during which the Seine froze over. The disturbances following the disbanding of the national workshops, days of rioting in which my paternal grandfather, a small-scale businessman, took part, his reward being deportation to Lambessa, in northern Africa, where almost a century later I was to play at believing I was something of a convict myself. The occupation of Paris by allied troops after Napoleon's fall, a memorable event for one of my great-grandfathers, I no longer remember which, because a Cossack who had been staying in his house was a little too forward with his wife, and my great-grandfather threw him out the window—though it was actually only a ground floor window. The great French Revolution, during which one of my ancestors on my father's side, a carpenter by trade, a regicide, and a member of the Convention, spent a large part of his worldly goods on outfitting a batallion that was to fight the Vendeans (I remember that in the house there was a miniature of him with his fat beardless face and his bare neck emerging from his Danton-style collar); at about the same time, a great-great-uncle of my mother's or some such relation, who was a priest or a defrocked priest, was forced to hide out in some woods in the region of Paris, one of his female relatives coming every night to bring him provisions. Finally, at the far end of our historic horizon, the Montlhéry Tower, which my brother Pierre and I saw and whose name, Mons Leherici, we liked to think of as related to our family name, as though that spot in the outskirts of Paris where a feudal ruin stood had been its actual birthplace.

Thus, passing from what I have authentically experienced myself to what, in this city of Paris where I was born, my ancestors experienced and I have also experienced to some extent through stories (in other words by proxy), then inserting all of it into the perspective of history itself, I come to the point of fastening my own time, which is framed by certain places and narrowly defined, to a much vaster time, one which has come from much farther off and which, unlike a river, which has a source, is not localized anywhere. An immense, echoing nave that reminds me of the "empty house," a name given by my brothers and me, in the Nemours days, to a group of rocks that formed a sort of natural dolmen: "empty house," a name that echoes the way our voices echoed under the granite vault and evokes the idea of a giant's deserted home, a temple of impressive proportions carved out of a rough, hard rock whose very coarseness seemed a gauge of its prodigious age, an old pachyderm the faded color of a mammoth under whose belly my brothers and I played.

With links half familial, half historical, I therefore hook my slim adventure onto the general chain of the epochs and situate myself—recalled to some sort of modesty—in the unfolding of a larger whole. Yet how much can I care about the sort of time that can only be a learned thing, the pale fruit of culture, that does not have much weight compared to my own time, so radically distinct from that parade of ghosts, the succession of the ages! Whatever attention—and can I also say respect?—I may give to the facts of history, I scarcely see it as more than a catalogue, sometimes picturesque but more often colorless, of events that have no real relation to me. For me to *feel* history, I have to transport myself, in my imagination, to the time when I was sitting on a bench studying it in school. The *oldest* thing, really, does not seem to be the thing that sits highest on the ladder of chronology; it is simply the one I have the earliest memory of, the one

I learned about or experienced the farthest back in time. One example—without even talking about sacred history—is the history of France, whose beginnings, at least, seem to me situated in a more remote time than the history of the ancient world, for the sole reason that the latter was only revealed to me later. Even more, certain memories that happen also to be sources of an indescribable sweetness, because they involved things experienced in my early youth and because this very intimate conjunction of something burgeoning and something faded, the matinal and the crepuscular, the fresh and the old, confers on such memories a quality that is unique for me and endows them with a marvelous, almost *sacred* halo, the halo of a chivalry romance or a fairy tale—so extremely present and yet separated from what I am today by such density. Sufficient evidence of this is the following memory, definitely one of the most moving of those I have retained, perhaps only because it is the most remote and remains as ill defined, as problematic, as though I were extracting it from some sort of prehistory.

I must be about three-and-a-half years old. My head is round, my hair curly, and I am still wearing a dress. (Obviously there is no question of my *remembering* all this, but this is how I see myself!) It is sometime around May. My mother is visiting a house (in a place reached from the Saint-Lazare Station, none other than Viroflay) that she wants to rent or has just rented for the whole summer. She is carrying me in her arms. We are in a room with closed shutters that smells of something like dust and perhaps insecticide powder. The sunlight falls through the horizontal slits of the blinds in broad slices of softly filtered light. The room is empty of all furniture. Outdoors, it must be rather hot, and insects must be humming. I am filled with a feeling of warmth, well-being, and safety as I watch the motes of dust moving about.

It is no doubt because of this peculiarly ancient quality that I have always been awestruck by things that seemed to say to me, "Once upon a time. . . ."

Sunday

Sunday outing in the car, through the Ile-de-France. Crossed Chantilly, Senlis, Compiègne, Pierrefond, Nanteuil, Mortefontaine, Ermenonville. . . . Met Sylvie, in the form of a very pretty blond shepherdess about fifteen years old, tall, svelte, with beautiful blue eyes and hair cut in Joan of Arc style. She was dressed in a long black smock with white stripes and was leading a goat to pasture.

The light in the Ile-de-France reminds me of the light in Greece, especially Olympia. It is the same thin mist or diffused light. The trees are of all different sorts, which prevents the landscape—not very hilly, but undulating slightly—from being monotonous.

There is a dreadful crowd of people coming by car to gather lilies of the valley. This is the petty bourgeoisie in all its horror; the world of shopkeepers. It is impossible to find one sympathetic figure among all these figures. Written on a banner in a little town decorated for a festival are the words: "All honor to the authorities!"

To cross Saint-Denis is always a stirring experience. One sees majestic factories with towerlike chimneys of a different sort of menace from those of feudal castles. On the Seine, people canoeing or swimming don't seem to care about that at all. It is as though the only decent people in Paris have stayed locked up in their houses or gone to demonstrate at the Mur des Fédérés.

Under the date May 26, 1929 (the day of the traditional demonstration in memory of the Communards shot down in Père-Lachaise), I find these lines in the square-ruled notebook with the blue cardboard cover where day by day—with intervals that can last for months, sometimes even years—I write this or that detail from my life to be set down for my own use, a dream from the night before, a reflection inspired by some external event, or by my state of mind at the moment. An album of memories, a keepsake, much more than a journal or collection of thoughts. An album almost in the same sense as an album of postcards or photographs. There are documents glued to many pages, in fact: separate leaves of paper scribbled on haphazardly and inserted just as they are, sometimes because of the fetishistic value I might have accorded these original documents (still quite steeped, in their very physical being, in the circumstances in which they were written), sometimes simply because I was too lazy to recopy them; pictures of women from the theater who embodied, at a given time, a type I felt to be particularly attractive or moving (such as Adelaide Hall, the black star of the 1929 revue, *Black Birds*, or Damia, the cabaret singer); publicity leaflets, like the announcement of Cervantès's *Numance*, produced by Jean-Louis Barrault with sets and costumes by my friend André Masson (an announcement followed by a few lines by Robert Desnos) or like the publisher's blurb from my book *L'Afrique fantôme* (which is really the private journal I kept when I was traveling in Black Africa on an ethnographic mission); a photograph of a painting by Masson whose subject is Narcissus and Echo and another of one of his oldest paintings, in which some men are sitting around a table over a meal of bread, red wine, and pomegranates; a piece of letter paper showing a pen sketch of a bullfighting scene, the work of a nephew of Picasso's, which Picasso gave me, knowing (and for good reason, since I was with him when I saw my first fight!) my love of corridas; the cover of a program for the film *Wuthering Heights*, with a picture of Merle Oberon in the role of Catherine and another of Laurence Olivier in the role of Heathcliff; a printed page of pale green at the top of which, under the title "The Lilac," is depicted a branch of lilac behind two circles, one circumscribing a ram and the other a crescent moon with its points to the right: a shoddy sort of horoscope given me by a maimed beggar one day when I was sitting at a table on the terrace of the Taverne du Palais with a person I had known for quite a long time through family connections, but whom I never saw very much of and who is himself almost an authority in matters of occultism and astrology; another horoscope—also on a green background—picked up by chance at a movie and concerning people who, like me, were born in April; a large sheet of square-ruled paper on which a clairvoyant woman (whom I once went to consult, without much believing in it, when I belonged to the surrealist group) summed up, in a series of reference dates and words as well as a diagram indicating the general arrangement of the lines of my hand, what had been and would be, according to her, the course of my life up to and beyond 1939. Glued to a double page at the very end of this notebook (on the back cover and the verso of the mauve end paper) is, lastly, a pencil drawing I did idly one day in 1928 and entitled "My Life, By Myself." At the top is a pyramid with the horizon behind it; then, to the left of the pyramid and looking at it, my profile; at the bottom, the eye of a woman whose gaze seems to rise toward me from right to left, the eye enlarged by the arc of an eyebrow and placed parallel to an oblique line that is the base of the wavy lines forming the hair. What seemed to me at that time charged with meaning in this drawing was the radical separation between this image of me and the imposing but geometrically cold shape it seemed to be looking at fixedly, and then between the woman's eye and my image, toward which the gaze of this eye rose from the very bottom as though the exiled creature who was casting it forth had vainly sought an impossible union, in the same way that my own gaze could only appraise—without leaping it—the distance that prevented me from reaching the pyramid, close but inaccessible.

This succession of images and other pieces of evidence punctuate my notes, whose general tone is rather pessimistic. More consistently pessimistic, obviously, than would be appropriate if I had set out to write my memoirs or collect in this notebook, relying only on chronological order, the elements needed for the composition of a portrait. The reason for this being that only during my periods of depression do I feel the need to pour out my heart to a future interlocutor (an almost imaginary partner) in these handwritten leaves of a journal that will not be published or even read in my lifetime but will constitute the last, posthumous message I address to those of my family and friends who survive me.

When things aren't going well, and especially when I don't feel up to real literary work, I readily resort to writing this sort of note, which is less satisfying, certainly, than the things I manage to give a shape to but satisfying enough to prove to me that my mind is still awake. During the long periods when I have to confess to myself that I am incapable of creative activity (whether all my attempts in that direction prove fruitless or I have even lost my taste for them, out of despair or simple laziness) these notes are positions to which I can withdraw. I am quite aware, of course, that I have no chance of attaining any sort of deliverance until I have formulated the thing I want to get rid of in a way that is fascinating to someone else and therefore capable of exalting me too, the orator priding himself on the sound of his own voice. But unburdening myself so massively of what weighs on my heart, throwing it down on the paper so unaffectedly, gives me a certain undeniable comfort, at least briefly, as long as my throat is still wet from confiding it—that is, not for much longer than the ink takes to dry on the page.

Sunday, the day of the *repos hebdomadaire* [weekly rest]—or the *"repos du dromadaire"* [dromedary's rest], as we said jokingly in my family—can very easily be catastrophic, at least for those not crushed by a thankless job all week long and for whom such a day is more than anything else a time when they are forced to confront themselves more squarely, no longer knowing what to do with these hours of idleness they have perhaps looked forward to but during which all sorts of occupations seem pointless the moment there is complete freedom to pursue them. An empty day (since the week has reached its end and has frozen into a period of immobility before starting off again), a hollow day (which essentially represents a vacation in the common as well as the pure meaning of the word), Sunday—the day of the Lord and the seventh stage of Genesis—periodically introduces into the calendar, not the pious figure of the creator resting on his laurels as one retires after having made one's fortune but instead a scaled down image of death and nothingness. This, the effect of an obscurely sensed allegorical correspondence, may explain the fact that Sundays—and all high festival days—tend to be so very depressing. They are reminders, at regular intervals, of that same menace in the face of which it becomes unbearable, for example, to think there are people who "retire" and buy or build houses so that they will have a place to spend the few days left to them in peace and quiet.

It is Sunday today, and what is more, Easter Sunday. Yet I would be lying if I said I didn't feel good. Since the war started, since we were defeated, especially now that the enemy occupation has become so oppressive, the fact is that things have changed a good deal for me. Now that life is closed off, the future only a black hole, now that one can no longer make plans except idly (because one always has to tell oneself some story), I yield less easily to these fits of moodiness, these attacks of depression. Since the present no longer dissolves into unreality as it did when everything was soft and easy, I keep myself closer to it and am able to savor it as long as it remains more or less livable. Nothing I may do can seem gratuitous to me anymore, in these times when such hideous things happen that it is impossible for anyone not to hold himself more or less responsible and not to assign to each of his actions a measurable significance.

Therefore, when I hear the bells of Notre Dame ringing I don't hear them as a knell, nor does the calm in the street seem to me to prefigure the calm that prevails in cemeteries. Even the rain, which has just begun to fall, is rather agreeable to me. If I am in better harmony with the parenthesis of Sunday in these oppressive years than when the world was still breathable, this is perhaps also due to the fact that since everyone, or almost everyone, is depressed every day, a "day off" does not have that flagrant absurdity about it of being, precisely, "off," that is, a day one celebrates by not working, by relaxing a bit, by doing one's best to be interested or happy as though it were not simply one more step toward the day when one won't be here anymore to experience the days passing. Now that Europe is worse than a factory, neither more nor less than one great labor camp—if indeed not a penitentiary—there is even something comforting in the thought that despite everything there are days when we escape from the yoke they try to impose on us by not working. Far from being the fissure through which nothingness seeps in, the parenthesis of idleness has become a breach in the wall, so that we don't suffocate.

> *Les Anglais le dimanche*
> *S'en vont passer la Manche*
> *Avec une chemise . . .*

> On Sundays the English
> Go off across the Channel
> With a shirt . . .

and, no doubt, a *valise*, because of the rhyme called for by *chemise*, in which I can still hear the slight crumpling sound of my father's starched cuffs as he slipped them into his cuff protectors or pulled them out, he who—given the weekly day of rest—was essentially, for me, the Sunday man, if not the man from across the Channel. This is the beginning of a song that is being heard again these days, since it is the famous "Viens Poupoule," a song dating from the Entente Cordiale that I often heard when I was little. Along with "Aoh, yes! Aoh do you do?" sung to my brothers and me by a certain Stéphane Ferranti, the son of a flautist of Italian origin who had been part of my father's artistic circle and whose own name was Lodoïs. Since Stéphane (also called "Sté") was preparing, or believed he was preparing, for a career as a violinist, the rest of us boys amused ourselves by rhyming his first name with *colophane* [rosin], lovers as we were of preposterous nonsense and also nicknames—like all children of our age—and having for a long time delighted, for example, in calling exclusively by the name of "Clown Pâté" (instead of "Claude Taté," his real name) a boy who lived almost opposite us, though I don't even know if he deserved this nickname by being especially corpulent.

Edifying, lightweight entertainment, listening to these two Anglo-French songs, "Viens Poupoule" and the song in gibberish sung by Stéphane Ferranti, who would adopt the manner of a professor of music theory or dancing master even though he wasn't accompanying himself on his violin. Pleasures that, when I look back on them from a distance, are permeated—as worn linen is with a starchy stiffness—with a flavor so stale, so familial, and so old that I can't conceive of them taking place on any day but Sunday. The residue of occasions that were no doubt jolly at the time but when they come back to me in memory now, seem scarcely different from certain old impressions today deduced to little more than a name associated with a smell or a special quality of light impressions that, though originally rather sinister, have acquired a kind of sweetness along the way, taking an opposite path to the one that leaves me with a melancholy memory of moments once so happy.

One of the people I was taken to visit on Sundays was a boarding school friend of my mother's, a round little person with graying hair above her florid face, and a hint of a moustache, whose placidity—proverbial among her friends—did not prevent her from being witty and playful. The director of a nursery school in some nasty neighborhood I can't remember exactly anymore, she lived in Saint-Mandé, and to go there we took the Ceinture [Belt] railway (a line whose name seemed to me justified by the broad leather strap—a kind of belt—used to lower and raise the windows of the doors in the railway carriages). One station on that line—the last or next to last before we arrived at Saint-Mandé—seemed to me like the vestibule of a particularly deserted and lost part of this outlying area of Paris, which almost always has something lugubrious about it. I'm talking about

Bel-Air-Ceinture, a station I can only see lit by a pallid light from incandescent burners, even though in reality I passed through it only by day, and in any case this was a time when stations were illuminated by even poorer means than gas. Mingling with this unwholesome dawn or dusk light falling upon the green of benches made by Allez Frères was a stale smell of smoke, the image of two slopes of earth on either side of a railway cutting, and also the image of the vast black hole of a tunnel entrance.

Another station name—one that could be read on the large maps in the metro—made me even more uneasy, not only because of the ill-famed neighborhood where it lay but also because of a boulevard very close by with a name that exuded the exoticism of an outlying district. On the elevated part of the Étoile-Nation line, which served the outer boulevards, the name of the Barbès-Rochechouart station, not far from Ornano Boulevard, which remains associated with a smell of chemicals (the smell of the disinfectant that was used in the metro then, it seems to me) and stinks of crime, in the same way that "Arcole" (from the Pont d'Arcole or Bonaparte at Arcole) is redolent of the pleasant smell of methylated spirits. I tend to think of this name, "Ornano," when I read in the newspapers that someone has committed suicide by throwing himself under the metro. As for the smell of disinfectant, I always imagine it emanating from the little shining specks one sees sprinkled on the stairways in the stations.

Visits to relatives or friends of the family, which were paid on Sunday or after dinner, were always, whether at noon or in the evening, framed within the part of our life dominated by my father. Spending all day at his office and only coming home at dinner time— even later when it was "account day" at the stock brokerage where he worked—my father, eclipsed the rest of the time by the figure of my mother, resumed all his importance the moment he was there again. It was enough for him to come home, his day finished, hang his top hat on the coat rack, and pull *Le Temps* from his pocket (his usual newspaper, besides *Le Matin* and *Le Journal*, which we liked to call *le journal Le Journal*, redundantly joining the common and proper nouns); it was enough for him to put on his slippers and gray flannel smoking jacket for everything in the house to fall into place. Even though he was the least authoritarian man in the world, once he was back home, authority was present, embodied in a simple gesture like holding the soup ladle as much as in the gravity of the name *Le Temps* spreading its gothic letters across the bluish newsprint.

With the same clutching at the stomach I get from the memory of the Englishmen crossing the Channel and the memory of "Aoh yes," I recall certain jokes—the sort that set your teeth on edge—which my father liked to indulge in affectionately. When, for example, he called my brothers and me *les éfants* instead of *les enfants* or when he conferred on us the epithet *Ostrogoths*—and I've always wondered whether the expression was peculiar to my father or common to the class of society to which my family belonged. There was also the *vase de Soissons** to designate the chamber pot, and *Michenne* in place of my real first name.

I don't know if I am pained here by a vulgarity that immediately shames me because it concerns my father and, indirectly, me too, or whether, instead, the shame only comes to me secondarily from the fact that I am yielding, as I remember these entirely pointless jokes, to a feeling of tenderness. Insipid attacks on language, as though for no other reason than to create a private slang and a feeling of solidarity among the few people who use it; plays on words whose aim is not so much to make the family laugh as to recognize one another, like initiates in a secret society, as members of the same family; purely conventional locutions, the heart of a pact sealed by the people who use them, sealed so firmly that it still proves effective, and even today I can't think of one of those miserable jokes without being moved (and embarrassed by my emotion) at being thus all at once plunged back into the old freemasonry of the family.

Their remoteness in time, the odd nature of words such as *Michenne* or *les éfants* tend to make me rather indulgent here. But as a general rule, I detest these family jokes, which are repeated on more or less fixed days and at more or less fixed hours. Among people who see each other every day, habits inevitably form. Each person becomes frozen in a clearly-defined attitude, the result of the conception others have of him. Each person also has his own specialties, his "numbers." This is what I can't bear, what I see as a sign of mummification and senility. I only submit to the use of slang with the greatest uneasiness, be it professional, friendly, or familial, for the use of slang—an easy means of complicity within a group—is one of the clearest signs of the herd instinct.

At the time when my father liked to call me *Michenne*—was it mockery touched with tenderness or pure and simple teasing?—I

* Play on *vase de nuit*, chamber pot, and Soissons, bean-growing area.

didn't yet have any particular opinion about these special languages. To tell the truth, I didn't even know what slang was. What I didn't like about this alteration in my name was that it affected me like an injury to my person. Even more than in the case of Rue Michel-Ange, *Michel* was associated with *Saint Michel archange*, and I saw it not only as my own property but rare enough so that I could justly be proud of it (the way some people may take pride in a noble title). Next to my other given name, *Julien* (which reminded me unpleasantly of *julienne*, a vegetable soup I didn't like because the taste of carrots dominated), *Michel* seemed to me a special given name, having something to do with an angel because of *Michel-Ange* and a good deal to do with an archangel because of *Saint Michel archange*, a figure all the more prestigious because he has the anomaly of being a saint who is not a man but an archangel. Furthermore, why should my given name be such that it comes before the title *archange* or *ange*, whereas one says *l'archange Raphaël*, *l'ange Gabriel*, putting the "archangel" or "angel" in front of the name? A celestial warrior attacking demons, a gate-keeper with a flaming sword guarding the earthly paradise after Adam and Eve have been driven out of it—such was the supernatural being with which it seemed to me I was in league, a nobler and more powerful protector than all the other patron saints. Such brilliance could only reflect on me, since the archangel and I had the same name. To change this word, my very substance, was therefore not only to change me in the very deepest part of myself but also to deprive me of some of that brilliance and take me down to a level almost as low as that of *julienne*.

Angel and archangel were associated with every day, including Sunday, quite unlike from Mass, which was associated only with Sunday. Mass was also associated with my mother, as were angels and archangels too, actually, along with everything else belonging to the domain of religion.

At issue in the Mass were, above all, Our Lord Jesus, the Holy Virgin, and the Good Lord. Their servants were the priests, whom I knew by name, some of them being my catechism teachers, and who were simply men rather different from others, men to whom I owed respect but who had nothing marvelous involved in their persons. Angels were scarcely a part of the Mass, and the only creatures spiritually present, aside from the Holy Family, were the saints. But saints, whatever their legends may be and whatever miracles may be attributed to them, are still half human, as all dead people are. Even though they are closely related to the Good Lord—more closely than the priests—they differ from us less radically than the winged species, the angels. Mass therefore remains a human thing, the ceremonious gathering of grownups expressing their goodness of spirit by giving to the collection plate and their piety by the seriousness of their behavior. Given these conditions, I wonder if the church we were taken to on Sundays, dressed in suits more handsome than the ones we wore during the week, was really the best place for mystical experiences, or if it wasn't rather at home that we absorbed our faith, in the bedroom where we were made to say our morning and evening prayers, where we knew the guardian angel was watching at the foot of our beds.

"My little Jesus, I give you my heart and promise you to be very good"—this was the earliest prayer my mother made me say when I got up in the morning, at a time when my main duty was to obey. I forget the formula she made me repeat every night—perhaps the same one?—after she had dressed me in a long nightshirt that enclosed me like a sack (because it could be tied at the bottom with a drawstring, so that when I moved around during the night, as I always did, it wouldn't ride up). When I was a little bigger and could learn longer texts by heart, my mother had me recite "Our Father" and "Hail Mary." One night—and I must have reached the age of reason by then—I added to my usual prayer (of my own accord or at my mother's instigation?): "My Lord, I thank you for having my father appointed managing director." Thanks given to the Creator for the promotion my father had just been awarded at the stock-brokerage where he spent his days; thanks which I offered with a fervent heart, since my own importance seemed to me to have increased a notch now that I could boast of having a father who, with the help of Providence in addition to his own abilities and love of work, had become almost equal to the great wealthy bourgeois who was his boss.

Neither rich nor poor, angels were angels, whereas the Infant Jesus and, even more clearly, the Holy Virgin had led the life of poor people on earth. As for the saints, they too were ranked with the poor, since for the most part they also went barefoot, without even a pair of sandals. Barefoot along with the saints and the Virgin carrying the Infant Jesus, the angels, at least, did not walk on roads, because they could fly and always, moreover, belonged to the category of invisible beings. Their feet, though bare, were not the feet of the poor, just as mine were not when I was lying in my bed, also wrapped up in a long white tunic. Not having bruises on the soles of their feet from outcroppings in the earth, not having a carapace of dust over them, these were especially luxurious feet, like the shining, curly hair, the immaculate robes, the wings with their orderly plumage: in short, everything that showed the angel belonged to a world where bread did not require the sweat of one's brow and where even having to eat was out of the question.

"Good as gold," "quiet as an angel"—I don't know if I deserved these epithets very often. But in those days, when the most important moral rule for me was to be docile, the insipid figures in holy pictures, baby-faced cupids playing with their bows and arrows, angels like the puffs of meringue in floating islands with their serious, young faces all seemed to me models for an unparalleled zeal, complaisance of character, and sweetness. To be good was certainly to perform charitable acts, to give pennies to the poor when one saw them in the street, if necessary to share what one had with one's little friends, but above all it was to make one's parents happy, to be pleasant and studious, to adopt toward them the attitude of an angel whose only concern is to serve God and love him.

Next to the Virgin, the mystical spouse of the Holy Ghost, there is the craftsman Saint Joseph, who appears to be an intruder into the Holy Family and is hardly more than a good, honest man with whom a half-angelic creature is joined in a strange misalliance. This was how my father seemed to me, since I knew that his early life had been difficult, whereas my mother had been rather well off in her youth and had received an education quite advanced for a young lady of her time. She spoke English fluently and was certainly more cultivated than my father, who left school at the age of thirteen or fourteen. But I owe it to him to add that she did not take advantage of this superiority and, having a deep love for the man with whom she had chosen to make her life, did not in any way behave like a woman who has married beneath her.

The area where the primacy of my father was most clearly evident within the little society of which he and my mother together formed the foundation was in his role as household provider. In his circle he was often jokingly compared to a pelican, and I think that in fact he would have gone so far as to give us his very entrails to eat if he had no other way to feed my brothers and me. In his eyes, any money he might earn was valuable mainly as it related to our "future," his dream being to turn us into young men in a position to direct themselves toward a career of their own choice and to embellish their minds better than he had been able to do. The greatest distress I ever caused him, I think, was when, at the age of eighteen, I undertook (unsuccessfully, moreover) to become a businessman, wanting to have at my disposal a little more money than I was given to spend on my own entertainment. He, who had failed to do what he wanted to do and became a stock broker in order to support his family (instead of an artist, as he would have liked—an opera singer or comic-opera singer, for which he really had the gifts), would have liked to see me continue my education, but at that time I was only thinking about immediate profit and troubled myself very little over the contradiction inherent in adopting a vocation that involved regularly sacrificing most of my time while I wanted only to be able to lead a life this very sacrifice would expressly preclude.

Certain objects seemed to me to represent physically, like emblems, the economic power with which my father was invested. There was his gold watch, which he wore hanging from a thick chain whose ends plunged into the fob pockets on either side of his vest. Hooked onto the same chain, there was, most importantly, his gold-purse, a small round box with two slightly convex sides, with a double bottom inside worked by a spring in such a way that the depth of the receptacle was automatically reduced as, opening the cover and pressing lightly with one's thumb, one slipped the louis d'or out of this gem of a strongbox. Twins of these two objects were given to me at the time of my first communion. I was also given a superb chain, which they first told me was only gold-plated (because one of pure gold would have cost too much) and then—having arranged this surprise—that it was well and truly a gold chain. These gifts, long awaited, long coveted because they seemed to be attributes of our father, these presents promised for a ceremony that is the first official step one takes in one's progress toward adulthood, offerings one sees streaming in from various directions like wedding presents, did not, however, succeed (despite the obligatory feast) in turning first communion into the "most beautiful day of one's life" they have so casually promised us without worrying about the fact that such a prediction will necessarily cause a disappointment inevitably affecting our future piety. After enjoying them for a few years (as proud owner of possessions which only those who have attained the age of manhood have a right to), I parted with these objects, or almost all of them, selling them at a loss as needed, at a time when hardly a day went by without my chasing after a little cash so that I could frequent the snobbish bars where I imagined—a schoolboy, really, still at the point of first communion despite female companionship and cocktails—I could least expensively lead something that resembled the heady life of gilded youth.

Scarcely two and a half hours ago—the day after I wrote the preceding paragraph (about which I will observe long afterward, I note here as an addendum, that it alludes indirectly to a black man, the saxophonist Vance Lowry, one of the first Negro musicians to come to France at the end of the other war, and to whom I gave my beautiful gold chain in exchange for the tiny sum of fifty francs)—I was, as it happened, leaving a bar, the Rhumerie Martiniquaise, unquestionably the one I like best of all the cafés in my neighborhood. There are fewer West Indians there now than formerly; the place is not at all picturesque now that its decor has become more opulent; but to sit on the red velvet-covered seats is comfortable, and they have punch still called *martiniquais* (admittedly less good than before because a different quality of rum is used, and it doesn't have lemon zest in it or nutmeg); you can get it at all hours of the day—despite the restrictions—and all week long except Thursdays and Fridays, the days when La Rhumerie is closed, in conformance with the regulations in force during this period, so strictly policed down to the smallest things. I had just paid for the drinks and was about to cross the doorsill with my two guests, one of whom, whose name is Khadidja, I feel very close to because of her name (the name of Mohammed's first wife and also of a girl I knew when I was a soldier in North Africa); because of her love of dance (which she has done professionally) and the spectacular bull-fighting *fiesta*, two arts on which my friends know I place a high value because of their violent, primitive quality; most of all because of her physical attractiveness and, in particular, the fact that although she lives in Saint-Germain-des-Prés she is an authentic Moorish woman, a native of Port-Etienne, the desolate desert village where my boat made a stopover on the way to Dakar, as I was preparing to face the heat of the tropics for two years or so. The three of us were about to go out of the bar onto the terrace (a sort of platform made of boards, as in seaside bars) and from there to the sidewalk on Boulevard Saint-Germain, where we were to separate, when we ran up against a bicycle policeman or rather against his bicycle, which he was holding

in front of him crosswise, barring the door. It was a raid. A call home
to tell them I would be late and the reason why. A wait of a few
minutes, then a step up, with the other customers from the café, into a
van with windows that had bars but no panes. The month of May
being quite gloomy this year, 1944, when the van started up we were
cold. We ended up at the central police station on Place Saint-Sulpice,
where we were released as soon as our papers were checked, but not
before our three names, like those of the other people, were put on a
list, which is very unpleasant at a time when one of the most desirable
things is to remain completely unknown to the authorities. On the
whole, everything went off smoothly (I have to admit). The only
disagreeable remark we heard was made by a secretary who answered a
man in a hurry by saying, in a furious tone of voice, that things would
certainly go much faster if we weren't all standing there crowded
against each other "like a flock of sheep." To hear her, we were the ones
responsible for being penned up here like animals after being packed
into a van.

This trifling incident—absurd, since in these days so many very
serious things are happening—this unexpected but fortunately fleeting contact with the reality of the police occurs as a reminder that the
earth continues to turn and life to go on in a bad way while I am
remembering and, as best I can, writing.

I have almost always considered to be atrocious (if indeed I can form
any idea of it) the situation of people who have no money and for
whom there isn't even any difference between Sundays and weekdays
because they have lost the relative wealth of having a job, and all their
days seem to them equally empty and miserable. Even apart from
those ravaged by idleness and hunger, there is a certain level of
poverty at which even love no longer seems possible. A sad situation,
that of people for whom there is nothing luxurious about carnal
intercourse, for whom it is a simple necessity; who don't find each
other beautiful (worn out as they are by their difficult life); who don't
promise each other any happiness; who simply sleep together, make
love without any mythology (because it is in the nature of people to do
it), mingle their weariness by resting against each other. Thus, a few
years ago on a street in Paris, I saw a very poor young man sitting on a
bench with his female companion and sleeping with his head on her
shoulder, while she had her arm around him in a motherly way. It was
one of those things that ought to give everyone cause for reflection.

Shortly after I turned twenty, during the period when I became committed once and for all to the literary life, I felt a certain romantic attraction to poverty, conceiving of it as the indispensable sanction of genius; but what was involved here was not so much true poverty as the ostentatious rags of bohemia. I have to confess, also, that I never did anything that might deprive me of a certain level of financial comfort. However, I don't remember, except in my early childhood, ever attaching any importance to money as such, and the fact is that it doesn't represent anything for me, outside of the pure and simple possibility of spending.

Until my first communion—and maybe even a little later, as long as I didn't receive a monthly allowance from my parents—I put away in a money box everything I received for New Year's Day gifts, on birthdays or saint's days, for good grades in schoolwork, or desirable placements in exams. I'm not very sure what use that money was to me, or if it sometimes happened that I would dip into the sum I had amassed for the price of something I wanted to buy. When I think about it, I am more inclined to believe I didn't do any such thing but confined myself simply to hoarding it—the only time in my life when money really had a value for me, one independent of what it could be converted into.

Louis d'or, ten-franc pieces (smaller and thinner), large *thunes* of a hundred *sous*, brand new *gros sous* that I kept because of their glitter, which was like the glitter of gold (when we were all three still very young, the older of my two brothers extorted a ten-franc piece from me one day, giving me in exchange one of those beautiful gleaming *sous*, after captivating me with its color)—these were the different denominations that lay together in my money box and formed a treasure for me whose sum, even after the New Year's gifts (that is, at the moment of my greatest wealth), could hardly have been more than about fifty francs.

My attitude toward all these coins was not so much that of a miser in love with his gold but that of a numismatist who sees a coin not as an instrument of exchange but a medal having a value in itself. In this I was like other children for whom a coin is to such an extent an *object* that one of their most common amusements consists of reproducing its image on a sheet of paper, first arranging the disk of metal under the thin flat surface, then, while the pressure from the fingers placed on either side of the coin keeps the two in close contact, passing the pencil lead over it, bearing down slightly: an amusement almost as enticing as that in which one rubs with the edge of a coin the apparently blank page of a special kind of notebook to make a drawing appear on it whose meaning will become clear as one extracts it piece by piece.

Besides these tangible coins stashed in a gold-purse or locked away in a moneybox, I knew that there existed other forms of money. Before becoming managing director—as though promoted to commander or colonel—my father was stocks cashier in the firm where he was employed. I had a vague idea of what stocks were: large, thick pieces of paper different from banknotes (which were still money). I even knew that my brothers and I owned a few that my father had bought for us and was keeping at his office, the place where plots involving money were hatched. For several months, we enjoyed following in the newspaper *Le Temps* the fluctuations in price of the Santa-Fé, some shares of which the head of our little household had one day announced that he had bought in our names. "Playing the stock market" was another thing we often heard him mention with obvious disapproval. Given his profession, based on traffic in values, our breadwinner certainly must have speculated occasionally; but those prudent moves on the part of the head of the family had no relation to what I sensed were the plays attempted by these gamblers, who could lose or win a fortune in the space of a day and whom I imagined sumptuously dressed (in topper and jacket, not forgetting the cigar) until the moment of their ruin, when they had no other recourse but suicide (like the leader of the gang of counterfeiters who, in one of the first films I ever saw, blew his brains out deep in the woods where the police had tracked him), unless they were simply reduced to begging (like my father's former colleague who after being quite well off, had lost everything he owned at the races and now humbly asked my father to lend him a hundred *sous* when he met him at the Bourse).

A horror of gambling, which inevitably led to debt, an inclination to thrift and hard work coupled with a love of perfect honesty, a manifestation of pity for those who had not been smiled on by fate, the avoidance of greed, modesty in one's dress, as in one's way of life (not excluding bodily cleanliness and hygiene)—these were the great moral principles that my parents, through teaching and by example, tried to inculcate into us with regard to money and what immediately derived from money. In all of this there was no questioning the validity of the distribution of wealth in our current form of society. The rich are rich, the poor are poor. He who is lucky enough to count himself among the first is only required to behave like a "good" rich man, and if there are clearly "bad" rich people, it is just as obvious that certain poor people are "bad" poor people. To each his lot in life, to each his virtue: to the rich man, not to be greedy and to give; to the poor, to wait with resignation for his misery to be relieved and, through the dignity of his bearing and the strictest probity, to merit what he may be granted; to all, whether or not they are needy, to show themselves to be "disinterested."

Poles apart from the benign blind man with his white beard and poodle, as from the starving man with the bad luck to get caught just as he is stealing a loaf of bread from the baker's stall, the bad poor man is the one who in a bitterly hateful tone demands what he regards as his due, abandons himself to some vice, such as alcoholism or just plain laziness, does nothing to cleanse his filth or patch his ragged clothes. The bad poor are also members of that amoral underworld such as were sometimes seen by my mother's friend who lived at Saint-Mandé and became the director of a nursery school. Among other anecdotes intended to show what social circle many of her pupils belonged to, she would tell—depicting the emotion she had felt about it as a pleasant amazement—the story of a little girl whose mother sent a man to pick her up every evening when school was over, a man the little girl would call "papa" without seeming surprised that almost every evening this "papa" was a different individual.

Very close to the bad poor man—situated scarcely above him on the steps of the social ladder—is the bad working man, the one who does his job against his will, goes on strike only in order not to work, dissipates the whole of his pay in bars on Saturday night or Sunday instead of taking it home or even acquiring a savings-bank book for his wife, his children, or his own benefit. The typical specimen of the bad working man: the day laborer who becomes brutishly drunk and once he's drunk, lays his wife out with blows from the empty bottle; no weekly rest or happy leisure time for her, whose Sundays and days of freedom are the most difficult days because of drink, the manual laborer's only pleasure. "Day laborer": a professional label that didn't tell me what its corresponding work was, anymore than "metal polisher" did for a woman, but which I knew, as I knew the latter also, to be the name of a person one of whose most obvious occupations consisted in figuring prominently in the brawls and other acts of violence described in the news briefs of the local paper.

Yet another event—but this one very important—comes rapping at the window between two of my sentences: on the morning of June 6

Les Anglais ont passé la Manche

The English have crossed the Channel

—at last, the famous landing!

There is certainly something laughable (some people wouldn't even hesitate to call it odious) about my determination to go on with this investigation, which has no direct relation to the tragic crisis the world is going through now. But isn't it just when everything is being called into question that one feels most urgently the need to take stock of oneself? It is now or never, in fact, that I must know what I really value, what my life may be worth living for, in what respects I do not want to be blameworthy—in other words, the image of myself I attempt to impose on others, at least *certain* others whom I love and respect, who will be my chosen witnesses. An image that must resemble me and more importantly, that I must try to resemble. For what is the good of being present in the heads and hearts of other people if I know I exist in them only under a borrowed aspect? Like the lover who is anxious to be loved only "for himself," it is myself as I really am—and not a stranger—that I want people to accept. It would be pointless to pay the bill with counterfeit money, it would be pointless to try to mislead people: I must, literally, "put myself on the line" if I have struck this bargain that is a form of commerce with myself as much as a transaction with someone else.

"Work is freedom," "He who pays his debts will be rich": useless axioms that attempt to misrepresent boring, thankless tasks as paths to freedom or positive gain. I never believed in them, even when I was a child and hardly questioned what older people said. True, I think these maxims were offered to me with very little conviction and only cropped up in the conversation as dictums one quotes mechanically, without putting too much faith in them, even with some irony, surrounding them with quotation marks as truths whose only guarantee is that they are traditional, truths to which, however paradoxical they may be, one must pay homage (or pretend to) without venturing to discuss them, since they emanate from the wisdom of the ages.

The opposite of the bad poor man was the bad rich man, hardhearted, pitiless toward the sufferings of the underprivileged. An example being one of the most important people at the office where my father worked, who, if he gave his young son a few pennies, never failed to say to him: "We must be *thrifty*," regarding it as part of his duty as teacher to teach greed. A step higher on the ladder of wealth—and perhaps also of evil—was the American multimillionaire living in France, a Vanderbilt, I think, who, I found out from the newspapers, was involved in an automobile accident in which his chauffeur was killed. Going at sixty miles an hour, which at that time was very fast for a nonprofessional's car. And I felt uncomfortable thinking about this rich man, some kind of maleficent pleasure seeker whom I held responsible for the death of his employee, since obviously he had been the one to give the order to go so fast in that limousine, lolling back on the upholstered seat, freshly shaven, wearing a top hat, and smoking a fat Havana cigar clamped between his lips like a little brown dirigible (or like—exactly like—what my brothers and I, devising the opposite metaphor, used to call a "cigar balloon"). For a while this preoccupied me when I was trying to go to sleep, because all the accidents I knew about frightened me, and this particular one—the specific image of a race toward death ordered by an imperturbable man padded with banknotes—had all the necessary qualities, in its guise as a drama involving high society in white or butter-colored gloves edged with black like a death notice or the headline at the top of a newspaper announcing the most catastrophic kind of news.

At one point I thought that my family (though it was really very much of the middle class) was to some extent laying itself open to the very accusation people made against the "bad rich." For some time we had a maid named Marthe in the house, a neat but graceless person of thirty-five or forty who came originally, I think, from the Sarthe. Very clean and hard-working, she unfortunately had an extremely bad character and because of this had been threatened with dismissal many times by my mother, who was an extremely gentle woman. Marthe often gave vent to her bile by making great speeches about what she grandly called "the new era," a time she said was coming any day now and would be marked by a complete reversal of social relations, especially where the positions of masters and servants were concerned. My mother would let her have her say, waiting patiently for this flood of words characterized by a vague idea of revolution to abate, or if the session threatened to go on forever, she would request our servant to do her the favor of sparing her further explanations and return to work in the kitchen or pantry. Another subject on which Marthe liked to expatiate in her fits of voluble exaltation was that of suicide, an act she savagely condemned, indignantly declaring herself against the foolishness of those who committed it, whenever she happened to read the story of an intentional death by coal gas or some other means in the *faits divers* of one of the papers. One evening, an uncommonly violent scene (as they say in proper newspaper style) erupted toward the beginning of dinner, right in the middle of the dining room. Having found a hairpin in his soup, the older of my two brothers pointed this out to Marthe; she replied sharply that it had nothing to do with her, and gradually the argument became acrimonious. Suddenly getting up from the table, my brother, red with anger, declared to my parents that they would have to choose, for if the maid—that liar—didn't leave, he himself would go. Obviously, if she had stayed he wouldn't have done anything. Nevertheless, Marthe was given notice (for my mother had already put up with too much from her), and as soon as she left us she returned to her own part of the country. But she soon regretted it, because not long after she wrote my mother asking for her job back. My mother answered that that was out of the question, in view of all the ranting and raving she had done. More days went by without any other news of the woman whose tiresome character had resulted in her permanent dismissal. Only a few weeks after she left my mother's employ, however, we did have news of her, news that upset the whole family. A letter from Marthe's sister informed us that our former servant had deliberately drowned herself, broken-hearted at not having been able to get her place back and also because she had just suffered a rejection in the matter of her affections. Of these two motives, my mother especially stressed the first, the one she had to confess she was responsible for, however legitimate it might have seemed to her to be inflexible toward a person who was so bad-tempered, whose stay with us had been marked by so much untimely complaining and so many unsuitable declarations. As for me, for a long time I was haunted by the image of that surly creature who, after months under our roof, had been reduced to putting an end to her life by throwing herself in the river. I pictured to myself that dead face—eyes closed, features even more pinched than usual—the body all stiff, and the clothes wet, as she had just been fished out and was lying by the edge of the water, very clean, very neat, as though starched or dressed up in her Sunday best, in the midst of a smiling landscape and a buzzing heat that I couldn't separate from the idea of the country at that time, when my only brief contact with rural life was during the summer vacation. Behind this face, more stubborn than ever, there was something like a reproach, the continuing articulation of a grievance. Whether it was the bitterness of an unhappy creature from a lower class toward those who had humiliated her by giving her orders and paying her a wage and then, at the last moment, remaining impervious to all mercy, or whether it was the hostility of a maniac immured in her isolation, all the more cut off because she was hostile and all the more hostile because she felt walled up, forever incapable of breaking the circle— whatever the exact meaning I read in the face of our deceased servant as I imagined her in her suicide's apparel, there was something terrible about that face, frozen as it was in an obstinate rejection that could appear to have assumed the immobility of a lifeless thing only to express itself with even more intensity.

Arithmetic problems involving interest, discounts, rates (transcribed by a number followed by the hieroglyph % which I now enjoy locating on the typewriter because it reminds me of my exercises when I was a child), lessons about business concerning invoices, dividends, drafts, securities, letters of credit, or bills of exchange didn't in the least affect the vagueness, the unreality that the notion of money had for me. How could they, since they were simply number games scarcely more concrete, relating as they did to francs and centimes (which at least had the advantage of being immediately representable as money) than if they had related to units of the metric system? And how could these lessons have enlightened me, since their subject was hardly more than a ceremonial, a formality with complicated provisions governing a dizzying currency in which one's eyes became confused as they looked in vain for the money, just as in the three-card tricks you see near racecourses, in which so many people get fleeced, you try to keep track of the card with the different color.

Besides the poor examples offered me by the coins I kept in my money box, the tiny sums I was given for my Thursday half day, or the bonds I knew were lying in my father's desk, for me money was something necessary to life, as necessary (or almost as necessary) as the air our lungs absorbed; but it was of almost the same immateriality. Of course I knew that some people had a large amount of money while others possessed or earned very little. But this large amount of money was a kind of intrinsic quality clinging to the persons of those said to be rich, just as other people could be said to be lucky or to *have* good health. Wealth seemed to me not so much an enumerable sum of goods, distinct from the man or woman who owned them, as an attribute inherent in the individuals who belonged to a certain category, the category of rich people, as there is a category of famous people (catalogued in the series of photographs entitled *Les Célébrités contemporaines* published by the Félix Potin publishing company), a category of great men (whose attribute is glory), and lastly, a category of saints (recognizable by their haloes).

To have a town house, to be served by one or several male servants, to drive one's own car—for some years, these were to me the most patent signs of wealth. I can say that in a sense they *were* wealth, the visible insignia of the rich man, the incarnation of his prestige, just as the throne, scepter, and crown embodied the power of the king. Undependable signs, however, for I was aware that there were "flashy types," and people who lived on a grand scale without having "the means" to do so. Behind the external signs, then, there was nevertheless some notion of solid incomes distinguishing the true rich from the high livers as the legitimate sovereign is distinguished from the usurper. But in the high liver's manner of being, in the way he gets himself up, in his excessive jewelry, and even in his person (with his hair too tightly curled or too brilliantined, his skin too sallow), aren't there a number of signs showing that his wealth is only make believe, in the same way that the tart's elegance is not true elegance and the supernatural powers of Simon Magus are a sham compared to those of Simon Peter, the only one accredited by God for performing miracles? Thus money seemed to me the necessary condition to cut a figure honorably or to show, as they say, a certain "face." Whence, no doubt, the fear I have always had of being without money, as though such a lack did not simply create an uncomfortable situation but led to a profound diminution.

There was a time in my life when I was surrounded by boys for the most part richer than I and thus felt myself in a marked enough state of inferiority to look back on this period as one of unrelenting humiliation. I was about twelve and had just entered the Lycée Janson, where I was in the fifth class. There many of the other students belonged to families who lived in Passy, a more fashionable neighborhood than mine, Auteuil (which was also close to the Bois de Boulogne but at one end adjoined the frightful Point-du-Jour). Whether out of thoughtlessness, the vanity of young parvenus, or pure and simple malignity, some of the boys would attack everything about me that indicated that I was less favored than they where money was concerned—just one of the many forms of teasing to which I was subjected as a "new boy." One day, when I was standing in the recreation yard dressed in a shabby, faded overcoat with frayed cuffs that couldn't have looked very good on me even when it was new (assuming it hadn't been passed down to me from one of my older brothers), one of the boys had tried to rouse a few other students into a mob spirit: "Look at Leiris! He's like an old beggar!" Another time, my mother had come to get me, dressed very simply as she always was (concerned above all with saving money, which she believed was necessary in order to assure my brothers' and my "future"), and one of my tormenters asked me the next day, with an innocent air, whether it had been my mother or my governess they had seen waiting for me at the door of the school. Like a coward, I said, "It was my governess," thus denying—and I still feel remorseful about it—the woman who had called me her "treasure" during my early childhood, infusing into this word everything that seemed to her, because of the great love that filled her heart, unique and almost magical in the fact that she had not only borne me but nursed me, as had not been the case with her two other sons.

I am inclined to think that one result of the vexations I endured in the course of my adolescence was, as a sort of thirst for revenge, the desire to be well dressed that I have consistently and for so long now done my best to satisfy. But in seeking the cause of this desire, touched with uneasiness and combined with the feeling that I have failed somehow, a desire that makes me want to buy my clothes from the greatest tailor in the world (an English tailor, naturally) so as to be able to tell myself that no chance of success has been neglected and that in this area I have gone as far as I could, it would no doubt be more accurate to look farther than this schoolboy teasing, which only wounded me so deeply because the question of clothes was a ticklish one. It was certainly harder for me to tolerate these gibes at the mediocrity of my appearance and at a tic of mine that consisted in blinking or screwing up my eyes as though they hurt (a form of ridicule that involved my flesh even more closely than the other), it was harder to endure the scorn brought down on me by my physical appearance and also my mother's, than the other forms of bullying I was not spared—far from it!—during my first year at the lycée. I can't find any deeper reason for this special kind of raw sensitivity than a certain misunderstanding between me and my body (which even today still feels as though it is a sort of costume in which I am uncomfortable), an uneasiness that grows when I am under fire from the eyes of another person or whenever I face someone who is judging me and sizing me up.

If, when I was very young, I was in the habit of making a scene when I was given a new suit because I thought I looked grotesque rigged out in a way I wasn't used to; if, when I was a little older, clothes that were too worn out made me feel ashamed; and if, today, I am quite likely to dress less well on Sundays than during the week so that no one will suspect me of having chosen that day in particular to dress up—in short, if the idea people might form of me from my clothes has always tormented me, wouldn't it be because, too preoccupied by my body not to feel vulnerable and too little at ease with it not to be mortified by this assuredly visible deficiency, I have always been liable to feel dominated by other people so that if someone gives me a look in which there is no amiability it always has the effect of a direct attack? Thus I remember another pupil at Janson whom I knew in the second class and who must have felt the same as I, that unfriendly looks scorched him, even though he always had handsome clothes and nothing in his physiognomy was of a nature to attract attention. Didn't I see him pounce on one or another of us several times for no reason and ask him furiously what he was doing looking at his shoes? But since this boy was Jewish and at Janson, where there was no lack of anti-Semites (I know something about that because for a while I was called "yid" as a result, I think, of a misunderstanding that might have arisen from my name), that could have been reason enough for him to have acquired this frenzied irritability. I had a different reason; I was merely uncomfortable and awkward in my body, which at the time I was being subjected to these insults was a little too plump (enough so that a person my father knew referred to me one day as the "little fat one" to distinguish me from my brothers, something that hurt me very much when I heard about it), of a roundness and softness that, it seemed to me, were perhaps increased by the secret pleasures I indulged in at night or in the bathroom. So I was forever in the position of an accused person and felt I had to drag around with me everywhere the most overwhelming incriminating evidence.

In the scenarios of the two insults I regard as the most deadly of all the ones I suffered during my first year at the lycée, dress was in a certain sense symbolic. It situated me as far as wealth was concerned, wealth itself being the measure of a certain social rank, that is, the position I occupied in relation to all the others. Because of the disgrace of my clothes, and my mother's too, I had to endure seeing it made obvious to everyone that this rank was not one of the highest, since at that time I was incapable of imagining that it was up to me alone to make up for it by becoming superior in less crude areas (areas that had nothing to do with those issues of wealth and rank, which I now know don't mean very much). I was also incapable of grasping the fact that by itself elegance in clothes, a matter of taste at least as much as of money, can only be interesting, when all is said and done, as an objective expression of a sort of moral elegance. But in another, much more immediate sense, the clothing that covered me when they called me an "old beggar" was, literally, the *face I showed others*: party wall, contact surface, protection screen, which I needed to be much more beautiful because then the gaze of the other person would have shattered against it and dissolved in envy, instead of using it to gain an advantage over me and cut me to the quick, the way a lance pierces a badly-made shield.

A few years later, at the Ecole des Baccalauréats, a stinking hole of a preparatory school on Rue de Passy where I was in the first class, my position was a little more glamorous. Inherently so, but especially because I was in a squalid setting that I didn't have any trouble looking down on from my lofty position: on every floor, a smell of toilets, walls that looked as if they might have leprosy and even seemed contagious; a courtyard to which it would not be possible to allude except to note its pure and simple absence; the most dismal sort of director, as grossly vulgar as a poor restauranteur; teachers not one of whom I can remember but who, I will swear without the slightest hesitation, were all filthy; indeterminate students from a variety of backgrounds, among others a Rumanian (with a charcoal gray moustache out of place in his too young face and a perfectly sinister expression under a bowler that clashed with his threadbare suit), a redhead who smelled of Cyprian wine and always tried to paw my buttocks when we were sitting side by side in a class, a few dunces of the most classically anodyne sort, and a trio of boarders with the mugs of dead men who boasted all day long about the reciprocal buggery they indulged in every night under the eaves, true or untrue feats in addition to which two of them—who, in order to look like soldiers (for this was in the middle of the war), would wear the uniform of the Fédération, the military training club—also chased women, strolling in their khakis and leggings up and down the sidewalks of Passy, which were then as now packed with thriving shops and fruit and vegetable vendors attracting around their carts a crowd astonishingly animated for this neighborhood, so calm and starchy almost everywhere else. In these surroundings, where I would have had to be quite perverse to feel in the least inferior, there were really only two boys I associated with. One, who had a Polish name, was probably Jewish (a fact I have only thought of in retrospect, now that the hideous crisis of anti-Semitism that has occurred in Europe has had, among other sad results, that of habituating people, even the most rebellious, to include adherence to one religion or another among the reference points they use to situate people roughly). He was a well-educated boy whose calm and affable manners stood out in contrast to the crudeness of those of so many of our fellow students. I remember once going to have tea at his home, a pleasant apartment on Place d'Iéna, and four or five years later meeting him on the threshold of a shop in the Poissonnière part of town where he had become a fur dealer, while I myself was studying chemistry after having unsuccessfully tried to go into business. The other boy was a quite ordinary bohemian who impressed me for reasons completely the opposite of the ones that caused me to appreciate the society of the first. He had been around, he dressed sloppily, and he had the air of someone who could handle women. He told me he had written songs and plays, talked about his tours, the chansonniers of Montmartre and elsewhere whom he treated as colleagues. That he had had such associations impressed me, because I had just discovered nightclubs like La Pie Qui Chante, La Lune Rousse, and Le Perchoir and had become infatuated with them, being at that time at the height of the awkward age and delighting in the most vulgar sort of smutty stories and the most dismaying jokes, like so many other schoolboys for whom the understanding of these lame pleasantries has the effect of separating them from the mass of the profane because they are among those whose minds and whose language are nimble enough to grasp their piquancy.

At this same school were two other students I hardly associated with at all because even beyond the fact that they were a little younger and therefore not at the same point in their studies, I had nothing in common with them. Since they lived not far from me, we sometimes walked home together. I took no pleasure in these walks, but they were the ones who sought out my company, even to some extent clinging to me because, I think, I looked down on them as much as others may have looked down on me. True, at about that time I had just discovered American bars where people drank cocktails, and I was proud that I could refer, for example, to the New York on Rue Daunou, where you could meet aviators, a place that seemed to me the very last word as a spot for elegant drunkenness and debauchery. Having never had a taste for lying, I didn't boast about women and did nothing to make my life seem other than it was, a life that hadn't yet reached the stage at which active love of someone else, taking the place of solitary pleasures, gives one the illusion that one has become a complete man. But it wasn't the same with alcoholic concoctions; too young, of course, to be a real drinker, at least I had lost my virginity in this respect, and I could in good faith sing the praises of the creamy sweetness of a port flip, for instance, the tart limpidity of a manhattan, or the bracing quality of a good whisky grog served with a slice of lemon stuck with four cloves. Nothing more was necessary to make me seem important in the eyes of my two idiots, who got the idea from my rambling conversation, uttered without any deliberate intention of dazzling them, that I led a life of luxury rare enough to arouse their envy, since they had never set foot in such places and their worst orgies consisted of downing a few completely French aperitifs, such as vermouth-cassis or picon-grenadine (here I'm naming at random), unless they simply had a resinous white wine, as we did together one time, in one of the little open-air cafés that existed at that time near the Auteuil station, below street level on Boulevard Suchet.

Not only did these two boys—whom I found childish, indiscreet, and vulgar—bore me with their conversation, but their physical appearance made me uncomfortable. The older of the two was actually hunchbacked and with his hat worn over his ear and a snickering mouth in a pallid face, looked at once cunning and self-satisfied. Also very pale and with puny arms and legs, the younger boy, less loquacious than the other, even taciturn, followed him like a shadow, his face sad under his felt hat with its broad, turned-down brim, his feet dragging, his torso leaning a little forward (in contrast to the swaggering of the hunchback, who did his best not to lose one inch of his small height) and loitered along the sidewalk rolling his shoulders broadly, looking at everything and everyone with an impudent fatuousness spread over his bony face. What perhaps irritated me the most about my two neighbors was this very combination: the shabby chicness and artificial joviality of the first and the servile admiration of the second, always at his heels and seeming to delight in playing the part of his faithful lieutenant or stooge. I took no pride in the good opinion they seemed to have of me, and every time I could do it without seeming too flagrantly hostile, I contrived to shake them off.

After I left the Ecole des Baccalauréats—where I stayed only one year, just long enough to pass my Romance languages baccalaureate (the section regarded at that time as the easiest, preferred by lazy students)—I completely lost track of the hunchback and his companion. Recollection of them would no doubt have more or less disappeared from my memory if there hadn't occurred, some time after I left the school, an event that struck me vividly and that might make the painful quality of my contacts with the two acolytes seem like a presentiment. One morning the newspapers announced that two boys from Auteuil had killed a jeweler during a robbery, entering his shop in broad daylight and knocking him out with a rubber truncheon. The names of the two authors of this crime, which was described quite appropriately as "sordid," were printed in full, and I immediately recognized them as the names of my two pests.

A rubber truncheon: the weapon of a crippled man if there ever was one. Why not a crutch, the wooden leg of a one-legged man, a rubber-tipped cane for ataxics or lame people? I can imagine the hunchback with the murderous lump in his pocket, palpating it, caressing it as though it were an orthopedic part of himself, a false limb raised to the dignity of an accessory to a tragedy after having been simply a medical implement. A revolver—I believe this now—would have been less horrible. In a drama involving the explosion of gunshots, instead of a silent murder, two extremely important elements would have been lacking: on the one hand, the almost direct contact between the killer's fist and the victim's skull (isn't a club like the very blow itself, materialized?); on the other hand, the astonishing conformity between the device used for the execution and the physical particularity of the person who uses it. Compared to a truncheon, marked by a prehistoric brutality, the revolver is unquestionably a bourgeois weapon. Even now, isn't one of the most typical examples for me of that class of instruments (whose quality as infernal machines is especially revealed by the slang words using "fire" to name them) my father's revolver, a 6.35 caliber Smith and Wesson of nickel-plated metal, stowed away in a gray suede or chamois holster and carefully locked in one of the drawers of the secretary where our family papers were put away, or in the night table next to my parents' bed? A token of security for the house, the attribute par excellence of the pater-familias, which no one but he had a right to touch and concerning which I was told how one evening when they were young, as he was returning home with my mother, he had pretended to check the gun by the light of a gas streetlamp to see if it was ready to fire in order to intimidate a couple of prowlers whose behavior worried him. This had happened on Boulevard Richard-Lenoir, a neighborhood they lived in during the early part of their marriage and which my mother always talked about as though her only memories of it were painful or unpleasant. It was there that the little girl who should have been our older sister died very young; it was there (an incident I often heard her recall, to show how unsafe was the part of Paris where her parents-in-law lived) that my mother was accosted one day when she had gone out by herself and kissed full on the mouth by a murderous type. The death of her little girl, she told me very recently, was what drove her to settle in Auteuil, choosing a part of the city far away and very different in character from the one where she had never been really happy to begin with, one that had become grievously unbearable to her now that every aspect of it seemed calculated to revive her mourning at every moment.

Apart from the horror I felt because I had come into close daily contact with the authors of an act that was all the more inexcusable because it had been committed, at least to all appearances, in the absence of any pressure of necessity, I also felt uneasy when I contemplated what my two former schoolmates had done. By thoughtlessly talking to them about the pleasures I enjoyed—pleasures of relative luxury but still too costly for them—hadn't I deposited in their hearts the leaven that would soon work the dough and swell that soft and troubled substance with a greed that called for crime? These two ex-pupils of the Ecole de Baccalauréats may have been of weak character and limited intelligence, moved by base desires, they may have been cancers, failures, even authentic jailbirds. But it is still a fact that I had, not without some complacency, played the part of the well-off young man in front of them and that my behavior toward them—even its negative and distant quality—could only have made them feel their lamentable mediocrity more acutely and developed in them, like a stabbing pain, the desire to cut a better figure. That they should have chosen such a brutal and absurd way of triumphing over their condition as this heinous, low-grade crime could well testify to a perversity that one could believe was natural to them. Nevertheless, in giving them a taste for smarter places than the ordinary cafés of Auteuil where they went to sip their indeterminate apéritifs, I had contributed, by intensifying their snobbery, to increasing their need for money, and therefore I had to recognize, in the end, that I was not entirely dissociated from their deadly decision.

For a few days at most, and without ever giving it a prominent place, the newspapers spoke of the affair. Then there was silence. Either the families, ashamed, had persuaded them to hush the thing up, or a murder surrounded by such unspicy circumstances was felt by the editors of the crime news to be without interest. As a result, I never knew what became of my two sad companions. Since they were minors, they were probably sent to a reformatory. After that, at least for the one that wasn't crippled, it was perhaps the French disciplinary battalion and then—who knows?—prison again, whence their unlucky stars would not be able to get them out, one might imagine, except to put them back into the penitentiary. As the years went by, a feeling of pity, added to the sharpened consciousness of my unwitting but tactless influence on the fate of my two fellow students, ill-favored and unfortunate in every respect, took the place of the repulsion with which I had reacted at first. By now I have come to believe I was distinctly guilty in relation to the hunchback and the so very colorless shrimp who was his inseparable friend, just as every man who enjoys a certain wealth must be regarded, whatever he does, as guilty in relation to a man poorer than he.

Among the figures I used to see during the one school year I spent at the Ecole des Baccalauréats, there is another I haven't forgotten and whom I would like to be able to raise to the peculiar mode of life of statues and portraits: my literature professor, a tall man, dry and brown, whom at that time I placed in the family of the Edgar Allen Poe type, probably because he had wild hair and the face of a mystic. Later I borrowed his features for the bohemian Heathcliff when I read *Wuthering Heights*. He was careless in his dress, and the classrooms reeked from his malodorous feet (shod in thick shoes misshapen by wear) and his eternal cigars. In a lycée like Janson, his gaunt face, his dirtiness, the tired look of his marly or olive-colored clothes, the fire that burned in his eyes, and everything about him that seemed romantic, ravaged, would have made him quite unsuitable. In the miserable hole on Rue de Passy one could say, on the contrary, that he had discovered surroundings that fitted him completely. There he seemed at his ease, taught his courses conscientiously, clearly, and without going beyond the strict limits of the curriculum. But sometimes he talked to us—and at these times a spark of enthusiasm

would show through his indifferent manners, the manners of a man
for whom what he does has value only as a way to earn a living—about
poets who don't usually figure in the official teaching. It was through
him that I encountered Rutebeuf, whose two famous lines I remember
having taken down in dictation from him:

> *Ce sont amis que vent emporte*
> *Et il ventait devant ma porte*

> These are friends the wind brings
> And the wind was blowing before my door . . .

It was he who quoted Théophile de Viau's "Ode": an odd work, in
which unusual juxtapositions are created without any disturbance of
the lyricism at all, and one of the first clear examples of surrealist
poetry in France:

> *Un corbeau devant moi croasse,*
> *Une ombre offusque mes regards . . .*

> A crow squawks before me,
> A shadow clouds my eyes . . .

Perhaps it was also through him, though I can't swear to it, that I
heard of Maurice Scève for the first time. I have retained a very
imprecise memory of this course in literary history taught by
Masclaux—for that was my professor's name—and I can't do anything to remedy its lack of clarity because as soon as I had taken my
exams I got rid of the notebooks containing the notes from all my
classes. Nevertheless, I remember with what interest I listened to him
teach his class—especially the part having to do with lyric poetry—
and how much I appreciated the fact that he really wanted to help us
discover authors whose names I hadn't even known before then. Some
years ago now, I happened to be reading the *Nouvelles Littéraires*, to
occupy my eyes almost as much as my mind, when I saw an announcement of his death. On the same occasion, I'm pretty sure, I learned
that he had published a study of the symbolism of *Faust Part 2*. This
seems strictly in keeping with what I imagined about him, as he
endeavored to lead us out of the much too beaten paths of literature:
something fantasmagorical, a subtle vapor mingling with the effluvia
exhaled by his feet and the smell of old cigar that clung to his clothes,
as the odor of cooled incense clings to the soutane or surplice of a
priest.

In all fairness, a disinterested observer might think of my teacher as no more than an educator slovenly in his dress, a visionary spirit, a failure like thousands of others. However, I am reluctant to admit that this was all he was, and I don't believe, anyway, that one can describe a person as having "failed" if one doesn't know what his goals were and one isn't sure that it was not part of his intention from the very start to be precisely what one sees that he now is. Aren't the worst social downfalls often the fruit of a sort of vocation, and what is a man whom one describes as "successful," if not someone whose ambition lay within the limits of possible mediocrity?

During the strange roller-coaster week the people of Paris have just endured—a week that saw the city and its suburbs liberated from the oppression (still so recent when I began writing the present book)— the pious expressions of the folk who live in the sixteenth arrondisse ment or elsewhere and who regard themselves as "successful" because they have a little money or work at a so-called liberal profession, seemed to me more ridiculous than ever. During those days, when each person felt his personal destiny merge with the future of a rebellion, the only thing that mattered was the excitement of the parts of the city in revolt, and everything seemed lifeless as soon as one left the places where open battle was being waged against the rem-nants of the occupying armies.

One of the things that leaves me most thoughtful, among all that my eyes were obliged to register in these memorable circumstances, was the way the figures passing each other in the street tended to assume a classical quality, not so much the moment victory was achieved but when it was possible to sit down in relative security. Insurgents in their Sunday best—this was what I saw when I looked out my window at the crowd of people out walking in the afternoon on the first somewhat peaceful Sunday. Quite a few men who were still carrying their rifles and hadn't yet gone back to their normal way of dressing still bore the mark of their recent seditious past. But this had a stylized, well-groomed look, in the process of becoming fixed, as though to establish a fashion or a uniform: in nice, clean shirtsleeves and sharply creased pants, with a forage cap on their heads, a frankly military attribute added to the tricolored armband, which during the preceding days had been the purely civilian badge of the irregulars. I found that there was something moving, of course, but also a little sad, in the dress of these men who were little by little returning to a codified life after the exceptional week when they had been heroes. If a good many of them must now be prisoners of their everyday occupa-tions once again, there are others who have completely committed themselves to the path of war. For them, even though they have renounced the romanticism of the barricades, there can be no question of either security or settling down. Yet their militarization represents a transition to a norm, and where they are concerned, too, one may lament the fact that the wheel of history didn't stop at this phase, where the streetfighting had a directly perceptible revolutionary meaning. True, I am talking about this from a comfortable position, I who haven't fought and have been content to occupy my workplace— the Musée de l'Homme—in the sixteenth arrondissement, which seemed to me so uninvolved every time I left it to steep myself once again in the feverish atmosphere of the neighborhood of Rue Dauphine, the part of the city where I live.

Picasso exhibiting at the Salon d'Automne (the first time he has given pictures to a group show since he began living in Paris) and the paper *l'Humanité* announcing, on the eve of the opening, that he had been in the group of men fired upon (as though to point out that it was certainly because he had become a communist that he agreed to see his art descend into the street). The Mur des Fédérés demonstration in memory of the resisters shot down by the Germans (I was there on Sunday, October 8, as a member of the Writers' Committee, marching a few steps away from Picasso and not far from Maurice Chevalier, who was greeted by the crowd massed among the graves with applause and shouts of "Vive Maurice!" delighted to see in their midst the star whom the Front National had so recently taken over). The arrival in Paris and the move into 53 *bis* Quai des Grands-Augustins of the relatives for whom (in order to stow their furniture here, because it was threatened by the anti-Jewish regulations) I had rented this apartment (which since their arrival can no longer trouble me—far from it!—by its overly ample size). The inauguration of Rue Danielle-Casanova (named after a patriot murdered in Silesia, the wife of a man who made a profound impression on me when he hid in my home for a month and a half during the occupation, although I did not know at that time who he was). The work involved in preparing a journal for publication that is to include on its steering committee Jean-Paul Sartre (whose *Being and Nothingness* has given me so much to think about since I entered the labyrinth of this work, groping my way forward toward a problematic outcome), Albert Camus (editor-in-chief of the daily *Combat*), André Malraux (now a colonel in the east), and a few others including myself. The selection of texts and arrangement of a presentation for a matinee that the Théâtre des Mathurins is devoting to Max Jacob (who died in the Drancy camp and to whom I certainly owe this homage, not only in general but because it was he who led me to take my first steps in my literary career). The rousing of the Spanish Republic, which is beginning to stir and which, one may well believe, will soon be rid of this bloody species of arriviste, the dictator Franco. Such, enumerated in chronological order insofar as possible, are some brief or lengthy projects, events in my personal life or of historical importance that have interposed like so many opaque shutters between me and the task that seems to me most pressing of all: the development (left hanging for a long time) of the paragraph in which I will broach the question of career, sequel to the memories I was describing here when the uprising exploded and that are contained within the period when I was finishing my secondary school studies without any signs whatsoever of a vocation (and still less, the idea of exposing myself, possibly, to eating black bread and generally roughing it).

Pour choisir une carrière [choosing a career]: there was a book with this title in the house, a book whose precise interest was plainly marked by the use of the word *pour* followed by the phrase indicating what exact benefit (namely, making a judicious, utilitarian sort of choice) one could derive from it. I can still see this book, with its tan cloth binding, in format and size a little smaller than a small Larousse dictionary, its pages of thin paper on which one could read, printed in close-set lines and divided into two columns, information relating to all the respectable professions to which sons or daughters in average or humble circumstances could think of aspiring. *Pour choisir une carrière*: a guide for young people whose parents did not intend to let them launch themselves casually but wanted to provide them with all the desirable safeguards, as they were about to make a decision that they could, of course, always find a way of retracting, but on which, in theory, the economic progress of their whole lives would ultimately depend.

As for the general conduct of my own life, I don't see that the deliberate choices (or choices assumed to be so) of career that I would make from time to time as a young man had the least influence on it, except indirectly and without the linking of causes and effects being in the least foreseeable. All the more reason why I don't think the book *Pour choisir une carrière* could have been of the slightest help to me, and I would be inclined to suggest that those who need an advisor of this kind in order to commit themselves to a trade or profession are a little like the people who get married with the help of the advertisements one used to find in *Le Chasseur Français*, in what was, according to the people who knew, one of the most widely read sections of this periodical (which was published by the Manufacture d'Armes et Cycles de Saint-Etienne, also the publisher of a voluminous catalogue in which innumerable extremely useful or pleasant objects were featured and described).

Among the various professions on which my choice could have settled when I reached the age when it is suitable to prepare a future for oneself, some had been implicitly eliminated from the very beginning. That of clergyman, for example, toward which one of the curates of my parish tried to entice me shortly after my first communion when I was still studying with some assiduousness the "continuing" catechism, as it was called. Taking me aside one day as I came out of the confessional and asking me to sit down next to him in an empty chapel (the chapel of the Virgin, I'm fairly sure, close to the cubicle where I had just been accusing myself of my sins), the priest in question—a big, good-natured man with a bearish red face who was my usual confessor—delivered a little speech to me in an affectionate, earnest tone, a speech that can be reduced, in substance, to this: "My dear Michel, I have been watching you carefully: I see that you have the signs of the vocation. I am sure that you would make a very good priest." This flattered me because I imagined I was some sort of chosen person, at the very least a boy capable of being singled out by a churchman and of earning his respect. But in this I was quite naive, and I discovered it later! Having told someone about what had happened to me, someone who, I thought, would find it intriguing that a priest had thought of recruiting me, I learned from this confidant—a sincere Christian and, what was more, one very well versed in the ways and customs of the Catholic clergy—that my director had undoubtedly simply been performing his duty as conscientious propagandist, and that far from having spoken to me by virtue of some secret understanding, he had approached me, in all probability, just as he must have a number of my friends, those who had shown any contemplative leanings at all in the exercise of their normal religious duties.

Although at that time God still seemed to me to represent something alive, worthy of being designated by a name whose initial capital classed it among the names of persons (whereas now I no longer see him as anything more than the central figure in a certain number of curses), to devote myself to him body and soul every day of the week did not appeal to me in the least. I was not altogether without fervor, but I had far too little of it to think of becoming one of those people who spent most of their time in prayer wearing a soutane as though to express even in their clothing that they were cut off from the world. Most importantly, those who entered the orders were obliged to be chaste and prohibited from marrying. Already in a position to have some glimmering (from the childish adumbrations of it that I knew) of how intense the pleasures of the flesh could be, how would I have been able to give up, not only the joys I had up to then only tasted so imperfectly but also the form of communion, totally unknown to me, that marriage seemed to be, a seal set on what appeared to me to be the most natural goal in one's life: a shared love?

Another career I never thought of aiming for was military service. Like most children, I adored gold braid, medals, shoulder knots, stars, and other decorations, frogs and loops, plumes, piping—in short, everything added onto a uniform. When I was very young, I had been impressed by the stature and martial expression of Prosper, the sergeant in the colonial troops, an authentic soldier but the only one in my family and (I must say), given his weakness for before-dinner tippling and his parasitism, not a very encouraging example or one that could serve as a model for me. Also, being a reenlisted sergeant was not all that wonderful; it did not really constitute a "career." Prosper was more like a watchman on a public square, or a policeman, or even a stationmaster or department store deliveryman. If one adds to this my complete lack of combativeness, my little taste for any sort of physical exercise, one will have no trouble imagining that as an adolescent I felt perhaps even less attracted to a military career than to a life that consists, among the other duties assumed, of hearing confessions and officiating at the altar.

There was actually another soldier in my family, but I didn't know him. An admiral, he was a cousin of my mother's whom she saw only at long intervals. I knew only a few things about him. At the start of each crossing, he locked himself in his cabin for a few days and did not show himself to his subordinates because he suffered from seasickness, an affliction he could not get rid of despite his being so very accustomed to navigation. Later I had reason to believe he was an opium addict, and that he had acquired the habit in the Orient or in Toulon, as was frequently the case among men in his profession. A sailor, and what was more, a sailor who had the rank of admiral, was more flattering as a relative than a noncommissioned officer in the colonial troops who loved pernod rather than opium and was a Don Juan with the housemaids. Who can say? If I had known this cousin, maybe I would have thought of becoming a sailor too. But the fact is that I only met him later, when the die had been cast. Besides, I didn't want a career at sea. Voyages to distant places certainly allow you to see the world, and that isn't bad, but they last a long time, during which you are separated from the woman you care for. Then again, a sailor has to know how to swim, and I have always felt a great repugnance for swimming, incapable as I am of having enough confidence in the liquid element to abandon my body to it, lie down in it with my feet almost on the same level as my head, and let myself float without feeling dizzy. Finally, there was that accursed seasickness that appalled me until I saw, when circumstances led me to go out on the sea, that I didn't suffer from it. The wonders of the exotic, therefore, which would at a certain period play such a role in my life, at first had no more power than the wonders of gold braid to bring me to a decision. I didn't think of becoming a sailor any more than I wanted to become a priest or a soldier, and it was only much later, in a roundabout way and almost for the very reason that it frightened me, that I came to travel on the seas.

Below the *vice-amiral* [vice admiral] is the *contre-amiral* [rear admiral] (like Contrexéville, a watering-spot smaller than Vittel). It was the rank of rear admiral that my mother's cousin had achieved, having—I suppose—started from the level of cadet to become a sublieutenant, then a lieutenant, then a ship's captain. One can be more or less certain that he never passed through those two strange ranks my brothers and I believed had their recognized places in the hierarchical nomenclature and were situated somewhere, though we didn't know where, in the vicinity of ship's lieutenant: the rank of captain of a *frégate* [frigate] (a seagoing vessel as well as a marine bird, rhyming with *la plage Houlgate* [Hullgate Beach] as well as with *cravates régates* [narrow sailor-knot ties, lit. "regatta ties"] and that of captain of a *corvette* (a skiff whose only resemblance to a *crevette* [shrimp] is its small size). It is quite certain, also, that he had never had a rank as low as that of quartermaster (a man with a beret with a pompon on it, the sort one could find in the department stores), since for him the navy was very much a "career," chosen deliberately but in a rather bourgeois way. And one could infer from the bourgeois nature of this choice (for such was the background of my mother's cousin, as of my mother herself) that he had graduated from the Ecole Navale.

Foremost among the professional training colleges I could have chosen were the Ecole Polytechnique and the Ecole Centrale. But the prospect of a career as an engineer was out of the question for me, given my complete incompetence in math (an incompetence that I, like quite a few boys of my age and social milieu who were supported in this, foolishly, by their families, sported as an affectation, as though literature were more distinguished than the sciences). It was also out of the question for me to be a doctor. The professions of physician and surgeon were certainly noble ones, but when one studied medicine one had to dissect cadavers, and the horror I have always had of dead bodies was enough to discourage me. Another fine school was the so-called "free" Ecole des Sciences Politiques. Young people went there to prepare themselves for *the* career, the one that is sufficiently defined by the word "career" (as though there were no other): that of diplomat. What barred me from taking that path, which also tempted me only slightly despite the hints of luxury and brilliance I saw in it, were my parents' limited financial means. At one point there was some thought of my becoming an agronomist, but that would have obliged me to live in the country, and I have always been a confirmed city dweller, however strong an attraction I have to nature. Business, a simple means of earning money, and banking, which my father considered the millstone of his life (as he was dying, he murmured, "I've got thirty Rio's pulling me down," one of the few delirious sentences that issued from him during his death throes), were just as much out of the question for me—even though in theory there was nothing against my choosing them—as, for a man of the ancien régime, a profession that would have made him lose caste. What was left, obviously, was to enter some ministry as a civil servant.

Neither my parents nor I ever regarded this as more than a last resort. And yet, little by little, it was a civil servant that, in actual fact, I became. A civil servant of a certain kind, of course, and not a government but a museum employee. Nevertheless, I have to say that with regard to what I have finally recognized as my true vocation, there is, when all is said and done, not much difference between working in a ministry and working in a museum. Whether one belongs to one of the organs that constitute the very body of the State or to one of the cultural institutions that constitute its adornment, whether one writes administrative reports or erudite studies, in both cases one has the same shut-in office life where the calendar holds sway as master. There is the same use of language for ends opposed to the implementing of the imagination and, with a practical aim that forces one to rein it in, the same formal exercise of one's ability to express oneself. In sum, a domestication of life walking hand in hand with an emasculation of speech, something like the lion changed into a poodle carrying a wooden bowl, well known to readers of children's magazines.

The model for a government employee in my family was another of my mother's cousins, one whom we saw quite often. Suffering from a clubfoot that obliged him to use crutches, and also augmented by a strange "wen" that developed on his bald skull, Louis l'Infirme had a florid complexion and a large fan-shaped beard. Easy to get along with, occasionally a sponge, heedless of the financial embarrassment in which he vegetated with his wife and three children, he painted a little—his wherewithal more or less assured by some job or other in the Ministry of Finances—and wrote some art criticism. A few of his works (discreet landscapes, barely touched by a hint of impressionism) were permanently exhibited in the office where he held his meetings, hanging next to a few acquisitions, reproductions, or gifts from friends among the traditional green cardboard that kept one from forgetting the administrative nature of the place. Orthodox, he declared that when he went to church he was incapable of communing with himself if he was not face to face with some pretty religious statue. He was convinced he was an artist and underneath his apparent simplicity was complacent enough so that one never mentioned him in the house without calling him the "master," a nickname bestowed on him by my mother's brother, who sometimes elaborated on the joke by calling him, superlatively, the "past master." His propensity for doing nothing and addiction to hanging around cafés had once saved his life. One day when he came to the house for dinner, the whole family was poisoned by a cream tart from a pastry cook who was responsible for several deaths in the neighborhood that evening. My brother Pierre retained a lingering memory of that poisoning, which I myself happened to avoid (because I was too small to be present at the meal): the sensation of having "teeth made of cotton," as he said, which he had felt for several days. Louis l'Infirme was the only one of the party who felt nothing, except perhaps a little indigestion; so that my parents, when they found out that after leaving our house he had joined some friends in a café and emptied a considerable number of glasses of beer with them, thought the beer he had quaffed had had a healthy laxative effect on him. Such was this other cousin of my mother's in all his infirmity, complacent laziness, and optimistic piety—a pen pusher who wore, if not the loosely knotted bow tie of an artist, at least a wide-brimmed felt hat. His example was no sort of propaganda for me, either in favor of the government or the fine arts.

Thus, disdaining a military career as well as a career in the clergy, the army as well as the church, and not wanting to become either a sailor (any more than a colonial, another profession involving remote places) or a doctor (maker of mischief involving dead bodies), or a speculator, tradesman, engineer, stock breeder, or farmer, regarding "*the* career" as barred to me and the career of government employee as the end of everything, never having dreamt (I'm not sure just why) of becoming a teacher, and also having none of the gifts that allowed my older brother, for example, to study interior design or my other brother to work at being a virtuoso on the violin, eventually, with my family's agreement, I settled on the idea that I would study law. But things were finally decided differently. Once I had received my baccalaureate I wanted, as I have said, to earn a little money, and decided to try my luck first in the Paris buying department of the Peter Robinson department stores of London, then with a mercantile agent of the Cité Paradis—Max Rosenberg, who soon changed his name to "Rosambert," better suited to the spirit of the years that followed the armistice of 1918—a firm I had been sent to by a relative by marriage of our cousin the admiral (to be precise, his brother's brother-in-law, a doctor with whom our relations were less irregular than they were with the sailor and whom we sometimes consulted medically). However, this didn't work out because it took all my time, was tiresome and humiliating for the budding snob I was (reduced, as apprentice tradesman, to the most subordinate position); besides, it earned me very little. One of my close friends at that time was studying chemistry and told me that while one was taking courses at the Institut de Chimie appliquée one could (but now I wonder where in the world he could have looked for this work?) earn money outside by doing analyses, and I resolved to enter this branch of science, preparing for the entrance exam to the Institut de Chimie, then for the certifying exam in general chemistry. I met with failure after failure, not being very gifted in this sort of study (as untalented as in everything to do with the exact sciences, despite my old attraction to the *leçons de choses*) and also much too nonchalant, since I was too jealous of my leisure time during the week and my freedom on Sunday to be equal to the exams, which, though they weren't the most difficult ones, all the same required some seriousness. Furthermore, what interested me most in this branch of knowledge were the old theories, the outmoded doctrines that spoke to the imagination, and not the modern conceptions. I much preferred, for instance, the idea of *phlogiston*, the substance lost during combustion, to the new theory put forth by Lavoisier after his famous combustion experiment. As for the recent propositions about radioactivity and the structure of matter (constituted in such a way that nothing prevents one element from changing into another since they are all, finally, no more than aggregates of particles in motion), these attracted me only as they related to alchemy and transmutations. Dense as I was when it came to mathematics, and incapable of making the effort that might have allowed me to catch up, I took an exclusively qualitative view of these sciences, as though in that domain measure and quantity weren't primary.

These studies, which lasted a good three or four years, but which I pursued without any application, have left little trace on me. I didn't retain much on the level of theoretical knowledge, and the required laboratory work did not make me more precise or skillful in my way of moving. And yet objectively they had a great influence on my life.

It was because I was a student of chemistry that I was able to carry out my military service, when the time came, under more comfortable conditions than I could otherwise have hoped for. What I wouldn't have dared do in time of war, I had no scruples about doing in peace time. Having first been granted a deferment, I was able, thanks to someone my father knew, to enter the company of chemists of the 13th artillery regiment, a company that was later integrated into the 22d artillery batallion when the artillery workers' units were formed. After a stay of several months at the Aubervilliers fort (where we were put to work salvaging old masks and destroying stocks of poison gas left from the great war), I was detailed, on the recommendation of a member of my family, to the Institut Pasteur, where I finished my two years, leading a civilian life and theoretically preparing for the certifying exam in biological chemistry. In the end I even gave up this semblance of a justification and refused to sit for the exam, because in that year, 1923, I had other ideas in my head (the ambition of becoming a poet) and shied away from the few weeks of work I would have had to do.

This recourse to using the influence of friends and family—which is all too well known and seemed completely natural to me then—has gradually become a sort of original sin in my eyes. More perceptive now than I was at twenty, having learned to judge myself and be

realistic about the advantages I gain by being a member of the
bourgeoisie, I can measure the extent to which my civilian life—or
rather simply my life—was falsified by this initial injustice. When
the present war broke out, I was mobilized as a chemist, and not just
as a soldier but as a noncommissioned officer, profiting from the bit of
a stripe I had earned by mishandling the equipment—evaporating
dishes, balloon flasks, pipettes, test tubes, and other porcelain or
glass instruments—that I had used at the Institut Pasteur. Of course,
at Béni-Ounif (where I was sent with a detachment of chemists), when
they asked me what I could do, I didn't for a moment try to make my
talents out to be more than they were. But the die had been cast, and
what I ended up becoming, when I said I was neither a fully-qualified
nor a professional chemist, since they couldn't make me an artillery-
man either (seeing that I had had absolutely no military instruction at
all) and since unquestionably (because of the fact that I belonged to
the Musée de l'Homme, a.k.a. the "ethnological laboratory of
present-day and fossil man"). I had to be ranked, if not in the category
of chemists, at least in that of intellectuals and even laboratory people
(as though fate had wanted to make a wordplay on my behalf), was a
pen pusher, because I was attached to the general staff as a secretary
before being called upon—hardly less bureaucratically—to be an
armorer. So that my fraud, which is now more than twenty years old,
has never been rectified.

True, I made a vague effort to rectify it by writing home from
Africa to the director of my museum, describing the shocking aspect
of my situation, the deception I had perpetrated by prolonging a
misunderstanding to which I had tacitly consented much too long,
my hope of being employed in a manner a little more in keeping with
my area of expertise, even if that meant I had to come back to Paris (a
prospect I could envisage without shame, since Paris was actually not
as far away from the theater of operations as Southern Oran). On the
other hand, when I returned from Béni-Ounif after our mission and
had to fill out a form at my company's depot in which, among other
questions, we were asked where we wanted to be sent, I opted for the
East, thinking that by doing this I would at least be showing some
honesty toward my destiny, which seemed to want me to experience
the war in an exotic setting. But practically, all this came to nothing,
and the armistice found me in a forest of the Landes full of pine trees
and ferns, the location of the munitions depot to which I had just been
assigned as chemist when everything collapsed. A manly solution

would no doubt have been possible: to ask to be thrown into a fighting unit, any one at all, despite my lack of training as a fighter. But I was content with a half measure and did not stop using evasions. To apply for an assignment that was merely not improper or not absurd was still to make use of my prerogatives as an intellectual, therefore as a member of the bourgeoisie, to refuse to take the bull by the horns and go to the front line like anyone else. In short, my studies in chemistry had the indirect result of shielding me from two experiences that would have been of primary importance in my life as a man: first a military service carried out in the usual unpleasant conditions, then a war blowing me away like a wisp of straw among others, the logical sequel to that asceticism.

Here I am making use of natural chronological order in my research and plunging into the stream of the years as though to discover a Genesis in it. Wanting to know how I became what I am, professionally, today, I go back to my adolescence; I try to see what plans for the future I could have been forming at that time. And I see that in truth I wasn't forming any. Nevertheless, it is a fact that by profession I am now an ethnographer, and that, furthermore, the activity I prize the most is my activity as a writer. Can it be that what occupies the largest place in my life should thus have no apparent roots and no visible connection with any career dreams, however vague, I might have entertained as an adolescent? By going in the opposite direction—starting from the present and going back to the past—I might have more chance of discovering the juncture or turning point connecting my current occupations to old, more or less expressly formulated, desires. In the absence of explicit career ideas, in the absence even of any definable vocation, I will at least find a substructure and something to prove to me that my life is not entirely made up of random events.

Looking at it superficially, it was a fortuitous circumstance that turned me into a specialist in the sociology of black Africans. One of my colleagues at the journal *Documents*—a professional ethnographer working there to keep body and soul together after returning from a trip to Abyssinia—asked me if I wanted to join a new expedition to Africa he was thinking of forming, a proposal that came at just the right time for me, as I was so depressed that in order to force myself out of a state of mind that proved to be pathological, I had to resort to the help of a doctor. On top of that, I was racked by a fierce need for a change of scene. When I returned from that expedition, which occupied me from 1931 to 1933 and whose home port was the Musée de l'Homme (at that time the Musée d'Ethnographie), it was quite natural for me to find a place for myself in that institution and to set about getting the appropriate degrees for legitimizing what had become my de facto profession. And yet, in all this had I been merely the plaything of a conjunction of events? After weighing everything carefully, I say No. An opportunity presented itself to me, and I took advantage of it, but this opportunity came at just the right moment to satisfy something profound in me: a long-held desire to break open my horizons, an attempt to free myself that poetry now seemed to me sadly incapable of guiding, though for several years it had been the instrument of liberation par excellence for me. Later—and I am at precisely this stage today—I would return to literature when I had rehashed again and again a certain form of derision: namely, that ethnography only succeeded in turning me into a bureaucrat; that its nature as a science requiring objectivity and patience in the end flies in the face of my hopes (broken away from my armature of logic by contact with men living in obedience to other norms); last, that traveling, as I conceived of it (a solitary distancing), far from being a way of making oneself other than what one is by changing one's setting, is only the pure and simple displacement of a person who is always identical to himself, a nomad only in the spatial sense, who drags behind him—strengthened rather than diminished by his relative isolation—his narcissism, his worries, and his obsessions. A desire not to go away anymore that also came to me, as I felt old age and death approaching with the passing years and attached a higher price . . . to whom? To what? . . . I shrink from saying it, whether out of discretion, modesty, or an idiotic sort of compassionate respect that obstructs, not the most contentious of all the avowals I might have at the tip of my pen or on my lips but those that would make me look most like an average man, in other words reveal me as something I am determined to disguise either because its banality is humiliating or because this banality represents, better than any particularity I could admit to, my very innermost being.

An indirect consequence of my temporary adherence to the editorial board of an artistic periodical—this is how I think of the occupation from which I officially derive my income today. Even beyond that chain of material causes and effects, this other vocation seems to be a natural consequence of my condition as writer and has become, if not a reason for living, at least a social justification, a description that can be written on the white rectangle of my visiting cards. If at one time in my life I embarked on a long and presumably difficult voyage from which, yielding romantically to the itch for the exotic, I expected everything, this was the outcome of an internal evolution in which cultural elements also figured: a reading of Lévy-Bruhl that awakened my curiosity about the "primitive mind," an interest in Negro art (like so many people of my generation, whose disgust with classical art also led them to children's drawings, folk art, and the art of mad people), an admiration for the poetry of Rimbaud, and even more for his person, aureoled with the silence he drew from the quarries of Cyprus and the barbarism of Ethiopia. What remains to be discovered, since everything started with this, is how it happened that I, who had no vocation, realized one fine day that I was a writer, and what were the processes by which this activity chose me instead of my choosing it.

It is clear from the very way in which I am handling this piece of writing that I have always attached great importance to everything connected with language. Knowingly or not, I have sealed a pact with the world of words, which was revealed to me very early on as a book scattered with truths of the greatest importance rubbing elbows with the oddest maxims. It is not so much the love of reading—which never consumed me to such a degree—as this confused attraction to language per se that one must look to, I think, if one is trying to discover the earliest sign of my intimacy with literature, slow as it was to emerge. The fact that language, to which our whole mental life is attached, is so diffuse explains why this intimacy took so long to show itself. Whereas it is relatively easy to discover a bent one might have for a certain specific activity, the diagnosis is less easy when what is involved is something as universal as language. If one feels impelled to read and write one will quickly recognize that one has a vocation as a writer, but if one is faced with language in all its immense, sudden nakedness, the odds are that one won't recognize any vocation in oneself at all. This was the case with me, and it was therefore by groping my way forward, by successively eliminating other possible activities (in short, through a series of negations) that I turned to literature well before I learned (something that only came after a very long time and many detours and returns) that this was the only thing I could do.

Besides these numerous recollections I have involving experiences with language, I can, without straining, draw from my memory a small number of achievements that can be recognized without any accommodation as attempts—some well thought out, others less precise and also older—at literary creation.

In the late years of my adolescence, when I reached the age of earliest maturity that corresponds to the apparent dissolution of childhood, I wrote a few brief, insubstantial poems that forced themselves on me primarily because of a great need for effusion. Wretched pieces dripping nonsense, huffing and puffing, vitiated by the most ordinary aestheticism despite the burst of feeling that motivated them: so true is it that one must make use of a certain technique (the retort in which the substance one is handling becomes pure and proliferates) to achieve the true *cri de coeur*, the gush of feeling that wells up from the deepest substratum. I can also remember a translation of a poem by Whitman in praise of Manhattan's crowds of shoppers—a poem I had found in an English language book—and two or three prose texts, one of which was severely critical of Victor Hugo, to whom, influenced by the older of my two brothers, I preferred at that time Leconte de Lisle, with a pessimism expressed in alexandrines whose equivalent I see today in the sculptural polish of his cranium (bald though grassy) and cleanshaven face.

There were also the stories my other brother and I told each other as children when he and I relieved ourselves together every evening in the bathroom, stories that continued from one day to the next, serial installments featuring animals that we took turns inventing. It was in this place, where we met as though in a brigands' retreat or the den of a secret society, that we sensed a certain complicity most acutely. My brother sitting on the large toilet like a higher ranking initiate, while I, the younger, sat on a common chamber pot, a sort of neophyte's stool, both of us in the posture of visionaries, as though the spirit of the depths would reach us through the round hole that closed off an ancient system of valves, we tirelessly sought answers to the sexual enigmas that obsessed us and endlessly elaborated a whole mythology, resumed every night and sometimes set down neatly in notebooks, food for the most peculiarly imaginative part of our lives. Animals who were soldiers, jockeys, civilian or military aviators, who were thrust into competitions in war or sports or police intrigues. Sinister political machinations with attempts at coups d'états, murders, kidnappings. Plans for a constitution that would ensure an ideal government. Absolutely commonplace love stories that most often ended in a happy marriage followed by the birth of a swarm of children but did not necessarily exclude the final episode of widowhood. The invention of warlike devices, underground passageways, traps, and pitfalls (sometimes consisting of a simple ditch disguised with foliage, its walls studded with sharp knife blades and its bottom bristling with stakes, so that whoever fell in would be pierced and cut to pieces). Lots of fights, ferocious battles (on battlefields or in hippodromes). After each battle, detailed statistics including the exact number of prisoners, wounded, and dead for each of the opposing sides, which might be, for instance, the cats and the dogs, the first being royalists and the second republicans. All of this duly recorded in our notebooks in the form of stories, pictures, plans, sketched maps, not to mention summary tables and genealogical trees.

My brother and I were only amusing ourselves with this species of epic, born between four walls like a conspiracy we had fomented; we were only exercising our abilities as fabricators and not dreaming of creating a literary work. More ambitious were the poems I have alluded to, more or less imitating the little I knew of Verlaine and Baudelaire. Yet I don't think one can regard even those productions as anything but the vague attempts at writing that most adolescents indulge in with greater or less success, verbal outlets for the carnal and emotional desires that are beginning to torment them. It therefore seems I have to look upon such attempts as being like old-fashioned knickknacks that have no direct relation to the present: absurd, outdated objects you put away in a drawer because you think you would be failing your own past if you threw them in the fire, things that were once alive but are now quite meaningless except, precisely, insofar as they are "souvenirs."

The premonitory signs I am able to pick up when I go back through the more remote years of my life, signs pointing the way to what now seems to me sufficient to justify my existence as a civilized man, have therefore no value at all as proof: too impersonal and too vague to serve as the basis for any deduction whatsoever. But one element does provide me with a clue: the *negative* character of this vocation (or more exactly of this absence of vocation) which was not foretold to me by any particular little sign, even the most mundane. The only path open to me, the only way to use my time (which I would have liked to steal from more mercenary occupations as often as possible, but which I also wasn't willing to waste in idle pleasures), literature will in fact turn out to have represented the only goal worthy of my continuous application after everything else was eliminated.

Rejecting the various situations among which it would have been very simple for me to choose, myself rejected by one of them right away, without my really being tempted by it (the one for which the pompous title of *"the* career" is reserved), I came to the idea of adopting literature as my official reason for living to put an end to this series of rejections and refusals in which my will was only partly engaged. The passive rather than active outcome of a process to which I had been brought sometimes by chance, sometimes by whim, acknowledging myself to be a writer—accepting it as my lot to be suited to this and turning away light-heartedly from a field where I was really useless—was not only the affirmation of a positive desire but also a way of abruptly abandoning something I disliked as much for its effect on the facade I presented to society as for its influence on my innermost being. In the same way that in my pieces of writing, when they assumed some form, I manifested an especially intense need to ruin the architecture of logic, to free myself of the weight of the world by disputing the validity of the laws of physics (as though I wanted to escape my fleshly condition and deny the body with which for so long I had lived on bad terms, however attached I might be to it and however anxious to give it a dazzling appearance by the way I dressed), in the same way poetry, as social justification, may have seemed to me a way of situating myself on the fringes; of fleeing from something that would have immediately defined my place among other people; of annihilating, for myself, the menacing framework of ordinary professions; even of denying class separations or obliterating them by situating myself outside or in some way above them, perhaps in order to forget that by birth and fortune I was far from belonging to the highest class. (Just as people from the poorest classes can rise in the world overnight by means of sports, crime, prostitution, ascending to the rank of a god or a hero. As for me, if I had been a rich, handsome boy, if I had felt I was a candidate to be a great athlete, a Don Juan, or a brilliant man-about-town, perhaps I would have wagered on one of those cards, instead of on literature, to put me outside the common run.)

For me, then, poetry was essentially a *separation*, as much on the spiritual level as on the level of life in society, because it is a distancing, an escape from the norms (as traveling also seemed to me to be during a certain time). The eternally separate man—such was the image of myself that I wanted to form by aspiring to be a poet, and such was also the appearance I wanted to give myself when I made the drawing depicting myself with my eye fixed on a pyramid as though on a goal situated beyond my reach, while a woman's eye is fixed on me and all possibility of the two gazes meeting has been excluded in advance.

To dig in. To withdraw. To isolate myself from the normal arrangement of things. Not to enter any of the overly-respectable professions that brand the man condemned to forced labor with a number he will bear right up to the end. To interrupt the flow of time in order to return to the freedom of childhood, a sensation an adult sometimes has during travels, holidays away from home, or other parentheses carved into the uniformity of time, a sensation especially associated with the feeling that we had all the time in the world, time that included the present, in which we only had to let ourselves go on living (without being nudged by the knowledge that there was an urgent task to be accomplished), and the future stretching before us as far as the eye could see. When I, who had first thought of becoming a "Sunday writer" (writing in moments of leisure) and who in fact have become that "Sunday writer" (since I have had to accept paid work and count on Sundays, holidays, and other intervals of freedom for the work that matters to me), decided not to do anything but write, this was tantamount to rebelling against one of the things that seemed to weigh on me most oppressively: the division of my days into working hours and hours of freedom. If I was asking poetry to allow me to enter a land where two plus two didn't have to equal four (a sum that was only useful to accountants) and the clock did not rule with an iron hand, and since I regarded the poet as a sort of archangel (was I remembering the archangel Michael whose name I bear?), naturally it would have been a flagrant absurdity for me to have to devote only a part of my evenings to this art, dole out my time to it, when one of the clearest reasons I had for devoting myself to it was precisely that it would free me (in my imagination) from time as a category. As soon as I formulated a general requirement where poetry was concerned, there could be no question of bargaining. The practice of an art that I expected to transfigure all of existence was incompatible with a regulated life.

And yet it is a fact that the life I now lead is a regulated one. Though I am not a workhorse, I devote a large part of my time to the job I am paid to do. When I write, it is generally in the evening (unless I have an appointment or have to go out) or on Sunday (the day I have detested for so long) or during vacations. I have moved far away from seeing the act of writing as something sacred: a summons that could come at any hour of the day, for which one had to keep oneself constantly available, not accepting any task that would deflect one's mind from its prophetic role, prevent it from being pure speech whose truth would lie in its enunciation alone, with no need for any other guarantee.

Falling into the common rut which I had tried to avoid, in the end I resigned myself to taking a second job: at first as traveling salesman for a bookstore, because I had gotten married and had to have some sort of livelihood; then as secretary of the editorial staff of the periodical *Documents* and another art magazine; then as explorer (if one can use such a term in connection with Africa these days without laughing); and now as a museum administrator. This life, in which I must fight against my innate laziness every day, bothers me more and more. I write no stories and almost no poems now, tending to adopt the prose autobiography as my only means of expression. I don't know if I have to attribute this relative sterility to the life I lead, which is too orderly, or to the fact that I no longer have *all* my time (which, where poetry is concerned, could well amount to having none at all anymore), or whether, on the contrary, the fact that my poetic vein was already more than half dried up and my faith dulled led me to the habit of making a quasiscientific use of literature just as I was settling into my present profession. However this may be, and leaving aside all budgetary considerations, I have come to the point of no longer being able to do without such an occupation: a stopgap that colors my days gray but prevents them from being completely empty, wrests them from an idleness that I can't imagine without feeling afraid, knowing what gloomy, anguished self-examination would result from it, even if I would benefit from it creatively. Without this regular work, which, even if it only ties me down a little, strengthens me by taking me away from myself for a certain number of hours, I would live in a perpetual Sunday, without any barricade to defend me against the idea of death, as though the fact of being free and having all my time at my disposal, the fact of being wide open and empty would abandon me to the vertigo of *nothingness*, because of this very feeling of having *carte blanche*. I am so far away, now, from the paradise of my childhood with its happy nonchalance.

I have gone back up the river of time. To steer myself I have done a review, the way schoolchildren do at the end of each term. I have investigated the various elements in my history one by one, just as we recognize that the war of 1870, for example, had several causes, each of a different order, and that even though the immediate pretext for it was certainly the incident involving the Ems dispatch ("a red flag waving in front of the Gallic bull," as Bismarck said), we have to seek other, more profound reasons. I have tried as best I could to find out how I became what I am now, defined by the work to which I can't admit that chance alone has led me to devote myself. I have made a connection between the attraction I felt for traveling and studying so-called primitive peoples and literature, or at least the desire I felt, one day, to enlarge its horizon for myself. As for my love of writing, I have decided that it is based on a certain need for negation, as though my ultimate goal were to remove myself, to put myself out of reach, by inventing a world where all natural and human laws have been abolished and I sever not only my attachments to social classes but also the carefully woven rope passed around my neck by the civic state, which is the clerk—if not the executioner—in charge of everything to do with humanity engendered, subjected to forced labor, and unconditionally buried. Briefly, I have pointed out how eventually, because of a certain dryness or a certain abandonment—as though poetry (or what I knew of it) had been eaten into by the *no* it paraphrased—I scarcely wrote anymore except to put myself on the grill, anxious that my only somewhat solid ground should be the image I might draw of myself. Along the way, I mentioned how important to me, even above and beyond its being a social prejudice that drove me to embrace a condition apparently not circumscribed by petit-bourgeois mediocrity, was the depressing feeling I derived from the fact of having a body I could not forgive, not only for the mediocre position it assigned me among other people but for being subject to physical laws and consequently liable to die.

Tormented by an obsession with time and a preoccupation with decrepitude, not only in relation to myself (destined as I am to decline and disappear) but in relation to the opinion of others (who before too long will be the witnesses of my decline), I have looked for some way to put obstacles in the path of the things we lose by remaining alive, first through a curt refusal to believe that the general arrangement of our world is valid, then through a scheme to compensate, by an intellectual activity which I would do my utmost to make pres-tigious, for the ineluctable diminution that age would bring to me, notably in the domain of sex, that most precious treasure in a person's life, and soonest threatened. If this fear of decline is, in the end, what determines what I do, is it surprising that shaping my own statue should have become the conscious goal of my literary attempts? As one wastes away, the need to protect oneself becomes more and more urgent, and the most immediate protection is, probably, to cover oneself with beautiful clothing.

Theoretically, therefore, the comfort I manage to find in literature—however suspicious I may be of it—tallies with the idea everyone shares that there should be some compensation for old age. Most people believe that a normal life should be rewarded by an increase in the material well-being to be enjoyed by the interested party himself or by his descendants. What I see as the palliative for the end of my own life is the establishment of a spiritual capital that could make me worthy of, if not fame, at least the possibility of having some prominence and not sinking, once I am dead, into total oblivion. It goes without saying that I don't reject the idea of having a certain fortune in my declining days that would allow my old age to be accompanied by as few pains as possible (there is no comparison between the end of a wealthy bourgeois and that of the person for whom the poorhouse lies in wait). But this isn't the most important wish that I have, nor is fame, moreover. I have an aversion to appearing well-to-do, as though looking like a rich or important man is just as much a sign of old age as wrinkles are.

The statue I say I am shaping (and that I was merely tracing out in a rough sketch when I penciled that fragment of silhouette positioned between a woman's gaze and the lines of a monument) is therefore not simply meant to give someone else proof of my capabilities any more than it is meant to display me, to those who see me from outside, in what I feel to be the most interesting sort of light. Nor is there any question of its merely serving as an effigy in some funeral arrangement. If I am determined to create this figure (which will perhaps be no more than a ludicrous idol, not even suited to a wax museum), it is also because I am in some sense shaping and strengthening myself as I go along. Here I come back to language, to the powers of detection and exaltation I attribute to it, to the use of writing as an instrument for achieving heightened awareness and therefore for influencing oneself and for fabricating.

Since I started this chapter—a somewhat listless phase of my stubborn attempt at self-fabrication—a number of events have taken place. Some of a public nature and others strictly private. I noted the landing of the Allied troops, then the Liberation (which, once the excitement of the first few days died down, left me, as it did many others, rather disoriented in the face of our reconquered freedom: *all* problems once again arise, whereas under the occupation, since the enemy was there, with his specific menace, there was no room for any but immediate problems, and Good and Evil were easy to tell apart). I didn't mention a second trip I took to Africa (to the Côte d'Ivoire and the Gold Coast), nor a bereavement that affected me very closely and made me sorry that I had written, with a touch of irony, that now I could no longer deplore the too spacious dimensions of my apartment on Quai des Grands-Augustins. Camus and Malraux, whom I thought of very specifically during a trip I have just made (of the first when we stopped at Algeria, which is his native country; of the second when the plane flew along the coast of Spain, which was a favorite country of his, as it was of many of us) no longer belong to the editorial staff of the magazine *Les Temps modernes* because it took too much of their time, and time is not something that can be squandered. I have completely lost track of the Mauritanian named Khadidja with whom I was arrested in the raid on the Rhumerie Martiniquaise when the Germans were still in Paris. Finally, at a recent performance of *Richard III*, which he was playing as only the English can play Shakespeare (without affecting a stylized kind of acting any more than a naturalistic one but by *embodying* the character, with an undefinable humor as hard to imitate as an accent), I applauded the actor Laurence Olivier, of whom I had saved a photograph showing him with Merle Oberon in their respective roles as Heathcliff and Catherine in the film *Wuthering Heights*. In short, it is as though I am being constantly outdistanced in the race between myself and time that has been entered in the course of this chapter, as though my pen is vainly trying to pursue a reality that is running away from me. The fault lies with the slowness of this pen, which always labors as though to move mountains, when I would like it to be so swift.

It would seem, on the whole, that when I write my quarrel is primarily with time itself, whether I am trying to give an account of what is happening inside me at the present moment, reviving memories, escaping into a world where time, like space, dissolves, or trying to acquire some sort of fixity—or immortality—by sculpting a statue of myself (a real Sisyphean labor, since it always has to be started all over again). Whether it is the time comprised within my life itself or calendar time punctuated by Sundays and holidays, whether it is a historical fresco or a gallery of my private life, I am at odds with time, crushed as I am by my fear of death and unable to see time wearing the beneficent aspect endowed it, despite the ravages it works on them as well as on everyone else, by those who believe that the world obeys the law of progress—in other words that as time passes it improves, "makes progress" like a schoolchild during his year of studies. (Rationally, however, such a belief should be less and less widespread, since these times are hardly of the sort to inspire one with optimism.)

Degré, Barèges, liège are the cards I lay out in front of me now, as I talk about *progrès. Degré* [degree, step] because the notion of progress—that is, a steady advance or ascent—necessarily implies the notion of an *ehelon* [level] or *degré* (which is a *degré centigrade* or sometimes just a *grade* [grade, rank, university degree] but rarely the step of a stairway). *Barèges* because of the Barèges bath, whose sulfurous smell for me impregnates the word *progrès*, thus contaminated by a second assonance, and because in a hot bath there is always a thermometer on which one can read the temperature, which leads back by another path to the idea of *degrés. Liège* [cork] because *Barèges* summons it by a partial echo, and because on the surface of the bath is this thermometer, whose float was, it seems to me, made of cork (unless that was the plug on the bottom) in the tubs of the establishment I was taken to when I was little. Thus, progress seems to develop in the emollient atmosphere of a steam room, smelling of rotten eggs and looking less like the steps of a front stoop or curbstones than the cork with which not only plugs are made but life belts and the protective helmets that only a few colonials do without altogether.

Progrès, like so many words with wise and reassuring purport (*honnête* [honest, upright], which is a little simpleminded, like the kind of gingerbread known as *nonnettes, pudeur* [modesty], whose unfortunate beginning almost makes one think of some derivative of *puer* [to stink], which isn't the case with either *pureté* [purity] or even *public* but is perhaps with *puberté* [puberty]), is for me one of those words that give a nuance of discredit to the idea they express, unless just the opposite is true, and it is the idea that gives them an unpleasant sound when they enter my ears.

What allowed me, for example, to hope—given the constant perfecting of medical and surgical techniques—that I wouldn't suffer as much as my father suffered during the last few months before he died: this was the concrete meaning I attributed to the word *progrès* for some time and that could have been read by anyone leafing through the personal dictionary I carry around in my head (as every person does). More generally, it was what gave my life a chance of being happier than my parents' lives—this was the meaning I gave it without even noticing, certainly seeing progress as something that went beyond me but almost never rising above strictly personal considerations when I thought of it specifically.

Perhaps yielding to an impulse to be coquettish (or to a policy of confession similar to that of announcing your age because it makes you seem frank and leaves open the possibility that you will be found to look young), I insist on the egocentric quality of my notion of progress. With an ambivalent feeling that might be a disdainful satisfaction in this display of egotism, a pleasure in talking about myself even if what I say is bad, a degree of contentment in stealing a march on the judgments I might be exposed to, or a rather bitter joy at consciously leveling accusations at myself, I see that a notion of such universal scope as that of "progress" nevertheless made its way into me through the little door, the secret stairway, of apprehensions I have always harbored about the sum of happiness I'm permitted to expect from life.

But is it different for people whose belief in progress has taken the place of a faltering religion? Doesn't a complacent expectation that there will be an almost automatic improvement in the conditions of our life through the gradual dissemination of knowledge as a result of compulsory education and the constant growth of our marvelous stock of "inventions" imply a softness of character similar to my own, when I thought of the idea in terms of comfort, an idea that can hardly acquire any nobility except to the extent that it expresses a possibility and, far from representing a completely planned career upon which one would like to see all of humanity enter, simply indicates that there is a direction in which it is proper, rationally, to try to go?

Considering the present state of things and what terrible blows have been dealt over the last few years to this blind confidence in a development that is purportedly the natural consequence of science's victories judiciously turned to profit by the industry of man (a reasonable animal, even if one cannot count on the purity of his intentions), I also don't see what idea of progress a sensible individual could form, if not precisely that of a path crowded with brushwood in which we must at all costs try to make our way forward. Just as I discovered in myself no vocation for any activity at all, man has no vocation for the harsh and often dangerous work he must take on if he truly wants to make some progress. Whence the indifference of the many people who simply replace the old lazy optimism in which so many others remained smugly ensconced by a vague "What's the use?" (which is also restful, since it excludes in advance all motives we could have for acting). As for me, I have to guard very carefully against this attitude because I would be only too likely to pillow my head on despair, decide I was going to lie down on it, and never move again. Also I am too inclined—after having been attracted, first and foremost, to everything "modern" (loving jazz and dancing fashionable dances to begin with, then becoming interested in the new forms of art that blossomed in the years following the other war: at first furniture, which I saw as a setting for life or a supplement to clothing, then avant-garde music because concerts and ballets are part of such a setting, and finally painting and literature), all of this attracting me because it seemed to situate me at the very forwardmost point of the period and because I, who so rebelled at the idea that one day I would no longer be young, felt a kind of need to adhere to the very latest creations of the time—too inclined to flee romantically toward the golden age represented by certain ways of life that are past now, which may be childhood (the childhood years before the so-called age of reason) or the state of innocence attributed—without its being investigated much—to primitive peoples not yet corrupted by our civilization or all peoples not yet touched by our passion for technology. If I could only tolerate the emptiness and inactivity of a perpetual Sunday, I would perhaps leave it at that. But immobility—and even the immobility of happiness—means nothing but monotony to me, a uniform time elapsing with no incident to block my gaze (the way the priest's soutane hides the scaffold from the person about to be guillotined), with no picturesqueness of any kind that would, if not blind me, at least catch my eye and keep it from turning directly on the inevitable death awaiting me at the end of the street.

For ten years or so, today's war, which was in preparation and which I dreaded not only as a collective catastrophe but because there was some chance it would lead to my own death, played the anesthetizing role of an event looming in the future like a screen between the present moment and the time I computed to be my end. Later, my eyes were obstinately fixed on the hope of liberation. Even so, I had an inkling that when I had weathered that storm I would find myself once again grappling with my everyday monsters. Today, with the war gone from our continent and the occupation ended, nothing is in front of me anymore, no wall of fire to cross, no solid door to stave in, nothing standing in my path and stopping it from running straight ahead to the ditch; perhaps I have never before felt so helpless.

I have sometimes tried to change the direction of my life suddenly. Not in order to change something that seemed empty into something full, to satisfy a specific desire or a spiritual need, but out of a hunger for transformation, a need to whiten the page as though for a new start, or simply the desire for something noteworthy to happen before my final decline. Yet the tactic I ordinarily use in my struggle against time would dissolve into the management of a series of minuscule undertakings, in one sense distractions or pastimes (as I suffer from a shameful incapacity to draw from myself the wherewithal never to be idle), but in another sense pledges I take against the immediate future, as though at each instant I feared time would slip out from under my feet and as though I wanted to force it, impose a path on it so rigid that it would be obliged to pursue its course, thus giving me the promise of my own continuation. Weaving a network of small plans such as appointments with friends, dates for meetings, decisions to see a show on a certain night of this week or another, I manage—so dominated am I by this idea of taking a day as one accepts a guarantee—always to live *ahead* of myself, unable to experience the present and piling up the dust from these plans on top of the dust from other plans, scarcely profiting from any, as though in the end I were making dates, not with people or positive pleasures but with time itself. So tyrannical is this need to arrange my days, at least the most imminent ones (for fear of missing something and because once the future has been mortgaged this way, all danger of annihilation seems to have been temporarily avoided), so absurd my mania, where the routine of my pleasures is concerned, for always keeping some of them prepared in advance (like a sum of money I have deposited in the bank) that it sometimes happens to me, for example, that I make a date with friends I like, and then, even before the date of our meeting arrives, begin thinking anxiously about whether or not I will be able, at the time of that meeting, to make a later date in the not too distant future. My uneasy expectancy taking precedence over all other feelings, I can be obsessed by it even during the meeting and can seem embarrassed, absent, not very talkative, so that a harmony I would have liked to be perfect will be tiresomely altered, and all the pleasure I had intended to derive from these few hours of mutual relaxation will be spoiled. So powerful is this preoccupation (in which there is on the one hand some greed and fear of being idle and on the other hand the anguish that drives me to keep looking ahead), so maniacal and intrusive, that at certain gloomy moments, an accident like my own death, or that of someone close to me, my descent or his into the hell on earth of a serious illness, ends up seeming like the stick that will be poked into the wheels one of these days, preventing my schedule from being kept, though this schedule has been arranged not so much because of the pleasures I anticipate from it or whatever strange urgency might be associated with these futile plans as because of my concern to imprison the future in a fine enough net so that misfortune won't find any hole to slip in. Thus making use of trifling plans to give myself the illusion that I am protected against the threat of death and misfortune, I eventually come to look upon death and misfortune as things that might interfere with my carrying out these plans. What was merely an artifice for escape has become something that makes me hardly care about the rest, all business grinding to a halt, something, moreover, that would not tolerate any sort of escape. For lack of a larger idea, a real ambition compared to which death would not count for much, I entrench myself behind a mountainous pile of little things, an inglorious rampart and an ineffective one besides; for in addition to the fear from which I had hoped to deliver myself by constructing it, there is the fear that it will be destroyed now that what was merely a vulgar means of evading the certainty that a day would come when I would no longer be alive has nearly achieved the rank of my main reason for living. A bungled conjuring trick, a naive ruse that resulted in the complete reversal of the situation since now the means has become the end, the accessory has become the essential part, the buttress has become the cornerstone, the protective activity has become the first thing to protect. All because I harbor such a terror of death, as though death, before actually killing me, would begin by killing my ability to direct my actions in a rational way.

Ahead of myself. Living not in the present indicative but (when I don't fall back on the past) in that absolute future into which one is precipitated by the fear of death. Clinging to the relative future represented by those plans made with the idea both of establishing a future and of erecting across my path a series of barriers that I will have to surmount before reaching the point at which there is no longer any *forward* or *back*. Depending on whatever reassurance I can inject into what is coming up *now* to avoid being crushed by the thought of what will be coming up at the far end of *after.* Ahead of myself. Living my own death or clutching at any event whatever, some event that is certainly part of the future but not yet death or its premonitory symptoms.

I am going to be shot by the Germans (this is a dream I have one night during the occupation). I accept it courageously until I learn that they will be coming to shave me in the early afternoon, the customary last grooming before the execution. Knowing precisely at what impending moment I will no longer be separated by anything from the execution itself (whereas the last grooming, an event on which all my attention was focused, had until that moment hidden the final event that the execution would be), imagining the imminent disappearance of that last screen placed between death and me by the ceremony of the shave, my courage is replaced by a frightful panic. I feel that I will not withstand the shock of it, that I will cry and howl when I am led to the stake.

The impossibility of looking death in the face, not indeterminate death (like a sort of background) but immediately imminent death, death when my back is against the wall, death when nothing more separates me from it. An unjustifiable propensity to attach myself to trifles (formerly the outfit I would put on, nowadays anything that allows me to substitute an anodyne comedy for the tragedy of existence). An attachment, nevertheless, to the idea of revolution, because our life really has to be transfigured, and no real progress in our world where work and money loom so important can be conceived without a complete upheaval of the very economic conditions that, I have finally realized, have had an influence on my own outlook that, in all good faith, I cannot term negligible. A call for the "new era" that Marthe-who-committed-suicide dreamt of, an era that, of course doesn't seem to me a golden age (the true golden age being necessarily the one in which the question of death would no longer be posed) but at the very least a state of things less absurd than that in which I delight in playing the fool or acting like a drunken helot. In the dream I described, the people who were to shoot me were those who opposed everything that could result in such a "new era" during the period when my troubled sleep made me imagine this.

I know more or less everything I will be doing tomorrow, which is Sunday, a Sunday in Auvergne, where I am presently on vacation. My day is almost as well regulated in advance as a schoolboy's. There is nothing excessive in it, nothing lacking. But I don't know if I will make love.

Among the habits I have acquired in my Paris life, little by little caught in their nets without being able to say just how it happened, is the habit of "making a sacrifice to Venus," as the vulgar circumlocution has it, on Sunday mornings. This, because Sunday morning is practically the only morning I am perfectly free to do as I like and because I especially enjoy making love in the daytime, no doubt because to abandon oneself to pleasure while the sun is shining (especially in the afternoon, when one deliberately goes to bed as though to defy the busy world outdoors) stresses the asocial nature I ascribe to erotic activity. When I go to bed at night, at an hour when offices are closed and most machines are at rest, it is because I want to sleep. Tomorrow, Sunday—a Sunday in the country, for which one may hope for good weather—won't be Sunday for me but a day like any other, since I am on vacation; and could this be the reason why I don't know if I will make love? Since there is no work to stop me from staying in bed late or taking a nap any weekday I like, this Sunday will be whatever my mood and physical inclinations make of it. I will study English for a little while, which has become my daily habit since the beginning of last month. I will work for a while correcting the proofs of a text on African ethnology that I finished a long time ago but that is only just about to appear. Perhaps I will put the last touches on this chapter and go for a walk. There is someone with me I don't want to name, but I can say I don't want to leave this person anymore to go off by myself to another part of the world.

A newspaper we received yesterday confirmed a fact that makes bantering out of place and means that if one wants only to take a comic tone, it is time to keep quiet. Robert Desnos, who was deported to Germany and was already—or almost—on his way home, has died. We will surely talk about him, because he was a friend of ours and one of the three great poets to pay the highest price for this period of horrifying regression. Remembering Desnos will make me ashamed of my foibles and affectations; maybe it will give me a little of his courage. I will look at the meadows and trees, and I will make an effort not to turn my eyes to myself too much. In haste, and without knowing exactly what to think of it, I will recopy—as though to close a parenthesis or regain a confidence that, in the course of the conversation, has been lost—a passage that I wrote down one Sunday in the notebook with the blue cardboard cover in which I keep my journal, the same Sunday when I described an outing in the car into the region of Senlis, a Sunday that dates from the time when I still had the clear conviction that I was an individual essentially superior to, or in any case very different from, other people.

Then—tomorrow having become today in the interval—I see that it is very nice out (and a little cool, as usual, because we are at an altitude of several hundred meters). I left my room to go to the toilet, and happened to find a bit of a torn magazine with the photographs of the British plays that were being put on a little more than a month ago at the Comédie Française. It was there that I saw *Richard III*, and that was what made me decide to study English again (something I had been thinking of doing anyway for some time, having felt humiliated that I spoke so badly when I was in the Gold Coast). Because, among these photographs, there was one of the actor Olivier in the role of King Richard, I was taken back, naturally enough, to *Wuthering Heights*, a work I found magical, as did so many others, and one whose power to charm can be summed up in a few words: it is the legend of a love that mocks not only social prejudices but life and death too, since it continues beyond the grave, and years later, the furious hatred that is its corollary turns on the generation after the generation of its heroes, the two lovers. In the same way, what is captivating about Shakespeare's play is the imposing image of an uncontrollably passionate man devoured not only by ambition but by the need to mock everything.

Finally—and no doubt my mind was already made up to do this when I was still pretending to be undecided—the feast of love for two was consummated, while most of the holiday makers in the village hotel where we're staying must have been sprucing themselves up to go to Mass.

Now the morning is nearing its end. A thin curtain of cloud has appeared, drawn geometrically across one part of the sky, so that the day is just a tiny bit less beautiful. But even so, it is the sort of weather that makes one feel at peace.

With the Eversharp pen that Sartre brought back to me from a trip he took to the United States (a pen whose body reaches into a sort of beveled cap that covers the pen almost to its nib, a perfect pen except that it holds very little ink, but the inconvenience is minimal for me, since I always write very little) I am preparing to recopy the fragment of private journal I mentioned earlier, as though to come full circle, to move things back to the point where I took them up, or rather, close the door behind me before going off somewhere else, because to retrace your steps, even when you are writing, is humanly impossible. When you are climbing a mountain and have gained a little height, you also like to survey the path you have just taken, spying the house or outcropping that is now much lower but, as you are surprised to discover after this long walk, still close to the point where you are now.

> *I am in my room right now. I hear phonographs and people bursting into laughter; also the cries of women being tickled. It's the most complete ignominy—the ignominy of sweat—even more disgusting when it arises from bubbly exuberance than when it is produced by work. All these people revolt me in their tranquillity and their indifference, their total unconsciousness. This afternoon I saw a region called Survilliers, near which there is a housing estate. Quantities of petit bourgeois families have settled there. The women knit, while the men work in the garden or finish building their obscene little house of boards or rubble. The children are hardly more likeable; one can sense all too well what this brood will turn into later. Not content with working all week long, these people have to go on working the few days that are granted them for resting. They only like to build, dig in the earth, make a burrow for themselves so they can come here a few years from now and sleep off the fatigue of a whole lifetime of incurable imbecility. I don't understand why these people, in all their "happiness," aren't worried by the prospect of the diseases that will afflict them sooner or later and make them suffer more than a thousand deaths before knocking them off for good. I don't ask them to be prey to the sort of intellectual anxieties that even I, after all, make fun of, but I am astonished at this animal peacefulness that is not racked by any anguish, even physical. I can't understand how it is that these people seem to have no idea that they are condemned to death, or at least seem to be resigned to it. I find this the height of brutishness and servility.*

One last piece of news to record here: Japan has just surrendered, so the war is over.

The Trumpet-Drum

Words ending in -*lan* tend to have a cheerful sound. Like *brelan* [three-of-a-kind in cards], *ortolan* [bunting (the bird)], *cerf-volant* [kite] (in the shape of a sharply pointed heart with—glued to the middle of the white paper—the figure of a soldier cut out of one of those Épinal pages showing lines of soldiers in uniform); like *l'Aigloplan*, another flying thing belonging to my older brother (shaped like an eagle, and made of brown cloth); like *Roland* (whose heroic fanfare is still ringing at Roncevaux), *Coriolan* [Coriolanus] (who also puts a horn to his mouth and turns it into a triumphal march in a tumult of banners). Of the same metal as these names—of which the last two shine a joyous light on the fate of the two men, tragic though it was—there is also *bataclan* [trappings, paraphernalia] (with its burlesque clanging of kitchen equipment, saucepans predominating) and *mirobolant* [staggering, stupendous] (superlatively hilarious with its bouncing clowns released one by one into a series of somersaults or other stunts amid a peppering of slaps and a hail of kicks in the rear end).

The configuration of such words not only has the brilliance of an eye lit up with gaiety or a heap of silky cloth but a clear sonority (the driness of the drum head on which the sticks beat their rat-a-tat-tat) setting in motion something bold and victorious. When I was quite young, every one of these words vibrated with a happy note; and now I think this was because of *jour de l'an* [New Year's Day], a time lit by the sparkling of costumes, toys, books with colorful bindings, and all the other presents that made this time of the year, like everything that reminded me of its name, a sparkling world drawn out of the surrounding shadow by a magical kind of illumination.

A combination trumpet and drum, a single object producing two different sounds by itself, an Arcole drum from which the touch of the drumsticks not only set off a rhythmic cascade of beats but also released a sound similar to the sound of Roland's horn but higher and more cheerful, a surprise toy whose insides seemed to contain a clever, secret mechanism causing this cylindrical body, like the bodies of other drums, to become a receptacle from which the sharp voice of a brass instrument emanated—such was the trumpet-drum I wanted for quite a long time, perhaps going so far as to look for it (but with no success) in the New Year's gift catalogues. This all started one day when I was out walking and heard this musical combination of blowing and beating, thinking it came from the apparently quite ordinary drum with which two children were playing, without noticing (as I was forced to admit later, thinking about it) that one of the two kids, playing along with his drummer friend, had a trumpet and was emptying his lungs into it.

Other toys delighted me: watches with no works but whose two hands, if pushed with a finger or moved with the winder, could show any time one liked; colored cutouts of animals, flowers, and people; transfers of delicate glossy figures that always surprised one by coming unstuck and remaining whole as they were lifted onto the sheet of paper to which they were applied after being moistened; compasses whose attraction lay in the narrow lozenge of metal always ready to oscillate on its pivot; little turtles with feet that moved, enclosed in cardboard boxes with covers made of mica or some other translucent material; postcards (but am I perhaps dreaming this?) that were also phonograph records. All these toys except the last remained docilely contained within the limits of what could be procured for me without any special search and, in any case, without an excessive outlay of money. But it is quite clear that the toy for which my desire came closest to being an obsession—whether because its twofold nature (like the trumpet-drum) made it rather odd and attractive to me, or whether the mere fact of imagining it without ever seeing it (or knowing it only by hearsay) conferred on it a value unattainable by any object that had come, even if only once, within the field of my senses, or whether I had imagined it precisely because of a certain tendency to reduce several things to one so as to be able to say I held in my hand all sorts of possibilities and was free to take up one or another of them, or whether, lastly, not owning a toy that was really most commonplace, I simply wanted it longer and thus see it today, quite wrongly, as an obstinately coveted grail—was the postcard phonograph record.

Of my childhood dreams, one of the most insistent—I noted it down several times, once the vision of a constantly shrinking future began to incite me to poke about in the past accumulating behind me—was based on this very simple theme: the search for a known object that had been lost for awhile and that I ardently wanted to recover. A dream of pure desire, which I still have now and then in various different forms and in which the object I must put my hand on again is usually a gramophone record. An absolutely marvelous record (most often jazz) that I recall having heard though I can't manage to find it in the heap of other records I have also listened to recently; a real record, but one that can't be found (even though while I am in the grips of the dream I have no doubt that it is close by); a single item lost in a collection comprising many other items not without value, though they are nowhere near comparable to the one whose lack is a severe hindrance—if not over a longer period of time, at least for a few minutes—to my feeling happy.

Thus, in the parades of phantasms that sometimes still cross my sleep dressed in carnival disguises, amid the ever-changing flickering of their torchlight procession, what appears to me as the most desirable thing is an object almost identical to this enigmatic postcard. Not that such a childish desire for a trifling object has remained stuck in me like a splinter to resurface in my mature years (that would be a very strange remnant, too easily rivaled, in filling my dreams, by many old desires similar to that one and, like it, still unassuaged). Not that, as I dream this dream, I exhume an ancient dissatisfaction, untouched since it first came into being and molded in the exact same container: a solid body without thickness, holding potential sonorities, even though in its design it is small enough to be put in the mail. In the dream I have now, the record itself doesn't matter and does not derive its special quality from the possibility of a dual function as it is used over and over again. No need for this instrument (without any real luster anyway) to be a tiny miracle, or for it to have any other meaning than that of music.

Balancier de ma vie [pendulum, balancing-pole, of my life]: a fragment of a phrase without any melodic attraction and, isolated as it is, almost without meaning, but which has been plaguing me for several days. I chew it like chewing gum, waiting for other words or phrases to join it to become a poem, a poem that will be able to turn just as happily toward the passage of time measured by the pulse of a pendulum as toward my perpetual oscillations or the principle that can be seen as making my tightrope walker's progress more sure and continuous. *Balancier de ma vie.* Since I have rejected in turn various different nouns, one of which could have been nailed to this bit of a phrase, serving it as an epithet (*amour* [love], *ennui* [weariness], *paresse* [sloth], and the concrete noun *Afrique* [Africa], a land toward which I am thrust by real life at periodic intervals), since the fire is stillborn that I had hoped to coax from striking it against the flint of two syllables (the number required for one of those cadences one forges for oneself by experimentally fitting words together and which are difficult to get rid of once they have slyly imposed themselves), it now seems to me that without forcing things too much I would be justified in preceding it by the noun *musique* [music].

Though it is not exactly a *balancier* (that is, a regulator), music has always had great power over me. So much so that I remember certain times of my life mainly by recalling tunes that seemed to establish a common measure between me and the world. Mostly dance tunes, in other words songs associated with abandonment and pleasure, melodies tuned to a breath so organic and deep in me that when I dream of them, their absence is synonymous with a loss I have to make good at all costs.

"Hindustan," in which there are pheasants and caravans (the pheasants spread their tails like fans, while in the caravanseries or palm groves the tired animals lie down), "Hindustan," the street stall of a colonial exhibition or a Thousand and One Nights, is the tune associated with the 1920s and dancing parties. With the clarity, almost, of a bad color print, I can recall the state I was plunged into one of the innumerable times I heard it. On a certain spring or summer day—a beautiful day like today, a Thursday in mid-Lent when I was on vacation—I was walking in the woods in the late afternoon, probably with the woman friend I spent most of my time with in those days, giving hardly a thought to anything else. No doubt we were walking along a path with a decent reputation, like the Allée des Acacias. At that hour, the tea dance hour, there came to us from a pavilion all of greenery and glass the soft murmur of an orchestra playing "Hindustan," the most popular, in those days, of all the numbers imported from across the Atlantic. What it provoked in me was a great desire for a fulfilling love, for an easy and elegant life, with just the dose of exoticism or nostalgia necessary for all of this to resolve into a vague emotion I would have to call poetic. Along with it (was this present in my mind at the very time of this walk under the leaves or have I added it now, my memories agglomerating like a snowball?) came the image, more remote in time, of one of my dancing partners, a brown-haired girl, rather plump, always high-spirited, with whom I had no other connection than the dancing parties (as one of her partners while she was one of mine, a relationship that didn't imply there was anything more between a boy and girl connected in this way than a technical sort of intimacy, a partners' agreement, a love of a concerted sort of abandonment—a pair of instruments well tuned in their dialogue—to a pleasure, if not an art, that they know they are drawn to by a shared passion). She was of no more than average height, with bright, dark eyes and a nimble step, and her name was Mary (pronounced in the English way). Definitely not veiled in mystery and not in the least a distant princess; quite the contrary—matter-of-fact, vibrant, inseparable, despite everything, in the Mother Goose of my memory, from the indolently oriental fox-trot I'm not even sure we ever danced together. Like many other tunes that always move me if I have a chance to listen to them, what I was offered by this fox-trot, adorned as it was—like an Indian dancing girl by her plumes or a rajah's turban by its diamond—by the showy name of "Hindustan," what it offered me because of the voluptuous-ness and distance it evoked was, in short, an illustration—even a portrait—of my own desire. Why, then, should I be surprised to see it ineradicably associated with this figure in a pink or pale blue dress, with no more background than a mechanical doll? A figure looming up from a period when the daily eddies of dancing merely expressed, in a carefully regulated display, the sensual storms I couldn't yet give way to, restrained as I was by shyness, and was waiting to experience. A figure that expressed my waiting and, soon, my regret. Within the bounds of those two words—formulas of the insidious acids that were eating away, that day, at a thin ribbon of vivid color: the presence of a woman friend by my side—lies the charm of that music, whose cadence my body wanted to match once again: waiting and regret. A belief in the future, always as a door open on the possibility of a new feeling; at the same time a retreat toward the days (at that time barely passed) when my life was still only a groping expectation, still on the threshold of a vista of galleries whose light seemed all the more dazzling because it was seen from the half light of the vestibule where I was waiting.

Other dance tunes cling to events or phases that are not as old: Liszt's "Liebestraum," a syncopated arrangement of which is still the sound in the background of a walk I took in Nantes, a prelude to four days of hibernation on the Quiberon peninsula during which I worked up into poems the stale odors of an excursion across that city, a city where several partisans were born, and before them the slave traders for whom the extremely beautiful gray stone houses were built; "Love for Sale," which is associated with the troubled period when I was working for the magazine *Documents* and, apart from this paid employment, was descending painfully to depths of passion haunted by half-gentle, half-terrible maternal furies; "Some of These Days," which was broadcast over the loudspeaker on the steamship *Cairo City* as it was getting under way at the start of a voyage to Greece on the eve of the last war, a voyage in which I would leave behind the beginning of an adventure that the great chaos of events that followed was to cause, first, to blossom and then, rapidly, to be repudiated. Still other American music, "straight" music, coming at just the right moment, as though to emphasize the pathos of a certain particularly moving scene in a sentimental film I was playing: inside a taxi that I had gotten into alone after severing a bond—cutting myself a little, too, in the process—that had threatened to unite me with a faded blue-stocking for whom—once my eyes were opened after a brief infatuation—I had no more feeling except anger (like the hero of a tragedy filled with horror by the incest), the unexpected outburst, in the taste of the curtain song "Go Ahead and Laugh, Pagliacci . . .," of a jazz melody playing on the radio with which my vehicle was equipped; at the Orsay station, where I was seeing a woman friend of mine off on the train, a woman to whom I felt strongly attracted—across the tangle of sophisticated phrases that my perpetual fear of coming straight to the point made me substitute for positive actions—by a love thwarted by the taste for failure I have always had such great trouble quelling, over the hubbub of the station concourse an outpouring of very tender and melancholy blues, as though a director arranging for the right atmosphere had decided to comment in this way on the familiar sadness of departures, at the same time providing a choice morsel for my morose delectation. On a completely different level, lighter and gayer, not unlike comic opera, an old tune—Scottish or Canadian, I think—played on the banjo by an

American in the streets of Montmartre, where almost every night we encountered him escorted by a gang of roamers of his own kind leading (at least to all appearances) the unsystematic life on which I placed such a high value because of its very incoherence: this occurring at about the time of my affiliation with the surrealist group, when I resolutely wandered around at night with a few of my recently acquired friends and regarded cabarets as comparable to the Stoics' porch or the caves that history and ethnography show us so often to have been choice places for initiations. When I try to recall this tune, hymn of a period I saw as being inherently profound with a frivolous exterior, what always comes to mind is a French tune, the song known as "Raspberries, Strawberries," of which I never knew more than a few scraps, this confusion of two different songs having begun way back when my friends and I liked to listen to the amateur banjo player walking at the head of his happy team of sprites of both sexes.

So jazz, which moves me now as though it were my true folklore, and some more or less popular songs, have been with me at points of my life of which it is hard for me to say whether they had any real importance or have remained sharp in my memory only because music happened to be mingled with them, a providential message delivered to me by the outside world. Isn't this musicality, which seems suddenly to be exhaled by things, so that it brings them into tune with me, the symbol of what I have desired for a long time: no longer to be in the position of a stranger in a world where I alternately doze off and stir myself in pointless agitation? And was I already counting on a miracle of this kind (a sudden gift from outside, of a sort to make one believe that fairy godmothers are lurking out there) when as a child I asked for postcards that made noise, drum-trumpets, or other unusual toys? Didn't I want these double-purpose instruments simply because, more than other objects, they stood for the wondrous object, the lucky find I longed for in the shape of products issuing from an almost supernatural industry? More of a realist today, but perhaps also more extreme in my demands, I no longer really expect to receive presents like that from the world, presents endowed with their own inherently fantastic nature. Rather, I expect a complicity to form between things and myself—fleetingly, stealthily—as though now, instead of the lucky find in the guise of a "gift from heaven," the pure and simple fact of my passing encounter with a world in league with me, for the time being, assumed in my eyes the value of a magical conquest.

A pledge—so this is what I am really looking for when I dream of the lost record I would like to recover, also when I dream (as I noted down nearly thirteen years ago) of a crucially important book I am looking for in vain, inspecting the wooden shelves of a room in the publisher's office, where I know it is arranged among other works, travel accounts or treatises on magic. A pledge, a permanent sign I can refer to forever, a brief, chance moment petrified the way the disk of engraved wax that can be held in one's hands is a petrification of music one can play for oneself any time, again and again.

A philosopher's stone or a flask containing the elixir of youth. The portrait with the ambiguous smile called *La Gioconda*, whose theft from the Louvre was in the news for such a long time. Mambrino's helmet, stolen by the ingenious hidalgo Don Quixote de la Mancha in the form of a barber's basin (a sort of full moon or halo, a bit of which has been cut away, like a pancake broached by the first mouthful, a jaw biting full into the middle of it with fangs set in a semicircle). The zaimph, a sacred veil masking the statue of the goddess Tanit (and which one can assume is made of taffeta or muslin like the slightly shiny, gummy-looking cloth protecting the chandeliers during the summer months when the masters of the house have gone off on their vacation), an untouchable veil in which the Libyan mercenary Matho wraps himself in Flaubert's novel *Salammbô* and in the opera scenes the musician Reyer made from it. All sorts of secret documents filched by spies (double agents or not). The vast succession of legendary treasures to be unearthed, extracted from among the roots of a tree as thick as the oak under which Saint Louis sat to administer justice. The serious or light books with illustrations of women partially unclothed or in the nakedness of pure savagery, books I would go and get from my father's bookcase (the big one, so high, so wide, so black, or the little one of lighter wood) at the definitely awkward age when poking through these two parlor bookcases occupied a good part of my time, if I was free during an afternoon spent at home. The fountain pen of the most unquestionably perfect style, so that at school the whole class envied me because of it and many other desirable riches were offered in exchange for it. The mug of inscribed silver that, when I was younger, I knew was *my* mug, the one given me at my baptism, and that I would demand, shouting "like a madman" if someone else happened to use it either inadvertently or to tease me. Any one of the bagatelles or precious possessions whose ownership, now, would no longer give me any pleasure, preoccupied as I am with the idea of how swiftly time passes: what, then, is this rare bird I hold in my hand, in my very evanescent hand of flesh? (And the fact is that I now like only the most ephemeral of inanimate things, whose fragility proves to be fashioned after my own: articles of clothing or the accessories of daily life that constitute, not so much a lasting *possession* as a seasonal sort of gear that gradually wears out, so that it seems to be in step with my own body and require an expenditure without any return, without the purchase of the sort of lasting quality that would satisfy a miser. And if this is the case, then so much for collections, museum pieces, knickknacks, and works of art, rare books and large-format editions for bibliophiles—in short all acquisitions whose stability can only remind me, by contrast, how temporary I am, in the same way that contemplating the horizon, the sign of a certain fixity, makes the seasick traveler all the more distinctly conscious of the motion that is nauseating him.)

Forcing myself, despite my lukewarm feeling for everything smacking of a reliquary or curio collection, to pin down here, as though to the pages of an herbarium, whatever samples I can collect of objects jealously kept or ardently coveted, specimens taken from the field of my direct experience or that of things on which I have only an imaginary hold (since my knowledge of them is only second hand, and they exist for me only like emblazoned curtains drawn through my head for a moment), I am obliged to recognize that—like someone who is actually gathering plants—I see nothing I can turn into more than a dessicated stalk, unless it is a flower about to crumble to dust. And when I embark on this hunt that only results in deceptive captures (thin phantoms of real things always trailing behind me and already wandering through ruins at the very moment I write), I reproduce, transposing it onto an abstract level, the search I so often make, both in dreams and daily life, for an *object*.

A few years ago, in particular, I was regularly overcome with uneasiness every time I stayed home alone for a while. In most cases incapable of occupying myself with anything, not even up to reading, so great was my anxiety—that anxiety in which I felt myself still more unpleasantly mired if no special social engagement had come along during the preceding days to entertain me and give the impression that it was an event—I would brood about my mania for wasting the few hours of freedom I could have used to write if I hadn't let myself be filled with discouragement. In order to escape from this idleness, which caused the blackest thoughts to proliferate in me—so that I would dwell on suicide, toward which, when all was said and done, I did not dare risk taking the first step (and each time I dwelt on it I had to endure the humiliation of this fact, which was yet another reason for depression)—I had to go off in search of an object; more broadly, for some point in the surrounding world to which I could attach my interest or apply my restlessness. This could mean going to see a woman I knew, telephoning a friend to make a date, or going to his house with the idea of telling him something important that would introduce a new element into our relations (or at least I had the illusion that this was so). This could also mean, as a last, insipid resort, abandoning myself to a drinking bout or amorous debauch somewhere away from my house with a stranger. This could even mean simply exploring my kitchen cupboards to find something good to drink or eat, or—at an earlier time when these periods of isolation and depression almost inevitably resulted in erotic daydreaming (with the paradoxical temptation to use my own body as a plaything to distract me from myself, a temptation to which I sometimes gave in, then feeling remorseful at having tired myself out so idiotically)— using a real, physical object in a fetishistic way, even though I have never been in the least attracted by the erotic passion based on the exciting contrast between the extremely civilized nature of a piece of clothing, which represents one's social exterior, and the state of nature symbolized by nudity or the act of love itself. Having made the rounds of more or less viable male friends and women (my address book in hand, if necessary), having mentally reviewed all the entertainment that could have been provided me by the collection of useful or pleasurable objects contained within the walls of my home, I would discover nothing. Then, as a rule—after having first, in good faith, looked for one I would have been fully satisfied to read at that moment—I would start poking through my books or, at a pinch, almost anything (letters, souvenirs, pieces of paper, anything that could be inspected and classified), with the vain excuse of tidying up—handling objects because I hadn't found *the object*. Or not having been able to put my time to any positive literary use, I would open a drawer in the frightful American desk that was my work table at that time and take out the thick, square-ruled note-book in which I kept my journal, and I would write something down in it—just to have blackened a little paper, at least, and also to take stock, as though I were clearing up my accounts in the same way that, just a moment before or on other occasions, I tidied up, imposed some order, to mask as best I could the absence of what I had been originally looking for.

Sometimes, however, I would be outdoors when I suffered one of these indoor attacks, these evil fruits of my chambered solitude. Alone in the street, finding myself unoccupied (on my way home, for instance, from the museum where I work, or after doing some errand, walking along not very eager to be trapped between familiar walls once again), my first impulse would be to use these moments of freedom simply to look around—relishing the people, the objects, everything that happened to come along the sidewalk or the street. But after a few steps—as though the perverse desire had descended on me to render my gaze harmless by blinkering it and as though, straining my ingenuity to rein in any inclination to escape, I was determined to keep my intellectual halter tightly strapped and recreate, even outdoors, a confined atmosphere—I would transform the walk I was taking (which nothing seemed at first to prevent from being a stroll in the open air) into a suspicious sort of loitering in front of secondhand bookstalls or bookstore windows, pretending to be a book collector in search of old or unusual books and sometimes ending up buying something, less to satisfy any real desire or need than because my wandering tended in that direction as though by definition, and also immediately regretting it as soon as I had done it. For if I take an undeniable pleasure in owning books, and if it clearly gives me a certain satisfaction to receive one from time to time, whether it conveys a friendly thought or comes through a publicity department from someone I don't know (the same satisfaction as when I get letters, mimeoed circulars, periodicals, or invitations in the mail: I feel I haven't been abandoned and also feel a touch of childish delight at being a sort of *interested party*), this satisfaction is always tinged with a little uneasiness, even sadness. Since I read very slowly and, because of that, very little, I know I will not be able to read all of them (even supposing they interest me), and I compute how many unread books, their pages scarcely cut and leafed through, their rows of spines wrapped in transparent paper or, more rarely, bound—will line my walls at the moment when, if I am still lucid enough, I will be forced to realize that my profession as artisan of language, however marvelous the power of words, has not in the least protected me from the fate common to all mortals. Thus, every time I yield to the desire to increase my library by buying a book, I inevitably think that this acquisition is only a sterile gesture, since the more certain, definite result will be to augment the sum of things that I will have been tempted to read for a moment but that, when I come to the end of the line, I will no doubt not have read.

A childish gesture, the greedy movement of my hand toward an object whose rightful use I am not considering but which my hand is determined to appropriate; the happiness I will derive, symmetrically, from ridding myself of a certain sum of money, as though in this case the act of spending were the abstract equivalent of a moment of debauchery (hasn't it happened to me many times, walking through the streets this way and feeling at a loss, as on the days when I moped in intimate commune with my pen, my notebooks, and my desk, that I buy a book after first being plagued by the idea of going into a brothel for a more obviously venal association), and as though, consequently, it was crucially important to me that there should be some *traffic* between the world and me: the gift of a little bit of myself, in a direct embrace or in the algebraic form of a payment, the acquisition of a security that may be the temporary use of a living body or the possession of a small piece of the inanimate world that I have decided, for lack of a more precious loot, to take back home with me. The act of writing a book and publishing it is the same kind of thing, though it goes in the opposite direction (just as the ebb of the tide is of the same order as the flow). I deliver myself, I bare myself, I compromise myself; in short, I indulge in a binge of another kind consisting of prostituting myself, doing commerce in myself in the double sense of the word—which not only has a mercantile meaning but a larger one implying a kind of relationship—I make coin of my own flesh and produce an object that will be security for my life to the extent, this time, that its fate is to escape me (since it is put into circulation in exchange for hard cash) and continue its career in the hands of others.

Hungers that, in the end, no subterfuge was capable of outwitting (subterfuges like those I resorted to in the first year of the occupation, when Parisians were suffering the worst hardships since they hadn't yet established any connections with the countryside, when, like an unlucky gambler chasing his luck with the hope, disappointed each time, that the next move would pay better than the one before, I would walk into not just one but a whole series of pastry shops to eat piece after piece of cake, an impulse I indulged at the time almost shamelessly but which, lonely as I was, I would never have given way to in the days when these cakes were nevertheless much sweeter to the palate and much softer to the teeth), appetites without either whimsicality or gaiety (quite remote from the sort of hunger pangs that make it a joy to go to the dinner table), changes in my condition that have nothing to do with physical thirst or an opportunity to feast (the sort of change that causes many alcoholics to drink alone and without pleasure), these avidities—I could just as well call them *aridities* or *vacuities*—which almost always take the same form even though they have different objects, drove me along the same uncertain course, always with the same lack of success, toward something I hoped would temporarily swell the skin that defines my outer limits or, inversely, tear me from it. In sum, it was a matter of triumphing over my spiritual distress by discovering something I could cling to, something that, for my heart, pounding at the sight of this evidence, would be a rich, hard concrete mass cropping up outside a place that had no substance. And in the same way, I usually grasp at some indisputable, concrete roughness (a specific memory from childhood or later) when, blocked or misled in the actual writing of this text, I look for a way to start up again or leave the mistaken path I feel I am traveling. A tactic I could—pompously—compare to that of Antaeus, who regains his strength when he touches the ground and consequently finds new resources in himself every time he clumsily allows himself to be knocked down.

(Such an image, however, when I examine it more closely, seems to me completely deceptive. Because what floors me is precisely the difficulty I have achieving these real contacts. So that it would be more honest to declare that this is simply a vicious circle. Only the impression of having an intimate commerce with a tangibly wonderful thing can rescue me from this spiritual distress, yet this uneasiness, arising from the divorce I sense between myself and the concrete, is just what leads me, through the sluggishness that goes along with it, to loosen my hold on or to refrain from grasping any quarries but those which are easier to capture but of ridiculously little density. All of this leads back to the rudimentary notion of exile, or being cut off, of a fault opening between myself and what I apprehend, a ravine that, taking my courage in both hands, I have to try to fill in, unless with one desperate leap I can succeed in crossing it. In an even more earthy way, it could be reduced to the harsh idea of privation or scarcity, of famine that makes one gnaw one's fists or chew on pieces of wood while gorging oneself on dishes that are completely hypothetical, albeit necessary, if one can't get any real food for oneself.)

Since I am preoccupied to this extent by the concrete, enraged to see it keep eluding me or dissolving, I see all too clearly that without delaying any longer I must broach a question that has been bothering me for a long time and try to resolve it as best I can. Is the path I am following—trusting these lines as guides that must lead me to a country where all creatures will seem more alive to me—really the right one? Or isn't it rather a deceptive thread coiling up and becoming tangled, keeping me away from the vital point I would like to reach instead of leading me there after a few inevitable twists and turns? Of all the things various people in my circle of friends may have said to me about what they knew of my work, of all the letters and newspaper clippings I have chanced to receive on the subject of the fragments of it I have already published (although I am still quite a ways from drawing a line across the page from one edge to the other or writing in fat, satisfied letters the words THE END—which, however, don't imply that everything is really over since it will be necessary to reread, then cross out, and cross out again), I will mention some remarks or judgments that very pertinently act as warning signs and force me to wonder if I have not shown myself to be a bad strategist and if there aren't grounds for amending my method.

First, a letter sent to me from Menours by my sister. Interested in the historiography of our family and inclined, at least as much as I, to collect memories, this sister—to whose special erudition I often appeal—insisted on letting me know in a nice way that I was mistaken about that Aunt Firmin whose husband, the victim of fits of breathlessness, reminded me when I was little of a large dog. According to what my sister wrote me, Aunt Firmin was not the daughter of a valet of my mother's father; she was indeed my father's first cousin. But her husband had met her when he was something like a head butler and she herself was a lady's companion or a governess, and so the fact that both of them had been, as one said, "in service," was the cause of my mistake. The housemaid who for years and years was my grandfather's only servant was a different person, one I also knew—certainly a fairly close connection of my family's but at no time regarded as a relative. A first point, then, that shouldn't be neglected: the fact that inaccuracies may alter or distort the earlier events that I recount. I am willing to admit that in this case, the mistake I made about a family connection that was real rather than fictional, as I had thought, is not important: the memory was not actually my own but something I heard someone say. Nonetheless, it means there is a touch of uncertainty about these events, whereas I say I am restoring them in all their integrity and refer back to them constantly as a solid base.

Along with the compliments of various people who live or have lived in the district of Auteuil-Passy (sensitive, I suppose—and this does rather worry me—to what may be properly "sixteenth arrondissement" [upper-crust] about what I write), along with a few friendly commendations (bearing especially on the quasiscientific rigor that may appear to mark this writing, in which one can in fact be sure that I haven't wanted to retouch, correct, or modify anything, whatever its involuntary deviations may be, in other respects) I received certain harsher criticisms.

One friend—a writer himself and a reader in the publishing house with which I am associated only as author—a friend to whom I gave the first six chapters of my manuscript more than a year ago now, observed to me courteously after reading them that it wasn't very clear where I was heading after the chapter that begins with the story of my move to 53 *bis* Quai des Grands-Augustins. I grant that there is some basis for this reproach, but isn't one of the goals I am pursuing precisely to find out where I am really going? (The target: that external thing, that delicate, undiscoverable object that must be defined—and to define it could perhaps be to discover it—that object the lack of which explains why my life passes in a state of anguish and idleness, of desire scarcely going beyond vague daydreaming; that object impossible to discover, the desire for which, anxious and needy as it is, is associated with my fear of death; that object I would be able to bind myself to, in which I would be able to forget myself. The target: here as in reality, aren't I moving in pursuit of the revelation of what I may feel makes life worthwhile—which in actual fact is summed up by the metaphorical obsession with an object as stirring as a piece of music? A target that, in a very long drawn out and laborious way, I am trying to make less indefinite so that I may at last aim at it.) Seeking to enlighten myself about where I am going, how could I organize my story so that the governing themes would clearly stand out before I place the last period after the last sentence?

The wife of this same friend reproached me, one evening when a whole gang of us were in a West Indian bar drinking and dancing, for having alluded, in the passage where I speak of how I used to love taking trips by myself, to someone who was the cause of my not wanting to go away anymore and declining to designate clearly who this person could be, for whom I gave up one of my main diversions (if not reasons for living), this person whose identity, moreover, could not be in doubt to any of the people who know me. A reproach likely enough to affect me, because what it challenges is nothing less than a characteristic of mine (real or imagined), which I prize perhaps more than any other: a concern to say as much as I can without disguising or curtailing the truth. A reproach that, nevertheless, seems to me undeserved. Like a physicist performing what is called the "calculation of error," haven't I taken care to point out what my reasons were, good or bad, for deciding to be reticent about this, whereas about so many other things I have laid myself open to being accused of immodesty?

I have also noted an article that appeared in *Le Figaro* a few months ago whose author declared—referring in passing to the fragments from the "Sunday" chapter printed by the journal *Les Temps Modernes*—that the act I had committed in disowning my mother (as I recounted it with other memories of my lycée period) was the "basest" act "a child could commit." It would be inappropriate for me to protest here, for if I wasn't aware that I had been guilty of a base act, would I ever have felt the need to confess it?

But other criticisms give me even more food for thought than the judgments I have just cited.

From the May 15, 1946, issue of *France libre* (a clipping that came to me by way of *Argus*, to which I subscribed when a book of mine was published for the first time in a form other than a deluxe or limited edition):

> MICHEL LEIRIS. Dimanche. *Variations ad infinitum on the theme of Sunday. What could have held our attention by its humor, here provokes only lassitude and boredom. Is Leiris becoming another Léautaud—though without the latter's style or facility? How much more moving we found* Manhood!

From the eighteenth installment of the *Cahiers du Livre* (a clipping sent to me by the same agency, which one would think was a blackmailing organization or hotbed of police intrigue, to judge from its name, which promises an omnipresent vigilance):

> *Nor does* Les Temps Modernes, *worthy continuator of* La Nouvelle Revue Française *and organ of the existentialist clique (February issue), provide us with a very healthy atmosphere. Pages like M. Michel Leiris's* "Dimanche" *can't do more than describe, as do most works of the imagination (?) appearing in the same periodical, schoolboy mischief-making, extremely vulgar escapades on sidewalks and in fashionable bars. This* "dimanche" *is strangely like a kind of penal servitude.*

Last, from someone I don't see anymore but with whom I was beginning to be friends when I left for Greece the second time and heard the blues song "Some of These Days," great trumpet blasts that pierced me to the very heart, a few months ago I found—in the box reserved for mail and papers addressed to me in the secretary's office of the establishment where I work—a short letter of which I have retained these two sentences: "When will you stop being a child? You should be thrashed for writing like that."

Naturally I was offended by these three hostile comments, though my ears don't burn more than is suitable when someone happens to heap me with praise; I am as sensitive to it as anyone else and need it, above all, to reassure myself. Vanity aside, criticism never fails to disturb me, opening wide the door to questions.

When I wrote *Manhood*, did I reach the farthest limit of my capacities? That was about ten years ago; I haven't done much since, and there is nothing to prove that I am not already—literarily as well as in all other ways—fairly far along on my way downhill. Is the work I am writing now only a flabbier and more verbose rehashing of the confession I once attempted, an undertaking one can perhaps manage only once in one's lifetime, barring new adventures important enough to furnish material for a second memorial that would not simply repeat the first from a slightly different point of view? Incapable of drawing from myself anything but memories and able only to exhume less and less interesting ones (since I have already collected the ones that meant most to me in another book), am I now in a condition similar to the mental bankruptcy that overcame the "man with the golden brain" whose story impressed me so as a child when I read it in, I think, Alphonse Daudet's *Lettres de mon moulin*: a story portraying a man whose brain is made of pure gold and who, living off this treasure, exhausts it little by little, so that one day they find him dead, his head empty and a few last scrapings under the fingernails of his clenched fingers? Am I also—since I really have nothing more to say but continue to push on as though at a task that has been imposed on me—like a schoolboy stumped by his French composition subject and chewing his penholder, moaning: "I don't have any ideas . . . I don't have any ideas . . ." as my brother would do in a similar situation, giving his circle of friends a comic performance that I am all too often, without being forced into it by any teacher or parent, driven to reproduce?

Besides my fear of having passed the point after which a writer only repeats himself or becomes insipid, another question torments me, which the second of the criticisms provoked by my reminiscences and reflections about Sunday prevents me from ignoring. Don't "school-boy mischief making" and "escapades on sidewalks and in fashionable bars" mean—when added to the parallel established with the writings of Paul Léautaud—that the stories (vulgar or not) that I tell have merely anecdotal value? Although I claim to formulate memories in order to increase the knowledge I may have of myself, have I fallen—through complacency or blindness—into the trap of depicting them no longer for myself but for their own sake, giving them exaggerated importance and seeing them only as material for stories?

Even more irritating is the summons represented by the letter in which I am asked *when I am going to stop being a child.* Turning more and more to my distant past, have I become not only a specialist (whether astute or clumsy isn't the problem) in describing the years of my youth but a sort of aged child, a prisoner of a bygone period and henceforth shut off from all action—even thought—involving the future? As for these pages I labor over, far from evolving a message that others and I myself could profit from, do they merely reflect my satisfaction in scrutinizing my past, and do they in the end tend to chain me—instead of releasing me and opening up a more manly future for me—to ancient toys and dusty fetishes that I ought rather to put up for auction once and for all so that at last I would live on something besides my memory?

I can't help concluding from these observations, therefore, that there is something dubious and deceptive in my way of proceeding: possible errors in the very workings of my memory, indecision over the direction of my whole undertaking, reticence in regard to certain subjects about which I would rather keep silent or only explain myself cryptically, the danger of a lapse into the inauthentic; if it is true that I am now no more than a teller of little stories, the glaring contradiction of wanting to be a lookout man—eyes always ahead toward the prow—when everything conspires to make one an embalmer of dead things.

As for the inaccuracies that may taint the facts I am reporting, it is obvious that I can do nothing about them and that consequently I don't have to worry about them especially. I must resign myself to cutting my losses, because this is an imperfection inherent in my nature as a man, and it would be a waste for me to rebel against it.

The matter of my reticence is trickier. If I deliberately remain silent or only partially explain what I mean about certain subjects, doesn't this indicate that there are things in myself I am avoiding, refusing to look at squarely enough to discern them clearly, if not to make them public by putting them down on paper? I have to keep constantly in mind the idea, at least, of these lacunae, to limit the damage and avoid viewing as negligible things that have been reduced to a sort of nonexistence by virtue of their being left more or less unformulated.

But the most serious matter by far seems to me to be the enticement I fear I may have yielded to, the sort that so easily leads one to transform what once had value as talisman or catalyst into an object of contemplation for oneself or trinket for someone else. Fragments of life I brought into the discussion not only because they came out of life as I lived it but because they could also represent the seeds of something active and alive; the tiny facts I try to collect tend to petrify as my quest continues. More and more, they are treated as culminations instead of starting places, so that the investigation I am making of my past imperceptibly becomes a refuge, a resting place, after having been no more than an inspection of my inner ground with a view to leaping off from it more surely. A rectification is called for here—since the very meaning of my enterprise seems to have been gradually compromised—and the most effective way of achieving it is probably to go back to the beginning and examine my original aim and how that aim has changed along the way, by almost imperceptible degrees but to such a point that I can ask myself if these various transformations really conceal a single, permanent core, notwithstanding the planned changes of course or the involuntary deviations.

For a long time I contemplated establishing in a literary way what I once called, trying to define as best I could a notion that was then quite vague, *corpuses of facts grouped according to a natural identity.* I had already attempted something similar by taking as my raw material not facts but words. I had only to join together in sentences the nouns, adjectives, and verbs I liked best, the richest for me in flavor and resonance, after writing them hastily on a sheet of paper and hardly changing them more than necessary for obtaining grammatically correct propositions; I had only to put them end to end, adding only the indispensable connecting elements and trusting completely in the currents that seemed to form of their own accord and cause the different islets thrown on the white paper to communicate among themselves; I had only to make them come together and form alliances according to their affinities, for each sheet of paper randomly strewn with these seeds of language to give birth to a poem. This was how a certain number of pieces were constructed (until I had exhausted the limited vocabulary furnished me by the words I felt were endowed with the radiance peculiar to things that have a, properly speaking, *poetic* value), pieces I collected under the title *Simulacre*, itself chosen from among those words. It seemed to me, in fact, that my way of proceeding—shaking the dice of speech as though in a cup to make ideas spring out of it instead of using them to express preexisting thoughts—was just that, a "simulacrum," a mental pantomime of the same order as the various symbols, dumb shows, and make-believes currently used in black as well as white magic, a pantomime intended to reveal to me the ineffable (image of the absolute) by copying on a lexicological level the physical action of a demiurge. An experiment that, when I tried it in the narrow domain of vocabulary (whose upheaval seemed to lead straight to the unsayable), gave me a grandiose feeling of *revelation*: whence the idea—at first purely theoretical—of reproducing it, not at all in an identical way (for nothing more would have been revealed to me if I had begun all over again what I had already done, my stock of key words being used up anyway) but by starting from a puzzle of facts and no longer simply from a puzzle of words.

For a long time, too, I have observed that in my hours of fruitless work I often behave as though I were adopting the following notion as a rule: a certain *ritual* (a certain *mise en scène*) is capable of making up for the weakness of a faltering imagination. Liturgy or sequence of moves in a ballet? When I felt unable to draw from my own material anything that deserved to be set down on paper, I would be likely to copy out texts or glue onto the virgin pages of my small or large notebooks articles or illustrations cut out of periodicals, applying myself to these mechanical tasks and executing them—even though doing this did not really fool me—with all the finicky meticulousness one can bring to actions rigorously prescribed by tradition and felt to be capable of setting in motion effects far beyond their immediate impact. The photograph of a gigantic anthropoid monkey with a startlingly brutal cast of features; a series of vulgarizing statements about dialectical materialism; a note concerning the theory proposed by the Soviet linguist Marr, for whom the earliest languages known to humanity were those belonging to what he calls the Japhetic group; an article about a discovery relating to the sonnet "Voyelles" illustrated by a drawing of a moustachioed Rimbaud (very much the "fierce invalid home from the hot countries"); unpublished work by

Stéphane Mallarmé (the man in the Scottish plaid, in the shawl whose checkered material corresponds so well with the mathematical image of the throw of the dice; other articles about the dreams of such strange content that assaulted Descartes when he was preparing to write the *Discourse on Method*, about Restif de la Bretonne and his associations with Illuminism, about the apocalyptic views of the Russian writer N. Feodorov (whom I have never read) concerning the resurrection of the dead, about bullfighting and other games relating to bulls played by the Cretans a few thousand years ago; a reproduction of a picture by Goya in which one can see a witch removing a tooth from the jaw of a hanged man; a planetary man taken from a treatise on hermetics or astrology. Selected at random from what I remember, these are some of the items placed side by side under the stitching of those record books that are like rough sketches for a visitors' book of my curiosity, and that I still sometimes leaf through even though I haven't added anything to them for a number of years. Contrary to the impression—certainly not very reasonable but firmly rooted in me—that physically bringing together two (or many) texts of very different provenances might set off a sort of deflagration, however little value these texts might have in themselves, no reaction was produced among the heteroclite documents thus confronted spatially, and no new light emerged from it. What remains, however, is the mechanical skill involved in these motions, which is hard not to enjoy even if one does not expect any sort of practical result: cutting with scissors, trimming, brushing a surface with glue, squarely applying one surface to another. Precise motions performed as though to prepare these various elements according to the requisite procedure, arrange each in its place, elements whose apposition (effected in a suitable manner) is the sine qua non for their magical efficacy. Motions performed more for show, in truth, but whose attraction I feel even so, because when I perform them, I undoubtedly rediscover something enduring that goes back to my childhood: how much I loved to make scrapbooks or notebooks for myself when I was young, bringing together within a limited number of sheets of paper or cardboard covers (or in drawers or boxes) what might please or interest me, to enclose what attracted me for various reasons in a compendium that is always available to me. I was obeying this same impulse when I formed a file for my own use in which I noted down on loose sheets of paper, afterward kept in the same envelope, the memories of my childhood or youth I didn't want to forget—brief fragments, hardly more than memory ticklers. It was the same much later, when I had the idea of systematically putting down on slips of paper (stowed in the same yellow wood file box and divided up into several series by means of thicker pieces of orange cardboard, each corresponding to the beginning of a chapter) the material I am using here. I was assembling—in a bureaucratic way, though it was related to a deeper rut than my (relatively recent) familiarity with administrative and scientific methods—this "puzzle of facts" from which I dreamed of flying up, choosing it to be my springboard.

At first there was no connection between my desire to renew, on a more down-to-earth basis, the operation I attempted first with words and my collecting—entirely empirical—of nodules relating to points in my life that I wanted to pin down, taking them from all sorts of different areas, unless it was the vague need I have always had to confront different elements, group them, bring them together, as though moved by an obscure appetite for juxtaposition or combination, probably analogous to what caused me to find a composite object like the "trumpet-drum" so attractive when I was very small. If a habit I indulged for so long without any clearly defined purpose (yielding primarily to the desire to fabricate my own archive about myself) was to change one day into an organized process directed toward literary ends and quite specifically toward the project I had longed to carry out for several years, it was necessary that the fascination exerted on me by language lead me to study its arcana once again by attaching myself, this time, to certain facts that stood out in my eyes against the mass of other facts for the very reason that they were *facts of language* whose primary stimuli were words.

Misapprehensions, errors about the very texture or the meaning of a word, phonic analogies creating a network of strange relations between one term and another (between *idole* [idol] and *plâtre* [plaster], for example, by way of *idolâtre* [idolatrous], which has a little of the lithic whiteness of statues, or between *plot* [plug, distributor point] and *complot* [plot, conspiracy], both of them matted and enigmatic), the evocative power of some vocabulary elements, the charm associated with the names of certain historic or legendary characters (like the Greek heroes Epaminondas, Leonidas, and Ulysses, who remind us of floral decorations), the double aspect of words that have a meaning for us that does not necessarily agree with the definition given in the dictionary, various types of accidents of language comparable to the natural *accidents* [undulations in the ground] that give a landscape its character or the tiny irregularities such as freckles, small scars, and beauty marks that heighten the attractiveness of a desired body—such is the group of fragile but intensely felt realities (especially in childhood, a time when the capacity for wonder is greatest) I was collecting and that formed—without my leaving, at first, the verbal domain that was still special for me—the original core around which the rest gradually solidified.

When my project took shape, still in this airy form—which happened (if I don't count the few old pages containing the early, rough descriptions of several of these facts) the day that, demobilized after the "phoney war," I tried to think of a long and exhausting task to plunge into while waiting for life to recover from its illness—I resorted to the expression *bifurs* [bifurcations, railway junctions], at first regarding it only as a pleasing word, to designate, in my own personal jargon, the materials so difficult to label that I wanted to amass and shuffle: somersaults, trippings or slippings of thought occurring as a result of a fracture, a dazzling flash (like the reflection of the sun in your eyes when a clever hand turns a little pocket mirror the right way), or some singularity or other, harsh or barely perceptible, manifesting itself in speech; losses of footing or leaps from one level to another by which the person who suffers them feels himself thrown into a state of particular acuity and which, by appearing to crack open his boundaries, cleans out his horizon; eddies, wrinkles, bits of foam, or other alterations of the (ordinarily calm) surface of language, which generate a very special poetry, alterations of which I want to note down the datable experiences I had, in order to isolate the drop of truth they seemed to me to contain and prevent their vein from drying up.

When I was at that stage, I did not so much mean, by "bifurcations," the possibilities words have of switching tracks, of branching off, which in the end form a permanent system of relations, bundles of fixed communicating lines like railroad tracks, which are undeniably anchored in the ground unless, riding along in the train, one sees the rails moving away from each other, moving back together (scissor blades opening and closing again) and telegraph wires rising and falling, a spectacle in which one takes a lively pleasure, making a game for oneself of watching the fictive animation of what one knows to be immobile. (Sometimes, too, one listens to the din of the streets and hears it organized into a piece of music. I recall, not a record but a cylinder entitled *Express-Orient* having some of those characteristics, a piece that enchanted me when I was a child and expressed that very mania, common to so many people who ride the railroad. Another amusement of mine, if the train was crossing the countryside at a fast clip, was to imagine a steeplechase whose competitors, jumping and sometimes tumbling head over heels, crossed roads, fences, arms of water, and all the other obstacles presented by the landscape I saw rushing past through the window of the railway car.)

By adopting the term *bifur*—which used to impress me a great deal when I read it in fat capital letters on a sign at the edge of a gravel railway bed—I intended, rather, to emphasize the very act of bifurcating, of deviating the way a train does when it obeys the switches and changes direction, and also the way thought does, sometimes taken by the rails of language toward something dizzying or blinding, carried along in a kind of movement, that could just as well be called a *biffure* [scratch, crossout], because we see an equivocation here, a miscalculation that we go back over, as happens in the case of a lapse in speaking (no sooner blurted out than corrected) when we say to ourselves "I've made a slip of the tongue," when one's tongue has gone off the track, at a fork in the road or a crossroads.

To limit myself to these *bifurs* as I originally had wanted to define them would not have given me much to work with; I soon had proof of this. Such experiences had been very rare (and this was another reason I valued them so highly): an infinitesimal group of exceptions difficult to join together into something that could be weighed, a dust of fragile, precious curiosities shining at the bottom of their box like pinned butterflies, immobilized in flight with their wings outspread. Furthermore, it appeared to me, as soon as I tried to be more specific about the notion of *bifur*, that it was fading away, becoming empty verbiage, an arbitrary construction based on a name that—at best— expressed only one of its qualities, a warping or curvature, which was another image that always attracted me. (Seen, for instance, many years ago, in the postcard depicting Captain Ferber's biplane, equipped, said the caption enumerating the principal characteristics of the machine, with a device permitting the warping of the wings; and, strictly conforming to the dictionary definition of the word "bifurcation"—a place where a thing divides in two—the distinction my brother and I established with a byzantine pleasure between the two types of gliders, "rectilinear" and "curvilinear," which we made with pieces of paper and which, released in the dining room, where they could land on the nice, smooth floor, competed in distance records considered either as *officiels* or *officieux* [both plural forms of "official"] depending on whether or not the flight had taken place in the presence of both of us, the thin dressmaker's tape of waxed cloth serving us to take their exact measure.)

The fear I felt because I had chosen to raise my construction on foundations that were too narrow, the need to add elements to my store that were more physical than these stories about language, the fact that I was obliged to examine from different viewpoints a notion decidedly unamenable to my efforts to grasp it—all led me to do serious violence to my original idea. Therefore, instead of limiting myself to regarding as *bifurs* only the unusual displacements in our minds caused by words or combinations of words, I also admitted as *bifurs* the similar movements triggered in us by certain convergences or disjunctions we believe we see, at certain moments, fully manifested in things as well. (For example—a mysterious doubling that challenged the very basis of identity—what I used to see as a child when I was taken for a walk in the Bois, and we went or came back through Rue Géricault or Jéricho: an advertisement for the invisible mending of damaged clothes, displayed, I think, in the window of a dry cleaner and consisting of two rectangles of cloth shown side by side, objects that were supposedly *one and the same*—in a strange sort of simultaneity—in doublets corresponding to two different moments in time, one when there was still a visible tear, and the other when all trace of it had been obliterated by the careful intervention of the experts. Or another example, in the opposite direction, being the troubling conjunction of two things in one, as in objects like the trumpet-drum and the postcard phonograph record—the first belonging to the domain of purely auditory sensations, the second primarily disconcerting because of its postal nature and the mixture of hearing and sight it implied, though I don't recall whether the card included more than anodyne ornaments framing the grooved part so that no image coincided absolutely with the sonorities contained in the opaque cardboard.)

Similarly, yielding to my desire to confront, to approach, to establish connections, I allowed my attention to go off track, not so much into the special experiences I intended to analyze as into the various ramifications that could branch out from them, routes down which I alone could set off and whose multiple resectionings had to end when I wove them into a network like those which establish communications between all the different regions of a country. Clusters of facts, feelings, and notions grouping themselves around an experience that was more colorful than the rest and acted as a sign or an illustration striking enough to serve me as a reference point—this was what these *bifurs* soon became, my procedure also tending to replace static accounts composed after the fact by something more stirring, something freer, which would itself be a series of bifurcations or *bifurs* instead of the mere description of what I had at first called by this name. In the end, therefore, the main part of my work consisted less in discovering, inventing, and then examining these knots than in entering into a meditation that zigzagged along with the writing, and, *bifur* after *bifur*, wended its way from theme to theme (these themes gradually became organized into bundles that were more or less separate but juxtaposed in a sequence of chapters constituting something like a number of successive episodes in a whimsical steeplechase I would be obliged to conduct, across hedges, streams, tilled fields, and other features of a most irregular terrain).

Proceeding in the cluttered, scribbling, note-taking way I have described—with the help of slips of paper whose quantities certainly increased as I went along (writing fresh remarks, sometimes on the same sheets, sometimes on others, remarks that are elaborations of what I have already collected just as often as they are new notations motivated either by recent reflections or events or by old events or states of mind suddenly perceived as related)—I have no chance of avoiding the asphyxiating, dusty side of scholarly work unless I regard my papers as I would view the indications determining the itinerary of a steeplechase or, even better, a rally: simple marks signifying roughly the course I must follow (a few of which may even be shifted, as happens when, inspecting my filing cabinet, I slightly modify the way it is arranged, some element suddenly appearing to me to be better placed in the sphere of influence of this cluster than it was when it belonged to that one). Also—treating the parts of my filing cabinet I haven't yet brought into play somewhat like a reserve of cards I will save for when I feel I can't risk my bet without strengthening the hand opening between my fingers like a shabby fan—I must above all imagine the connections that may reveal themselves within this stack with its many partitions, and contemplate, not what now has the dismal appearance of an acquisition but the meshes that will allow me to go from one slip of paper to the next, so that any free and vital quality in my work is really some sort of connection or transition, and the latter become thicker and thicker as I advance, until they themselves represent the true *experiences*, at the expense of those which fill my slips of paper and are no longer more than milestones set at long intervals to guide my ricocheting path.

In this way, having started from the infinitesimal cracks with which my mind (image of my continuity) still seems to me to be furrowed and which give off numbing effluvia (perhaps due to the fact that, made possible by such ruptures or deviations, in which a certain discontinuity manifests itself, what is exhaled smells faintly of death or the end of the world—a leap out of relativity) I have come to regard these *bifurs* or *biffures* (which I am tempted to call, even more suitably, *fourbis* [scraps, leavings], a term that has little enough value so that there would never be any need to overinflate it), to consider them, now—whereas they were once endowed for me with the brilliance of revelations—as no more than simple knots, each of which is attached by one end or the other to a theme that the gear mechanism of my writing, raised to the rank of reasoned articulation, helps me to describe more exactly by turning it under all sorts of lights and positioning it against other themes, the whole gradually emerging as a form previously unknown but now looming up out of a complex network of lines—bifurcations, meanderings, different digressions. (Some of the elements of that form would be: the primacy of language, my retreat into a past that is necessarily imaginary and constitutes a sort of original bedrock, my obsession with the mineral kingdom and the throb of the senses, the enhanced image of myself reflected back to me by the desert, clothes as armor, the guilt conferred by money, literature as a means of removing oneself from one's social class and escaping the grip of time, my need to combine several things into one, my hunger for a complicity with the world, where I always feel more or less a stranger.) So that if there are still *bifurs* or *biffures*, their true justification is that they are strange phenomena, misleading enough, in the proper sense of the word, to make the mind step out of its rut, induce it to seek its fortune off the beaten paths or to derail it, according to whether one's appraisal of these experiences and the speculations I brought forth from them lead one to describe their result with the first or the second of these familiar expressions.

However arbitrary and perilous my point of departure, what matters now is to continue illuminating and elucidating the themes already showing through my tangle of lines and make their interweavings crackle here and there, as though it were indispensable that I go ahead and form this corpus (into which even the most commonplace facts now enter, illustrating only one or another of my ways of being), that I join its component parts end to end after having done my best to give them at least some rudimentary order (at first summarily chrono-logical, in the case of what I call primary facts, meaning those around which the others clustered without regard for sequence), as though I also needed to tie these facts together by all these complicated threads—weaving in events that occurred even as I wrote (trumpet calls from the living world)—to use them, with the figures thus gradually sketched out, as the leitmotivs of a musical composition, so that from all this something will issue, still vacillating greatly, no doubt, but which will, I expect, when my task has come to an end, throw a little light on the creature I really am and on what this creature has a right to retain as the necessary basis for his activity. In other words, that I may be enlightened—after all these *bifurs* (or these attempts at prospecting in all directions) and after these many *biffures* (or successive eliminations of illusory values)—about my nature and my purpose, about what I want most deeply, and what I might create in my life that would be most valid and would most resemble me. (For example, to be a poet, with all that is implied by such an ambition, which cannot be limited to the desire to write poetry but inexorably demands that the poet turn himself into a *spokesman* in the strictest meaning of the word and with all the corollaries that the choice of such a function involves.)

Crucial bifurcations on which my life has entered, corrections I would have to impose on it for it to become a *destiny*—these are the last meanings (one of them still completely involved in the search for old traces, the other pointed at the future since it is a matter of preparing the way for a transformation) that I contemplated assigning to, respectively, *bifurs* and *biffures*, treating them like liturgical for-mulas whose spirit can change completely without one's resolving to modify their letter, or like those ancient buildings whose facades have remained the same though the buildings themselves have had a number of different functions (being used as convents, hospitals, prisons, and last, perhaps, museums, as though being put officially in the service of history were the only possible stopping point in their own eventful histories).

Measuring how much the gap increases day by day between what I had in mind at the beginning and what I am struggling to encompass—am I fighting against routine? superstition? the inabil-ity to detach myself from a word that creates an image?—within the magic circle of *bifurs*, I note that one single purpose has remained consistent for me: the act of bringing things together, confronting them, creating paths that join different elements together. I take satisfaction in connecting, cementing, knotting, causing things to converge, as though I were trying—however my efforts were applied and whatever my original materials—to group together in a single picture all sorts of heteroclite facts relating to my person in order to obtain a book that would finally be an abridged encyclopedia of myself, comparable to certain almanacs in the old days that inventoried the world we lived in (like the one put out by the publisher Hachette: a mine of different information under a cover depicting a serious profile with a laurel on its forehead) or the pocket book *Memento* designed by Larousse for the use of candidates for the primary school diploma, a small volume (much smaller, certainly, than the book that is motivating these reflections is likely to be) in which it seemed to me, when I was a child, the essence of mankind's knowledge had been condensed into a few pages.

And here I find myself once again seeking out something that could appear to be a sort of necessary, complete outfit enclosed in a small container. It used to be a watercolor box or a compass box. Now it is this library, which I have always tried to reduce to what seemed to be the essentials (the idea being to have all of knowledge at hand, preserved in the form of books I won't even necessarily read; and if I hate lending books, I especially hate it when it seems to me that by doing so a series will be marred; because of this, it has sometimes happened that I have preferred to lend, or even give away, an entire series rather than one volume; for what is always at issue is the idea of a whole, a whole that must not be violated once one has formed it by confining oneself to the bare minimum, and it is better, under the circumstances, to sacrifice one of its parts altogether than to endanger it or separate it temporarily by lending it: miserable image of a whole entity patiently built up and then preserved, accompanied by such a fear of risking even the least of its elements that forgoing one of them right at the start—and if necessary taking away even more—seems preferable to the threat of accidental deprivation).

Always a miserly pleasure in amassing, gathering, linking, as though the whole so solidly lashed together would become inalienable, so many bonds accumulating, so many proofs, that no part of it could be taken away. Always a profound joy in manipulating or holding and shaping with my hands, as when I was small and played with a railroad that belonged to one of my cousins, who had set it up in the garden of his parents' house in Viroflay: my satisfaction in heaping sand around and between the rails, in "making it nice and even" so that only the parallel metal lines emerged, just enough for the train to roll along; such a perfect sensation of the smooth sand when I leveled it with the palm of my hand; also the sort of miraculous reality this toy railroad acquired from being set up in the open air, a manmade product blending in with nature.

At the point I've reached now, what becomes of my hope of an exchange, my desire, quite simply, to obtain a token, a sign the outside world would consent to give me and not a value to be possessed? When I began this book, I was groping toward a discovery, then gradually, with my growing need to bring together elements that could be connected, the idea grew that I was making a *book*, that I was composing it, building it, assembling it part by part (as is appropriate for a manufactured article as opposed to a dream object). The exalted feeling that I was clearing new territory was gradually replaced by the maniacal excitement of the person dealing in secondhand goods who sees his stock of possessions increase. As the book became heavier, page after page, while I made my way with no surprises from one slip of paper to the next, most of them at the time seeming quite without virtue (since they were things known and already classified), I lost my initial enthusiasm. Soon nothing was left of the *bifurs* but the name, like the grandiloquent emptiness of a newspaper headline, and nothing much came from my desire to bring things together. So I have gotten bogged down in my task of piecing together slips of paper and find a more and more bitter taste in this perpetual rehashing of observations and events that all belong to a past as dead as it could be. No poetic fire blazes up; I lose sight of my ultimate goal, smothered instead of clarified by the profusion of details, and at every step I sink more awkwardly into my gloomy little routine of collecting.

This is why a few weeks ago I decided to break it all off without further delay. Since the literary work to which I am devoting myself with such difficulty seems less and less uplifting and no longer necessary (since it gives me nothing beyond what I put into it myself more or less deliberately), it would be better to abandon it and wait for a more favorable time. And right now the most serious hope I have for recovery is to let everything lie dormant until the anecdotal illness ailing me, which was diagnosed in such a timely way by at least one of my critics, has ceased to rage, and my brain cleansed by this period of repose, I can shed my old skin. To come into a new skin after a long period of obliteration in blankness, like a drum one has beaten too persistently and which, even though its body may still seem in pretty good shape, absolutely must have its vibrating skin replaced by a fresh one.

My book—now as idle as my life itself—has come to the very edge of the void and exists only as a silhouette, an outline almost without substance. For me this state of emptiness is accompanied by a true euphoria—unspoiled, so far, by the touch of vertigo mixed in with it. Physically, I feel lighter, more detached. I am now behaving like people who don't have any work hanging over them to make them worry about the next day and have only to let themselves live and take advantage of the present moment, moving freely about in a world from which (wrongly, of course) they expect only entertainment. Spiritually, I have an odd feeling of suspense: as though I would never have to die, or as though I were already no longer alive; as though this were an interval in a long vacation, no traveling, everything at a standstill, that is, the ambiguous moment when everything becomes a trivial game. Though I still go to my museum every day, I am at least squandering my free time remorselessly. When I am having a drink with someone in the late afternoon, dining with friends, or spending the evening out, I no longer have the depressing idea afterward that this prevented me from *doing* something and that my time could have been put to better use. I especially no longer believe that I diminish myself by not producing anything (or by producing only these few lines noting that the engine is in neutral, though running). Since at that moment I had ceased to find vital nourishment in working at the construction of this book, it is quite obvious that my decision to abandon it, in the end, cannot seriously injure me. By returning to the anonymity of people who don't write—if indeed such an eclipse must be final—I would endanger nothing essential. Dropping an activity that had become, some time back, only for show, at the very most I would run the risk of dimming the small fame I might have drawn from the publication of my other writings. And on the level of miserable vanity, won't I perhaps even gain in the exchange, bartering the habits of a needy paper-scratcher for this attitude of nonchalant detachment and choosing to keep silent rather than making myself blue in the face for the sake of this foolish chatter?

There may be, however, something insufficient and shameful in this renunciation. The passive acknowledgment of a failure without the sort of reflection that could lead to something else. A way of filing my pen as though I were filing my petition on the eve of a bankruptcy. The obvious mischief of disguising as supreme indolence an inertia that I am forcibly subjected to, instead of choosing it as though I wanted to be a do-nothing for my career. The recognition, also, of my inability to join together at least a portion of the sketches that fill this chapter, so that I will be leaving a total rout behind me if I can't even arrange into a semblance of a bouquet the various stalks I've so patiently uprooted with my own hands.

However great my haste to be done with it, I can't avoid—is this the last attempt I make before laying my notes to rest in their little wooden box?—an uncomplacent examination of the true motives that goad me to silence.

Since I can't hope to correct, except after a long intermission, what has been spoiled, I have made the decision to be quiet. Yet this decision—which is also in keeping with a desire I have been contemplating for a long time now to make a break in a piece of writing I soon saw would occupy me for a good many years, if not up to the very end of my life—this decision (an appeal for a silence more real than the silence into which one temporarily lapses between two volumes) only sanctions a growing trouble. Far from being either the result of something I simply want to do or merely introducing a conventional absence similar to that of an actor who leaves the stage, it is an admission of disappointment and weariness, a retreat before too many difficulties, difficulties that lead me to withdraw from the game for a period whose duration is impossible for me to predict.

I would have very little interest in literary activity, certainly, if I didn't think that in one way or another it was parallel to life—if I thought it was detached, shielded, as though accomplished in isolation, without anything in common with anything else, the performance of a star that follows its own path. Every line, however polished, traced by a pen must be open to chiromancy, and in every motion of every hand that breaks the new ground of the paper, one can probably read the whole of this person who allows his destiny to be mirrored in the calm or troubled surface of a gesture. As for me, then, I am quite aware that the pitfalls I encounter in writing correspond to the many traps I must reckon on in my daily life and that the most accurate of all the portraits I will have made of myself will perhaps be—much more than any one of the writings in which I have chosen

to depict myself—the one I draw, unwittingly, when I try to formulate an idea, any idea at all, no matter how far removed from my stock
of habitual preoccupations. All my inkblots, my hesitations, my
stumbling over words, all the crossouts or interlineations that accumulate in each of my sentences and that I am so likely to attribute to
clumsiness of expression in fact betray indecisiveness in my thought
and defects in my character, (especially) the deep fear that prevents me
from advancing except by sudden leaps, detours, and backtrackings,
as though each time I had to affirm something or myself, I flinch like a
horse who shies at an obstacle and can only be forced to jump by angry
kicks from his spurred rider. A tendency to evade that is paradoxically
satisfied by the constant use I make of the first person: the moment I
say "I," though I may seem to be charging straight ahead, what I
present is less compromising. For to display their subjectivity openly
this way greatly diminishes the scope of my assertions, reducing them
to being no more than peculiarities or opinions I propose not as
general truths but as strictly personal viewpoints. A tendency that is
partly justified by my obvious incompetence in handling ideas, my
embarrassing lack of dialectic, but which becomes (if I give in to it
too lazily) a real deficiency preventing me, for example, from defend-
ing my point of view in a conversation that is at all intense, so that
often, finding little or nothing to say in opposition to the person I am
talking to, I go along with him, even if I continue to have a contrary
opinion, and just barely manage to formulate a few theoretical reser-
vations with which I can save face when the dialogue comes to an end.

In every case where I have trouble setting my thoughts in order,
where I am pessimistic about my chances of expressing myself accurately, silence is obviously the easy solution. How many times have I
refrained in this way from taking part in a discussion even when I
knew it would not have been useless to contradict what was being
said, even quietly, with just enough conviction to have some chance of
winning people over! But what I no doubt lack most of all is conviction, and I have always found excellent reasons to keep quiet, feeling
my conviction dwindle the more effort I make to display it. A
horror—naturally!—of the risk of speaking without displaying much
intelligence, in the same way that when it comes to literature, I
sometimes write nothing (or almost) because most of the time I prefer
this nothingness to the risk of writing badly and, faithful to the
obsession that so often makes me resort to a radical excision in order to
avoid the risk of a partial loss, put up with a kind of peace that is

merely the absence of the anguish I would suffer if I had taken a risk. (Thus, in a completely different realm, it used to happen that in order not to have to confront the possible shame of being defeated by someone else, I would give up courting a girl or woman if I saw that I had competition. And in the field of literature too, isn't it a rather similar fear of competition that has also made me forgo writing works of the imagination to lock myself up in this autobiographical genre where, since I am discussing myself, it is easy for me to tell myself I am the only one in a position to do it properly?)

Since from a very early time I have almost continuously wavered between total inertia and this other form of abdication which is a retreat into the heart of subjectivity, it was quite natural that when I no longer derived anything but disappointment from this piece of writing (since to analyze myself all the time, describe my states of mind, weigh and dissect words without letting myself get intoxicated by their vapors or burned by the flames of things is certainly the surest way of not discovering anything), I should be inclined to hold my tongue, adopting out of habit and at first unawares, the negative approach of turning away from the problem instead of doing everything possible to resolve it and at the same time carrying to an extreme the impulse that I have always found only too attractive: to wrap myself in the comfortably padded carelessness of egotistic solitude. In my quest for a pledge of harmony it won't do me any good to put my pen up for auction if the transition from chatter to silence only signifies replacing a verbose way of churning myself up by another way that is just as complacent and even more limited, deprived as it is of even the semblance of result represented by the soliloquy. But what mountains have to be moved if I, who am just as unfamiliar with a mouth that is hermetically sealed (supreme dignity) as with a mouth that pours forth its monologue and never runs dry, am to succeed in composing a song that may find its way out of me and resemble those tunes that accompanied the moments of my life that I believe were crucial!

Weakness of character coupled with faintheartedness in the exercise of speech: two aspects of the same defect, which explain, in the realm of banal professional activities, the unconquerable repugnance I feel teaching a course, giving a lecture (the anguish of beginning a sentence, face to face with the audience, and suddenly finding it hanging there without knowing how to finish it, my mind empty, my heart drowned in a great blankness), a repugnance that in these two cases is added to the dismay I feel—I who am so incapable of deciding on a subject—at playing the professor (at being the person who "knows" and on whom his knowledge confers the importance of the mature or rich man; even more than the one who knows, to be the one who seems to know, to be the one who behaves *as though* he knows). They also explain the uneasiness that fills me every time I have to express myself in a foreign language (invent a sentence that I know will almost certainly be badly constructed and make people smile, to leap, in some sense, into an oral world where words will no longer have the affectionate padding of memory that provides company and support when one speaks a familiar language), and explain why, even in French, I am so often not talkative (powerless to rise above the terror of having nothing to say or of only managing to say it badly). The feeling of having my back to the wall when I am obliged to speak. Panic when faced with words that have to be linked together, as when faced with something that has to be done. Always beating about the bush. Floating. Evading. Tergiversating. How can I make all this crumble away? How can I destroy this Jericho? What drum can I beat, what trumpet can I sound to bring down the barriers of confusion and constraint that block my voice?

Though I haven't been able to do away with this contradiction, I see clearly that the stronger my desire to break down all obstacles to complete communication (and say something to someone else that helps him to live, help myself by sharing these words with someone else), the harder, the more finicky and paralyzing become my requirements for achieving both a discourse capable of moving and persuading others and a sufficiently accurate portrayal of my ideas carried out according to a rigorous, logical procedure. And no doubt this shows that what I'm really after is perpetual motion, or the philosopher's stone, or the squaring of the circle. How can I, in fact, reconcile the delight I have in vivid, colorful things, my concern for achieving an authentic formulation, and my desire to build myself a sort of system that would have some validity by general standards? How might I make these three components converge, without their neutralizing one another, in one work that I would foolishly love to see flash like lightning, whereas I can only pull it, scrap by scrap, and not without infinite precautions, from the tailings of my slips of paper? The work, not of an inspired alchemist but a lab technician—which I nearly became professionally and which, despite the little inclination I evinced for it, undoubtedly corresponds to a real aspect of my character, as may be seen not only by my early interest in this kind of occupation but by the fact that even now I pulverize, filter, determine quantities, perform experiments.

I can't hide it from myself—the terms I waver between are irreconcilable, and since I am thus torn, there is nothing surprising in my distress. The strange thing is that an attempt I have embarked on deliberately, in response, really, to nothing but my own pleasure, should have become so oppressive to me, like a task that I can't evade without incurring the sharpest reproaches, even the most bitter punishments. The absurd situation of the literary man who sees the thing he chose as toy or means of his liberation transformed into a job he has to do. Really, a classic trick of precipitating a thing into its opposite, just as, because of the newspapers, the printing press becomes a contrivance for making people stupid rather than for propagating knowledge, the apparatus of mechanization serves to perfect slavery, and science in general becomes a means of developing the most sophisticated sort of constraint and destruction.

It is quite clear that if I am determined to trace calligraphic festoons in a more or less satisfying way (making deeper downstrokes and taller upstrokes than the usual script), it is because for me this act seems to be an adornment or mask for my life, smeared with the makeup I can't do without if it is to be, at worst, tolerable. But the fact is, too, that this possibility of tracing calligraphy will vanish precisely when I need it most, when I am too unhappy to be able to go on composing a cosmetic plaster to hide from myself the horror of living. As a consequence, what is untenable in my position is now glaringly apparent: that I mistake for the plank of wood that will save me from drowning one that I know for a fact is rotten, good only in calm weather, and definitely of no help when I am truly in danger. An even more radical contradiction than the one I revealed a moment ago, this time inherent in my very reasons for writing and not simply in the way I write.

Beset as I am by so many forces militating in favor of silence, it would seem that the wisest, if not most basically honest thing— would be for me to give in and stop here, not adding one more word to this statement of my failure. But because for me "silence" is almost synonymous with "death" (my death: the thing I won't remember, won't be able to recount; the line that will always be missing from this drawing, necessary if it is to be complete; my death: the experience that may be my downfall and that will be as crucially important morally, since I will be afraid, as it will be physically), I can't resolve to be quiet, and I opt for a solution that is, according to dictates of a perhaps praiseworthy but ephemeral wisdom, the absolutely opposite course. To speak without rhyme or reason, which at least allows me to break the enchanted circle in which I have been enclosed by reason reasoning, discourse discoursing, writing writing. It requires a leap, if it is true that my inner state has reached the point in its evolution at which the fact of writing—far from infusing artificial vigor into a person who can't otherwise feel completely alive—does not even give the illusion of filling in the hole of what is missing. Being able to fill this hole (or do away with this emptiness)—isn't that what I mean, though translated into the negative, when I speak of discovering an object, that is, finding something full, a sort of vital pulp or concentrate of flavor? Poetic speech, the only type of speech one can call full-flavored, is certainly the only one that takes us in such a direction. With a possibility of success will I expect my distress to accede suddenly to this sort of furor, or on the contrary, is this distress so complete that I can expect only sterility from it, since no wave of a magic wand comes along to change a profound numbness into ardor? Having probably entered something equivalent to what the ancient alchemists or hermetic philosophers called "the path from which one never returns," it is no longer possible for me to find a way out except by going forward.

In my list of cheerful words ending in -*lan*—words that exploded like those brass fanfares I loved so much when I listened to tunes like the famous march from *Aïda* or from *Le Prophète* (the noisy and pompous sacred march that I took at the time for the very image of grandeur)—I forgot one. I neglected, in fact, to mention *gondolant* [sidesplitting], though it is one of the most exemplary of those words. Current usage endows it with a broadly comical meaning, and one would be hard put to it to find an adjective that was more chubby-cheeked, plump, florid, swollen with laughter before it explodes, when the belly begins to be traversed by waves almost of pain, and the person thus tormented shows, by the gradual brightening of his features and the sort of obliteration his eyes undergo, that he little by little is becoming prey to a phenomenon of an almost cosmic order.

It is not a ludicrous concern to keep myself intact and separate but only my surly humor that prevents me from ending here with a burst of laughter. Those luxurious toys I held in my hands or broke, those uplifting pieces of music I so often listened to with ambiguous pleasure—it is one of them that I will exhume from my slips of paper to orchestrate this finale, like an opera composer who, his overture a step away from the conclusion, reintroduces and intermingles the main themes he introduced in the beginning.

Thin, milky, translucent globes, so delicate that I broke all or almost all of them the same day I came into possession of the toy, these were the standard lamps of the train set that included such a beautiful station and, perhaps, switches allowing one to effect bifurcations or create make-believe disasters by letting the locomotives run into each other. These fragile spheres of frosted glass, hardly more durable than soap bubbles even though they were mounted on posts, were the most precious ornaments of a sumptuous gift given me, on the occasion of one of their visits to France, by the person my family called "aunt from England" and the rich old woman who employed her as lady's companion, who, we knew, lived in Wales in a large manor and whom we generally called *la Lady*. This "aunt from England," who was always the life of the party when she was younger, is now a starched octogenarian, a dignified alcoholic (for she learned to drink strong liquor during her years on the island). She lives at Saint-Pierre-lès-Nemours, in the house where my mother also lives, and given her age and the fact that she can indeed lay claim to the title of grandmother, we no longer call her anything but Granny. This relative, who made her home in a foreign country and whom we only saw, when she was in Paris, in the drawing rooms of grand hotels (the Continental, the Ile, and the Albion, or other old places on Rue de Rivoli, that street which—quite aside from any true resemblance—has always reminded me of London because of its Piranesian arcades sheltering a series of little shops), always used to be surrounded by a certain mystery for my brothers and me, because for some time we hadn't known that this half-Anglicized aunt—whose gaiety we relished so deeply and whose fat, blotched cheeks delighted us as much as her clothing, always a little too solemn—had one child, and this child was the very person we had thought for so long was our older sister and whom, for my part, I have never stopped treating as such. Our first cousin, as I have said, whom our parents had taken in to raise with us when her mother left for England, right after the loss of her husband, a younger brother of our father's, a talented engraver (apparently) and, to judge from the portraits his wife and daughter kept of him, a pleasant and handsome man who was accidentally drowned during a canoeing party.

Near the cutting of a railway track and opposite a commonplace church, the kind one sees by the thousands all over France, lies the property where, winter and summer, my adoptive sister now lives, widowed several years ago. A few feet away from the front steps, in a neglected garden (so that it has a somewhat wild look) stands a curious little structure made of wood and sheet metal that is actually a replica of a sedan chair. This is where, on nice days and when it isn't too hot, my "aunt from England" likes to retreat to read or embroider—to do nothing, perhaps, or only doze? A beautiful plaything with which she enchants her old age, the old age of a brainless creature who has retained, from the time when she lived on the fringes of the aristocracy, a taste for the furbelows of the court and everything that even remotely recalls the pomp and ceremony of a monarchy. In my sister's home, and in the room her daughter uses when she comes to Nemours, there are—in the midst of the jumble of old furniture and knickknacks that accumulate from season to season—a few objects one could make into playthings but that are kept there out of a simple antiquarian fervor: an old music box that still works almost the way it should and a player piano they often talk of having restored but to my great sorrow I have never been able to hear in working order. I am more enchanted and moved, perhaps, by such sound mills than by ordinary instruments worked by fingers or lungs, precisely because of their automatism, which confers on them a quality of inevitability and gives one the illusion of being in the presence of pieces of the outside world that might suddenly start speaking, and speak in a language of melody.

The player pianos of the streets of London and Barcelona—the first, full of a nameless despair (because their manners are so brisk under their shoddy finery), the second, full of vehement drunkenness, ocellated with passion; the kind of piano I also heard as a small child on a Flemish beach where it was carried about all day long by two women dressed as Bohemian or Italian peasants (each had a large red scarf over her hair and, perhaps, gold rings in her ears), one taking up the collection, the other turning the handle so that a tune would flow out, and this tune has followed me around for a long time. At first I thought it was called—incomprehensibly—"Les Chados," but then I found out it was none other than the famous waltz "Ma Jolie" (whose opening words, "O Manon . . .," I had distorted into the enigmatic title that remained the caption to the cheerful picture of the two pseudovagabonds who carried around with them such a fine sun by the side of the Northern Sea); orchestrions, also Belgian, of the sort one finds in the bars on Rue Haute in Brussels; but especially the traveling pianos of London, which I come back to because of their enduring melancholy, unrivaled by that of barrel organs (even when they play a piece from *La Traviata* or another Verdi opera), pianos I was so sorry not to find when, at the beginning of this summer, I went for the fifth time to the city that I picture as almost entirely composed of arches and passageways (as Rome is a city of terraces and stairways), pianos the last one of which I heard was pushed around by two men in top hats and threadbare overcoats, as raindrenched as the two charming, brown-haired women had been sunny when I saw them as a child in their costumes so reminiscent of that of Maddalena, the bully's sister, in the last act of *Rigoletto*, whose dress—theatrical even though intended to be worn in broad daylight—probably excited me because it was a disguise, like the costumes of the wine waitresses in Switzerland the year before at Interlaken, who scraped the tops off the overflowing beer glasses with wooden scrapers and whose busts were tightly imprisoned in black velvet bodices laced over their white blouses.

The waltz "Ma Jolie," whose title one sees written on many of Picasso's cubist still lives of the period when musical instruments, like packets of tobacco and other emblems of a luxury associated with total poverty, were among his favorite subjects. The London mendicants' pianos, less beautiful in form than violins or guitars and which I am all too inclined to want to remember, poking rather arbitrarily at a certain melancholy feeling, though I may well ask myself if it is anything more than a childish sadness caused by growing pains and a crisis of unsatisfied desires, excusable when one is too young to have any way of satisfying oneself—or even of diagnosing oneself and discovering exactly what one wants—but unpardonable when one has reached maturity and has had ample opportunity to get to know oneself, to find out what one wants, when the only reasonable motives for sorrow are life's actual setbacks, that is, the things that come along to thwart us in a material way. True, there is a special sadness associated with maturity, just as in childhood there was a special sadness associated with the time after four o'clock (which was teatime), when one felt the hour for bedtime drawing gradually closer (ten o'clock when I was about twelve, a fact that still marks that hour of the day for me, in winter and summer both—like a cape I still have to round every day); a premature retirement forced on you by your parents and which is like a foretaste of death, when you will have to withdraw while others continue—a retirement I dread terribly, I who still have such great difficulty accepting the fact that I have to go home when a party is over and even greater difficulty making up my mind to leave if others stay on!

Piranesian perspectives, all with immense vaults, spans, and stairways; jerky harmonies piling up around the player pianos of London (amid the muffled din of the street or the silence of squares like Brompton Square where Mallarmé lived)—at this point I can call up these images, whose juxtaposition eloquently expresses what I feel today. Along with a certain thirst for beauty and a vague longing for grandeur (the beauty and grandeur one loves to look at and with which one must also try to adorn oneself, as in love, which demands that one think oneself beautiful and grand in the presence of the very essence of beauty and grandeur) there is an equally obvious distress, however attached I may be to its charm, the kind of distress that characterizes anyone who lives in a city in the industrialized world. These are opposite poles between which I oscillate constantly, whether I am trying to make room for myself and take control of things (when I am very soon brought back to earth by the idea of a certain deepseated inanity), or the acute perception of the ludicrousness of man's condition—and even more the condition of being civilized—appears to me as poetry's true motivating force (and, because of this, as the means of access into that very beauty and grandeur with which I dream of identifying).

Black-and-white engravings showing ruined monuments or crazy, tiered structures rising in undefined spaces like that between the below-stage area and the flies in a theater. Pianos with black and white keys too, lugged about by persons who manage to look bourgeois but are strangely tarnished and ravaged, living wrecks, stiff under their cast-off clothing, the clothing of scarecrows or secondhand clothes-dealers' mannequins. Rome, a city that is golden rather than black and white (colors that belong to London, where what you see most of, in the elegant neighborhoods, is pale stone coated with soot, a substance that looks precious enough so that even though there is a great deal of brick, it is relegated to the background); Rome, which for a long time I only knew (except for what I learned from my secondary studies and novels about the birth of Christianity or decadent morality) through Piranesi's *Antiquities* and *Prisons*, but of which I had a positive experience a short time back, having had the time to walk around there, at first prey to a sort of anguish (the isolation that I feel more and more in large cities), then to joy before such a profusion of beauties (those different blocks of civilization heaped up in an extraordinary disorder, perching on top of one another and swarming the way I wish my imagination would swarm). London, a city with such a dark name, where so many opposites converge that it can't help being mythological: the symbol of a certain form of civilization, already outmoded but brilliantly structured, just as Rome was queen of the ancient world and is now, with its troop of priests in skirts, the center of Christianity. London, which I feel is the more sympathetic of the two capitals and which I certainly like better, in the same way that, when all is said and done, I prefer, over naked beauty, a certain romantic throb that can't exist without the sophistication of the modern Western world.

For if in Rome I saw a crowd of lofty archangels (ancient or baroque statues like those punctuating the bridge across from the Sant 'Angelo castle and looking as though they were diving into the Tiber every time a swimmer from a nearby bathing place threw himself into the water, without any need for the individual thus changed into a supposedly divine creature to make what is called a *saut de l'ange* ["angel's leap": swan dive] for the mistake to seem real), and if, outdoors at the summer opera, I have also heard human voices rising into expectant and regretful caryatids of sound while the stage lights artificially carved out of the block of night an alveola of day in which people and things stood out in an undreamt-of relief, don't my true archangels move, instead, through sad, gray commercial streets like the big and little streets of the City of London—in the vicinity of the pubs, the men's clothing stores, the lobbies of clubs or hotels, the public parks, and the docks, and not far, either, from Hampton Court with its enormous, crimson-canopied beds under each dizzying ceiling, beds that bleed with the copulation of a king or a Jack the Ripper—charming silhouettes with fading outlines associated with decorative elements that touch me without my putting any particular faith in them: archangels that speak into my ear over a background of threepenny music, archangels who dance before my eyes in an infinitely deep light and invisibly bring to life something that represents at once my consolation prize and my winning card, my shield and the adornment without which I am nothing, also the only thing in which I can find for myself a semblance of grandeur and draw from it the illusion of being to some extent someone "who is like God," the literal meaning of my first name—*Michel*—in Hebrew? A perfectly childish illusion of an absolute, I have to admit, which is perhaps comparable to the daydreams of my "aunt from England" sitting motionless inside her false sedan chair and which must be given some other content than what exists on paper, at the same time that what is (it seems to me) most essential about my life, should cease to be merely smoke rising, from time to time, to my head.

But clearly I must fall silent now. However mortifying it may be to conclude a book without having reached any real point of arrival (the disclosure of some truth that was not there at the beginning), I will stop, like a locomotive that finds the tracks obstructed and comes to a halt in the middle of the countryside after loosing a volley of whistle blasts. At the very most—if I insist on changing this forced halt into a semblance of a rest—I have a right to tell myself I am putting off until *tantôt* [later, presently] my preoccupation with going back over all this, armed with other images that I will manipulate in their turn like variously colored pieces of glass with different powers of magnification. *Tantôt*—a word that rang in my ears with such promise when I was a child, and meant the afternoon; *tantôt*—which, though touched with a twilight uneasiness, still tastes a little of cake, caviar, the New Year . . .

1940–1947.